THE HISTORY AND PRINCIPLES OF VEDIC INTERPRETATION

About the Author

Prof. Ram Gopal, the author of the present book, is now Kalidasa Professor of Sanskrit and Head, Department of Kalidasa Chair, Panjab University, Chandigarh. He is an eminent Sanskrit scholar of international repute whose numerous research publications such as *India of Vedic Kalpasūtras, Vaidika Vyākaraṇa* (in two volumes) and *Vaidika-Vyākhyā-Vivechana* have won world-wide fame. He is an acknowledged authority on the Vedic language, literature and culture. In recognition of his outstanding contributions to the realm of Sanskrit studies he was awarded the Independence Day Award, *Certificate of Honour in Sanskrit,* by the President of India in 1971; and the same year he was honoured by the Haryana Government also with the State Literary Award in Sanskrit and a Felicitation Volume. The Ministry of Education and Culture, Government of India, awarded him a literary prize of Rs.10,000 in 1981 in appreciation of his reputed research publication, *Vaidika Vyākāraṇa* (in two volumes). He has chaired several seminars, symposia and conferences connected with Vedic studies and was the President of the Vedic Section of the All India Oriental Conference in 1966.

THE HISTORY AND PRINCIPLES OF VEDIC INTERPRETATION

By

RAM GOPAL, M.A., Ph.D.

Certificate of Honour in Sanskrit,
Kalidasa Professor of Sanskrit and Head,
Department of Kalidasa Chair,
Panjab University, Chandigarh

CONCEPT PUBLISHING COMPANY PVT. LTD.
NEW DELHI-110059

ISBN: 978-81-7022-171-5

First Edition 1983

Published and Printed by

Concept
Since 1974

Concept Publishing Company Pvt. Ltd.
A/15-16, Commercial Block, Mohan Garden,
New Delhi-110059 (India)
T : 91-11-41101460
E : publishing@conceptpub.com, *W*: www.conceptpub.com

PREFACE

Every student of the Vedas is faced with the problem of their correct interpretation. As soon as he compares any translations or commentaries of the Vedas, he is baffled by the diversity of their inconsistent and contradictory interpretations. He wonders why the Vedic scholars, ancient and modern, differ so sharply with regard to the interpretation of these hoary scriptures, and inquires if there can be any rational and scientific guidelines to determine the meaning of the Vedas in an objective and systematic manner. Although the problem of Vedic exegesis has engaged the attention of Vedic scholars for more than two millennia, a comprehensive work throwing light on the root cause of the problem, dealing with the origin and development of different systems of Vedic interpretation, and offering a rational and scientific solution to the problem has long been a desideratum. The present work aims at meeting this need of the Vedic students.

An attempt has been made here to put the problem of Vedic interpretation in proper perspective. Difficulty in determining the correct meaning of the Vedas is largely due to three main factors: first, the archaic nature of the Vedic language containing a large number of rare and obscure words and obsolete grammatical forms which are not met with in Classical Sanskrit; secondly, the use of common words in a figurative sense in the Vedas; and thirdly, a wide hiatus between the ideas embodied in the Vedas and those contained in the later works. The attempts of the ritualists, mythologists, mystics, etc., to interpret the Vedas according to their own standpoint gave rise to various schools of Vedic interpretation in ancient India. The Nighaṇṭu represents the earliest lexicographical attempt to tackle the problem of Vedic interpretation in a systematic manner. Similarly the authors of the Padapāṭha, the Prātiśākhyas and the Nirukta have made significant contributions to the linguistic interpretation of the Vedas. The origin, development and characteristic features of different ancient Indian schools of Vedic interpretation have been fully discussed by us in the present work. This discussion is followed by a detailed account of the ancient and mediaeval Veda-Bhāṣyas which are undobtedly indebted to the ancient Indian schools of Vedic interpretation in several ways.

When the study of Sanskrit was first introduced in Europe towards the end of the eighteenth century, the Western scholars were pre-occupied mainly with the study of Classical Sanskrit and had no clear concept about the nature and scope of the Vedic language and literature. In the initial stage of Vedic studies in Europe Sāyaṇa's commentary on the Ṛgveda was the principal guide of the Western Vedic scholars. However, the nineteenth century witnessed a great upsurge in Vedic studies in the West. A number of eminent Western scholars, who made a systematic, critical and thorough study of the original Vedic texts, rejected Sāyaṇa as their guide and gave a new orientation to the concept of Vedic interpretation. Since then significant contributions have been made by modern scholars to the realm of Vedic exegesis in the form of Vedic dictionaries, grammars, translations, indices, concordances, and critical studies on the historical, cultural and linguistic aspects of the Vedas. The present work gives a systematic and chronological account of the outstanding contributions made to Vedic interpretation during the last two hundred years, and discusses current trends and tendencies in Vedic studies.

Some of the modern scholars launched a virulent tirade against the Veda-Bhāṣyas composed by Sāyaṇa and other Indian scholiasts, and declared them to be taboos for Vedic students. In order to dispel misconceptions about the Veda-Bhāṣyas the present volume makes a comparative assessment of the Veda-Bhāṣyas and modern exegetical attempts in respect of their merits and demerits, and concludes that the best features of both the systems should be synthesized and their shortcomings should be cautiously avoided.

On a thorough and dispassionate analysis of the Vedic interpretations attempted hitherto, we have formulated in the concluding Chapter of this work a set of fourteen fundamental principles for an objective, scientific and systematic interpretation of the Vedas,

The present writer will deem his labour rewarded if this volume could enable the readers to view in proper perspective the problem of Vedic interpretation and the various attempts at its solution, and if it could arouse the conscience of such amateurish readers of the Vedas as indulge in spinning out fanciful theories about these immortal scriptures on the basis of some vague and inaccurate translations without caring to ascertain their correct meaning from the original text.

My thanks are due to the University Grants Commission for providing financial assistance to me to complete the present work as an Advanced Research Project.

Department of Kalidasa Chair, RAM GOPAL
Panjab University,
CHANDIGARH

1st January, 1983.

LIST OF ABBREVIATIONS

AV.	Atharvaveda
Agni. G.S.	Āgniveśya Gṛhyasūtra
Ait. Ar.	Aitareya Āraṇyaka
Ait. Br.	Aitareya Brāhmaṇa
A. Pr.	Atharvaveda Prātiśākhya
Ap. D.S.	Āpastamba Dharmasūtra
Ap. S.S.	Āpastamba Śrautasūtra
Asv. G.S.	Āśvalāyana Gṛhyasūtra
Asv. S.S.	Āśvalāyana Śrautasūtra
Baudh. D.S.	Baudhāyana Dharmasūtra
Baudh. G.S.	Baudhāyana Gṛhyasūtra
Baudh. S.S.	Baudhāyana Śrautasūtra
Bhar. G.S.	Bhāradvāja Gṛhyasūtra
Bhar. S.S.	Bhāradvāja Śrautasūtra
B. (Br. or Brh.) Up.	Bṛhadāraṇyaka Upaniṣad
Bṛhad.	Bṛhaddevatā
Chh. Up.	Chhāndogya Upaniṣad
Drah. S.S.	Drāhyāyaṇa Śrautasūtra
Gop. (or G.) Br.	Gopatha Brāhmaṇa
Gaut. D.S.	Gautama Dharmasūtra
Gobh. G.S.	Gobhila Gṛhyasūtra
Hir. S.S.	Hiraṇyakeśi (Satyāṣāḍha) Śrautasūtra
H.O.S.	Harvard Oriental Series
J. (or Jaim.) Br.	Jaiminīya Brāhmaṇa
J. Up. Br.	Jaiminīya Upaniṣad Brāhmaṇa
JAOS.	Journal of American Oriental Society

JRAS.	Journal of Royal Asiatic Society
K. (or Kaus.) Br.	Kauṣītaki Brāhmaṇa
Kaus. G.S.	Kauṣītaka Gṛhyasūtra
Kaus. S.	Kauṣikasūtra
KS.	Kāṭhaka Saṃhitā
Kat. S.S.	Kātyāyana Śrautasūtra
Kath. G.S.	Kāṭhaka Gṛhyasūtra
Kaut. Arth.	Kauṭilya's Arthaśāstra
Lat. S.S.	Lāṭyāyana Śrautasūtra
M. Br.	Mantra Brāhmaṇa
Mbh.	Mahābhārata (Gītā Press edition)
Manu.	Manusmṛti
Man. G.S.	Mānava Gṛhyasūtra
Man. S.S.	Mānava Śrautasūtra
MS. or M.S.	Maitrāyaṇī Saṃhitā
N.	Nirukta
P.	Pāṇinian Grammar
P. Br.	Pañchaviṃśa Brāhmaṇa
Par. G.S.	Pāraskara Gṛhyasūtra
R. Pr.	Ṛgveda Prātiśākhya
RV.	Ṛgveda
SBE.	Sacred Books of the East
Sat. (or S.) Br.	Śatapatha Brāhmaṇa
Sankh. Ar.	Śāṅkhāyana Āraṇyaka
Sankh. G.S.	Śāṅkhāyana Gṛhyasūtra
Sankh. S.S.	Śāṅkhāyana Śrautasūtra
Skanda.	Skandasvāmin, Ṛg-Bhāṣyakāra
Sarvā.	Sarvānukramaṇī of Kātyāyana
SV.	Sāmaveda
T. (or Tait.) Ar.	Taittirīya Āraṇyaka
T. (or Tait.) Br.	Taittirīya Brāhmaṇa
TS. or Tait. S.	Taittirīya Saṃhitā

Vaikh. D.S.	Vaikhānasa Dharmasūtra
Vaikh. G.S.	Vaikhānasa Gṛhyasūtra
Vaikh. S.S.	Vaikhānasa Śrautasūtra
Vai. P.	Vaidika-Padānukrama-Koṣa of Vishva Bandhu
Vait. S.S.	Vaitāna Śrautasūtra
V. (or Vaj.) Pr.	Vājasaneyi Prātiśākhya
V.S. or V.S. or Vaj. S.	Vājasaneyi Saṃhitā
Vas. D.S.	Vāsiṣṭha Dharmasūtra
Venk.	Veṅkaṭamādhava, Ṛg-Bhāṣyakāra
VIJ.	Vishveshvaranand Indological Journal
Yaj.	Yājñavalkyasmṛti
Z.D.M.G.	Zeitschrift der Deutschen Morgenländischen Gesellschaft

CONTENTS

1

Introduction

The Vedas which are undoubtedly the earliest books of mankind and the sacred books of the Hindus occupy a unique position in world literature. In comparison with the Egyptian pyramids and other ancient monuments which inspire us with their mute grandeur and perpetuate the memories of their builders the Vedas which have most faithfully preserved the immortal words uttered by the ancient seers thousands of years ago have been inspiring millions of devout Hindus since time immemorial. The Vedas are the fountainhead of later Indian literature both religious and secular. All ancient Indian law-givers including Gautama, Baudhāyana, Āpastamba, Manu and Yājñavalkya regard the Vedas as the principal source of *Dharma*; and all Hindus look upon the Vedas as the supreme authority in all matters concerning religion, laws and social conduct.

Religion, philosophy, literature, art and culture of India bear an unmistakable imprint of Vedic influence. Even after a passage of many millennia, religious beliefs of the Hindus are saturated with Vedic ideas. Millions of Hindus perform their religious rites with the recitation of those very Vedic Mantras which were recited by their forefathers thousands of years ago. As *Agni* (Fire) was the chief god and centre of all religious activities of the Vedic Aryans in the hoary past, so it is today. No religious ceremony of the Hindus can be regarded as complete without the offering of oblations being made into the Fire with the recitation of certain Vedic stanzas. The devout Hindus recite Vedic stanzas as part of their daily prayers. The origin of important deities of Hindu pantheon is traceable to the Vedas. Although Hindu religion has undergone significant changes in the course of millennia, its infra-structure is still essentially Vedic in form and substance. All the orthodox systems of Indian philosophy regard the Vedas as the final authority on matters of dispute. The Pūrva-mīmāṃsā school of philosophy is mainly concerned with the interpretation of Vedic texts in respect of their application to the sacrificial ritual. The Uttara-mīmāṃsā or Vedānta represents a systematization of philosophical doctrines propounded in the Vedic Saṃhitās and the Upaniṣads. The Bhagavadgītā which is regarded as the essence of Hinduism is a fine epitome of the Vedas and the Upaniṣads.[1]

The influence of the Vedas on later Sanskrit literature is clear and positive. The works of Vālmīki, Vyāsa, Kālidāsa and Bhavabhūti bear an unmistakable imprint of Vedic influence. It is impossible to fully understand and appreciate the epics, Purāṇas, Smṛtis and other works of Sanskrit literature without an adequate knowledge of Vedic literature and culture.

It is important to point out that the traces of Vedic influence are discernible not only throughout the length and breadth of India but also beyond the confines of the Indian subcontinent. Although most of the vestiges of Vedic influence abroad have been obliterated by the ravages of time, the few that have survived testify to the extent of Vedic influence in ancient times. Some clay tablets discovered at Boghazköi in Asia Minor in 1907 shed a good deal of light on the spread of Vedic culture in that part of the globe. These clay tablets include the records of treaties concluded between the King of Hittites and the King of Mitani at the beginning of the 14th century B.C. The gods of both the kingdoms are invoked as guardians of the treaties; and in the list of the gods invoked there are found the names of important Vedic deities, namely, Mitra, Varuṇa, Indra and Nāsatyau among the gods of Mitani. In the opinion of Prof. Konow, the extension of Indo-Aryan civilisation into Mesopotamia took place after the bulk of the Ṛgveda had come into existence.[2]

Close affinities between Avesta and the Vedic language are too well-known to need any elucidation. Besides, Greek, Latin and other European languages which are considered to be members of the Indo-European family of languages share a large number of cognate words with the Vedic language. For instance,

Latin *ignis* and Lithunian *Ugnis* are cognate with the Vedic word *Agni*. Similarly Greek *Zeuspater* and Latin Jupiter are cognate with the Vedic *Dyauṣpitā*. Although a common Indo-European origin for all cognate words found in Sanskrit, Greek and Latin is postulated by modern philologists and Sanskrit is not accepted as their primary source, it cannot be gainsaid that the oldest form of cognate words has been preserved in the Vedic language. Therefore, no student of comparative philology can fully understand the historical development of the languages comprised in the Indo-European family without an adequate knowledge of the Vedic language.

Moreover, a knowledge of the Vedic language is equally essential for a thorough understanding of the gradual development of later Indian languages including Classical Sanskrit, Pāli, Prākrit, Apabhraṃśa and modern Indian languages. For instance, without a study of the Vedic language, a student of later Indian languages would be unable to appreciate the semantic metamorphosis undergone by the word *Asura* which was originally employed in a good sense "giver of life", "possessor of life" etc. in the Vedic language as an adjective of certain Vedic deities such as Mitra, Varuṇa, Agni, Savitṛ[3], but which later came to denote "demon" etc. due to certain historical causes and hence provided the basis for coining a new word *sura* meaning "god". Similarly the word *Mṛga* denotes a wild animal in general in the Vedic language, but in later Sanskrit its denotation is restricted to a deer only. The instances of this type are a legion.

A correct knowledge of the Vedas is imperative not only for a proper understanding of the religious beliefs, rituals and cultural background of India and her neighbours, but also for a balanced appraisal of the religions, cultures, languages and literatures of several other countries of the world.[4] It is thus obvious that the Vedas which occupy a unique position in world literature have got universal importance from the point of view of religion, philosophy, literature, culture and comparative philology. Hence a correct appreciation of the religious, philosophical, literary and cultural advancement of different peoples of the world depends upon a correct interpretation of the Vedas. It is, therefore, very essential to exercise utmost care in interpreting the Vedas so that no confusion is created in the minds of the people about the Vedas through their incomplete, incorrect, arbitrary and haphazard interpretations and vague translations. A few instances are cited below to illustrate this point. If the Vedic phrase *svasurjāraḥ* (RV. VI, 55,4-5) is literally interpreted as "sister's paramour" in consonance with the later popular connotation of the words of this phrase[5], such an interpretation will create an erroneous impression on the minds of lay readers with regard to the moral standards of the Vedic Aryans. However, those Vedic scholars who are acquainted with the nuances of the Vedic idiom and thought know full well that the real meaning of this phrase is entirely different.[6]

Another striking instance of a similar misinterpretation is found in the case of the Vedic compound *pṛthu-parśavaḥ* (RV. VII,83,1). Some modern scholars are inclined to interpret the compound *pṛthu-parśavaḥ* as "Parthians and Persians". If this interpretation is accepted, it will materially alter the geographical and historical perspective of the Vedas. But as we have discussed this question in detail elsewhere, there is no worthwhile basis for such an assumption.[7] Several Vedic scholars who take the Ṛgvedic word *dāsa* as denoting a non-Aryan tribe interpret a number of Ṛgvedic passages as describing racial conflicts between the Aryans and the non-Aryan people. However, a close scrutiny of internal evidence available from the Vedas does not lend any support to this view.[8]

In order to attempt a thorough and dispassionate assessment of Vedic thought and culture, it is essential to have a complete understanding of the history and principles of Vedic interpretation so that every gratuitous assumption concerning the contents of the Vedas is not regarded as a valid interpretation of the Vedas, and only a scientific and systematic interpretation free from bias, prejudices and preconceptions may be accepted as the basis of Vedic studies. It would not be irrelevant to point out that even in the modern age of scientific and rational thinking there is no dearth of such scholars as do not hesitate to put an arbitrary and baseless interpretation on Vedic words according to their pre-conceived notions. The Vedas face the most serious danger from those so-called Vedists, historians and philologists who seek to read their own pre-conceived notions into the Vedas without paying any heed to the unexceptionable principles and traditions of Vedic interpretation. It is sheer injustice and open insult to the Vedas to say, as som people are wont to do, that the Vedas are capable of yielding all sorts of meanings according to the whims and fancies of interpreters.

It must be admitted without demur that the seers must have intended to express absolutely definite and unequivocal meanings through the words employed in the Vedas which are undoubtedly literary compositions of a very high order. It must be the endeavour of every interpreter of the Vedas to arrive at the definite meanings intended by the Vedic seers. Therefore, the main object of the present study is to trace the history of Vedic interpretations and to formulate such principles as would help the future interpreters of the Vedas in their formidable task of determining the precise meanings of obscure Vedic words and passages.

Notes and References

1. *See* my article "The Vedas and the Bhagavadgītā", in *Modern India: Heritage and Achievement*, pp. 427-432.
2. Cf Winternitz: History of Indian Literature, Vol. I, p. 306, footnote 2.
3. Cf. RV. V, 12, 1; 42, 11; VII, 65, 2.
4. In this connection, F. Max Müller's following observation on the universal importance of the Vedas is worth quoting: "In the history of the world the Veda fills a gap which no literary work in any other language could fill. It carries us back to times of which we have no records anywhere, and gives us the very words of a generation of men of whom otherwise we could form but the vaguest estimate by means of conjectures and inferences. As long as man continues to take an active interest in the history of his race and as long as we collect in libraries and museums the relics of former ages, the first place in that long row of books which contains the records of the Aryan branch of mankind, will belong for ever to the Ṛgveda" (A History of Ancient Sanskrit Literature, Varanasi, 1968, p. 57). Pischel and Geldner in the Introduction to their well-known work "Vedische Studien" have aptly remarked: "No one can have the least doubt that all scholarly studies of Sanskrit attain their highest culmination in the Veda."

5. Griffith translates this phrase as "sister's lover", while Wilson's translation of the same is "the gallant of his sister".
6. In RV. VI, 55, the phrase *svasur jārah* is employed as an adjective of the god Pūṣan who represents an aspect of the Sun. In relation to the goddess Uṣas "Dawn" the god Pūṣan "Sun" is described by the Vedic seer as *Jāra*. In the RV. the word *Jāra* is often used to denote its derivative meaning "consumer" and it is sometimes employed figuratively also in the sense of "a lover", but only its literal meaning "paramour" is prevalent in later Sanskrit. See in this connection my paper entitled "Interpretation of Jārah Kanīnām" (RV. I, 66, 8) in VIJ., Vol. III, Part I (March, 1965). So the phrase *svasur jārah* means "the consumer of his sister Dawn", i.e. the rising Sun who consumes Dawn with his appearance. Dawn is figuratively called the sister of the Sun, because the Vedic seers believe the Sun as well as Dawn to be the offspring of Heaven; Cf. my paper "The Figurative Use of Duhitṛ in the Ṛgveda" in Kshetresa Chandra Chattopadhyaya Felicitation Volume, pp. 523-532.
7. See in my work *Vaidika Vyākhyā-Vivechana*, pp. 165-166, annotations on RV. VII 83, 1.
8. See my paper *Dāsa Varṇa in the Ṛgveda* read at the Vedic Seminar held at Aligarh Muslim University in 1976 and published in the Journal of the Ganganatha Jha Kendriya Sanskrit Vidyapeetha, Vol. XXXIV (1-2), pp. 1-12; *Vaidika Vyākhyā-Vivechana*, pp. 90-91; Pandit K.C. Chattopadhyaya: *Studies in Vedic and Indo-Iranian Religion and Literature*, Vol. I, pp. 206ff.

2

The Problem of Vedic Interpretation

The word interpretation means to bring out clearly the intended meanings of the words employed by a speaker in a particular context. The problem of interpretation is not confined to only ancient texts like the Vedas. It can sometimes arise in respect of the works of contemporary authors also. However, in the case of such ancient works as the Vedas the problem of interpretation is much more serious, because a large number of words employed in them are of doubtful meaning and their context is equally obscure.

The problem of Vedic interpretation is not of recent origin. More than 2500 years ago when Yāska composed his Nirukta (a commentary on certain selected Vedic words), the problem of Vedic interpretation was as intricate as it is today. Even prior to Yāska the meaning of numerous Vedic words and passages had become so much obscure that some persons began to doubt seriously whether the Vedic verses convey any sense at all. In order to refute this school of thought, Yāska refers to the viewpoint of one *Kautsa* who boldly declares that the Vedic Mantras convey no sense.[1] Yāska first reproduces the arguments advanced by Kautsa, then refutes them one by one, and finally proves his own view-point ridiculing Kautsa's gross ignorance about the Vedic lore.

Now the question arises whether Kautsa who openly decried the Vedic mantras as obscure, meaningless and contradictory was an historical entity or a fictitious name invented by Yāska to castigate obliquely the heretical critics of the Vedas.[2] In the opinion of Dr. L. Sarup, Kautsa was an historical entity and the leader of a movement which may be described as something akin to materialistic rationalism.[3] Dr. Sarup discountenances the opposite view that the name Kautsa has been invented by Yāska as a convenient method of giving expression to Vedic scepticism, for Yāska in Dr. Sarup's opinion could have very well employed such terms as *eke, ekam, aparam* etc. with regard to the above-mentioned controversy if it had not been associated with a particular individual, i.e. *Kautsa.*

An examination of Yāska's style of introducing controversial issues in the Nirukta reveals at least *three* different methods adopted by him. In some cases he mentions definite names of scholars advocating a particular view-point.[4] In other cases he refers to particular schools of thought,[5] whereas in case of still other controversies he simply alludes to divergent points of view in such general terms as *eke*, etc.[6] Śākaṭāyana and Gārgya whose views are cited by Yāska on controversial questions of grammar are well known authorities on the subject and there is no doubt about their authenticity.[7] Although Audumbarāyaṇa's view is not referred to elsewhere in Vedic literature, there is not much difficulty in accepting him as an ancient grammarian known to Yāska. The Bṛhaddevatā testifies to the authenticity of some other ancient teachers such as *Aurṇavābha, Krauṣṭuki, Gālava, Śākapūṇi,* whose views are cited by Yāska in connection with the derivation and meaning of certain words. However, the real difficulty arises in regard to the identity of *Kautsa* who is shown in the Nirukta as a detractor of the sacred Vedas, while elsewhere in Vedic and post-Vedic literature *Kautsa* is highly spoken of as a venerable teacher. Could a descendant of the illustrious seer *Kutsa* be so disrespectful to and ignorant of the Vedic lore as depicted by Yāska ? In the whole gamut of Vedic and epic literature there is no other trace of a *Kautsa* who denounces the Vedas.

In ancient Sanskrit literature we come across two conflicting traditions concerning *Kautsa.* According to one tradition which appears to be earlier, *Kautsa's* name is reverentially alluded to as that of a venerable teacher, while the other tradition speaks of *Kautsa* contemptuously and brackets him with a Śūdra. In keeping with the earlier tradition the Sat.Br.(X.6,5,9) mentions *Kautsa* as an ancient preceptor who was the teacher of Māṇḍavya and pupil of Māhitthi. The Asv. S.S. thrice refers to the opinion of a teacher called *Kautsa* on certain matters concerning the Vedic ritual.[8] The Gobh. G.S. refers to the view of a teacher named Kautsa on the performance of *Aṣṭakās*.[9] The Ap.D.S.(I,19,4) speaks of *Kautsa* as an authority on Dharma, and in another passage (1,28,1) of the same work *Kautsa's* view is alluded to along with that of Hārīta, Kaṇva and Puṣkarasādin on the definition of a thief. According to the Mbh., an erudite old Brāhmaṇa named *Kautsa* officiated as Udgātṛ priest at the snake-sacrifice of King Janamejaya.[10] Another passage of the Mbh. informs us that King Bhagīratha gave his daughter Haṃsī in marriage to *Kautsa*.[11] The Raghuvaṃśa of Kālidāsa mentions Varatantu's pupil *Kautsa* who on completion of his education approached King Raghu for gifts to be presented to his teacher Varatantu.[12] *Kautsa* mentioned in the foregoing tradition is explained by the commentators as a descendant of the seer Kutsa.[13] It is inconceivable that a descendant of the famous seer Kutsa reverentially alluded to in the above-mentioned texts could have denied any value to the Vedas and characterised the Vedic Mantras as obscure, meaningless and contradictory.

Now let us turn to the other tradition which speaks of *Kautsa* contemptuously and brackets him with a Śūdra. The Bhar.S.S. cites an earlier text (probably a lost Brāhmaṇa) which says that Soma stalks required for a Soma sacrifice should be purchased from a Kautsa,[14] and according to another view mentioned in the next sūtra of the same text Soma may be purchased from a Śūdra.[15] The same rule regarding the purchase of Soma is found differently worded in the Kat. S.S., and Vaikh. S.S. which lay down that the seller of Soma may be a *Kautsa* or a Śūdra.[16] The Ap. S.S. allows the purchase of Soma from a Kautsa or a non-Brāhmaṇa who in this context is interpreted by the commentators as a Śūdra.[17] The Man. S.S. contains the same rule as given in the Kat. S.S. etc. (see note 16) but reads Kutsa instead of *Kautsa*.[18] As regards the derivation of the word Kautsa employed in connection with the sale of Soma, Dhūrtasvāmin and Rudradatta, the commentators of the Ap. S.S., explain it as a person of *Kutsa*-gotra, i.e. a descendant of *Kutsa*, whereas Karka, the commentator of the Kat. S.S., explains Kautsa as a person doing contemptible acts :

"*Kutsitam Karma karoti iti Kautsaḥ.*" However, Gopinātha Bhaṭṭa, the commentator of the Hir. S.S. offers both the above mentioned explanations : "*Sa Cha Brāhmaṇaḥ Kautsaḥ Kutsa-gotraḥ kutsita-karmā vā.*"

Since the act of selling Soma has been condemned as sinful and blamable in the Smṛtis,[19] it is obvious that the word *Kautsa* in the context of selling Soma has been employed by the Sūtrakāras to denote a contemptible person of a higher caste (probably a Brāhmaṇa) who was engaged in the blamable act of selling Soma. But this role of *Kautsa* is incompatible with the use of the same word in the other works of ancient Sanskrit literature to denote a venerable teacher and acknowledged authority on matters of Dharma. This consideration prompted the commentators to suggest an alternative explanation of *Kautsa* as a person doing contemptible acts. However, the alternative explanation offered by the commentators appears to be arbitrary and far-fetched, and the obvious explanation of *Kautsa* is a descendant of *Kutsa.* It leads us to the inference that the word *Kautsa* denoting a contemptible person should be derived not from the celebrated seer *Kutsa* but from another *Kutsa* who is alluded to as an adversary of Indra in the RV. and the Brāhmaṇas. Apart from the seer *Kutsa* and his descendants (see note 13) favoured by Indra, another *Kutsa* who incurs Indra's wrath is mentioned in ths RV.[20] According to a legend narrated in the Jaim. Br. and P.Br., *Kutsa Aurava* murdered Upāgu Sauśravasa who offered a secrifice to Indra in violation of *Kutsa's* proclamation.[21] According to the Jaim. Br. version of this legend,[22] *Kutsa Aurava*, who closely resembled Indra on account of his birth from Indra's thigh and who went to Indra's wife Śachī in the guise of Indra due to his close resemblance, was dismissed from Indra's service as a charioteer and turned into a *malla* "wrestler".

It is quite clear from the foregoing that according to Vedic traditions there were two distinct *Kutsas* in ancient times. *Kutsa Āṅgirasa* was a famous Vedic seer who enjoyed Indira's favours and whose descendants (*Kautsas*) were highly respected and regarded as authorities on matters of Vedic rites and customs in the Brāhmaṇas and the Vedāṅgas; whereas *Kutsa Aurava*, who hailed from a family of *mallas* (wrestlers) and abhorred Vedic sacrifices, had an antipathy to the Vedic god Indra who is said to have humbled him on several occasions. This fact raises a strong presumption in favour of the view that a *Kautsa* who is mentioned in the Śrauta-Sūtras as a despicable Soma-Vendor and who is ridiculed by Yāska as an ignorant person denying meaning and authority to the Vedas may be regarded as a descendant of the wrestler *Kutsa Aurava.* Sanskrit literature yields no evidence in support of Dr. Sarup's thesis that *Kautsa* who denied all value to the Vedas was an eminent scholar or some great personality or the exponent of some philosophical system or the leader of a movement of materialistic rationalism. All available evidence points to the conclusion that Yāska has purposely chosen an ignorant and contemptible wrestler *Kautsa* to ridicule obliquely those pseudo-scholars who make pretensions to learning and denounce the Vedas without acquiring any knowledge of them. This inference is evident from Yāska's concluding assertion in refutation of Kautsa's contention, where Yāska emphatically asserts:[23] "It is not the fault of a post if a blind person does not see it. It is the fault of the person concerned. Just as among the country-folk a man with some technical knowledge becomes distinguished, so among the scholars of the traditional Vedic lore only a scholar of profound knowledge is worthy of praise."

Although Yāska cogently refutes the arguments advanced by *Kautsa* about the meaninglessness of Vedic Mantras, yet frequent allusions in the Nirukta to the divergent interpretations of Vedic words and passages show that the problem of Vedic interpretation had already assumed serious proportions.[24] Had there been no difficulty in the interpretation of such Vedic words and passages, their interpretation would have been unanimous. But it is not so. Moreover, it was due to the difficulty of interpretation that the Nighaṇṭu was compiled as an aid to it. In two stanzas quoted in the Nirukta Yāska censures those persons who have learnt the Vedic texts by rote without understanding their meaning.[25] It shows that by the time of Yāska the Vedic texts had become so obscure that it entailed special training and efforts on the part of learners to understand their meaning. This is why Yāska declares that it is not possible to understand the sense of Vedic Mantras without a study of the Nirukta.[6]

Difficulty in understanding the meaning of the Vedic Mantras arises mainly from the fact that the Vedic texts contain a number of rare, obsolete and obscure words which are not met with in the later language. Two hundred and seventy-nine such obscure Vedic words have been compiled in the Fourth Chapter of the Nighaṇṭu.

It appears that Yāska and his predecessors did not inherit any uninterrupted tradition of Vedic interpretation handed down by ancient teachers. It is doubtful whether any definite and dependable system of Vedic interpretation had been evolved in very early times. Even if any such system or tradition had ever existed, it seems to have already become extinct prior to the composition of the Brāhmaṇas, because due to the lack of any definite tradition or system of Vedic interpretation the Brāhmaṇas advance fanciful and wild conjectures with regard to the meaning of Vedic passages.[27]

Another important problem of Vedic interpretation is that since the language of the Vedas and especially that of the Ṛgveda is highly developed, polished and often figurative[28], any attempt to present a literal translation of the Vedic hymns according to the meanings assigned to common words in the later Sanskrit is bound to lead to a gross misinterpretation of the Vedas. The seers have carefully and purposely selected each word of their hymns after a thorough consideration of the subtleties and shades of the meanings of appropriate words. The seers are very fond of employing figurative speech, and the use of metaphor is quite common in the Vedic language. This peculiarity of the Vedic style has been noticed in the Brāhmaṇas which observe[29] that "the gods love recondite speech and abhor direct statements".

It is mainly due to the figurative use of the Vedic idiom that even, when there is no doubt about the literal meanings of the words employed in the Vedic verses, their real import remains vague and doubtful. In this connection Max Müller has aptly remarked[30] : "The Vedic hymns on the contrary, even when we understand every word of them, remain very obscure in their structure or construction." It is obvious that if the

Vedic verses are literally translated in accordance with the usage of classical Sanskrit, such a literal translation creates confusion, and results in sheer absurdity. A literal translation of the following Ṛgvedic verse would amply illustrate this point:

Chatvā́ri śṛ́ṅgā tráyo asya pā́dā
dvé śīrṣé saptá hástāso asya.
Trídhā baddhó vṛṣabhó roravīti
mahó devó mártyā̆ ā́ viveśa. *(R.V. IV, 58, 3)*

Although there is no doubt about the literal meaning of any of the words employed in this verse, yet the import of the verse is far from clear and its literal translations attempted by several scholars have failed to convey the real sense of the verse. For instance, H.H. Wilson's translation of the verse is as follows:

Four are his horns; three are his feet; his heads are two, his hands are seven; the triple-bound showerer (of benefits) roars aloud: the mighty deity has entered amongst men.

R.T.H. Griffith's following translation of the verse is not much different from the above:

Four are his horns, three are the feet that bear him; his heads are two, his hands are seven in number. Bound with a triple band the steer roars loudly; the mighty God hath entered into mortals.

Similarly K.F. Geldner's translation of the verse is almost identical with that of Griffith. It is obvious that so long as the allegory implied in this verse is not clear its literal translation is of no avail. Since very early times the allegorical implication of this verse has been interpreted by the commentators and translators in various ways according to their predilections and preconceived notions as we shall see below.

The tendency to interpret the Vedas according to one's own inclination in utter disregard of the predominant tenor of Vedic thought and usage is the greatest obstacle to their correct interpretation. In fact it is this chronic tendency of subjective interpretation which has given rise to various schools of Vedic interpretation since very early times. So Yāska in this connection mentions *Yājñikas* "ritualists", *Nairuktas* "etymologists", *Aitihāsikas* "mythologists", *Parivrājakas* "mystics" and *Naidānas*. Besides, some ancient authorities on Sanskrit grammar and law also seem to have tried to project their own view-point in Vedic interpretation, as we shall see below. Most of the ancient Indian commentators generally follow the ritualistic and etymological schools of Vedic interpretation. However, the views of the other schools of interpreters are also briefly alluded to in their commentaries.

As regards the Western interpreters of the Vedas, in the beginning of Sanskrit studies in the West they regarded Sāyaṇa's commentary on the Ṛgveda as their principal guide, and H.H. Wilson's English translation of the Ṛgveda based on Sāyaṇa's commentary is a telling example of this attitude. However, as Sanskrit studies made further progress, critical Western scholars discovered the shortcomings of Sāyaṇa's commentary and decided to strike their own independent path in the realm of Vedic interpretation. The celebrated German scholar Rudolf Roth who successfully collaborated with O. Böhtlingk in the preparation of the seven-volume *Sanskrit Wörterbuch* was a pioneer in this field. Rejecting ancient Indian commentators as reliable guides in the matter of Vedic interpretation, Roth propounded the thesis that the Veda must be interpreted with the help of its own words and therefore an interpreter of the Veda should endeavour to ascertain the original meaning of the Veda intended by the seers themselves. With this object in view, Roth compared relevant Vedic passages to determine independently the meanings of obscure Vedic words. The results of his researches are embodied in the *Sanskrit Wörterbuch*. Deductive method of Vedic interpretation is accepted in principle by all modern scholars, and all the Western translators and interpreters of the Vedas who came after Roth claim to follow this method. However, the translations of the Vedas attempted by modern scholars do not fully justify their claim of objectivity and leave much to be desired.

It has been frankly admitted by eminent modern scholars that the translators of the Vedas fail to convey the real meaning of the Vedas intended by the seers. Max Müller makes the following observation in regard to his own translation of selected Vedic hymns:[31] "I feel convinced that on many points my translation is liable to correction, and will sooner or later be replaced by a more satisfactory one. It is difficult to explain to those who have not themselves worked at the Veda, how it is that we may understand almost every word, yet we find it so difficult to lay hold of a whole chain of connected thought, and to discover expressions that will not throw a wrong shade on the original features of the ancient words of the Veda. We have, on the one hand, to avoid giving to our translations too modern a character, or paraphrasing instead of translating; while, on the other, we cannot retain expressions which, if literally rendered in English or any modern tongue, would have an air of quaintness or absurdity totally foreign to the intention of the ancient poets. There are, as all Vedic scholars know, whole verses which, as yet, yield no sense whatever. There are words the meaning of which we can only guess."

A very telling example of sheer absurdity resulting from a literal translation of a Vedic verse is cited below. In a pre-wedding rite described in the Śāṅkhāyana-Gṛhya-Sūtra 1, 6, 6, the Āchārya places a vessel full of water on the head of the bride and blesses her with the formula: "*prajām tvayi dadhāmi, paśūn tvayi dadhāmi. . . .*" H. Oldenberg has translated this formula as follows:[32] "Offspring I put into thee, cattle I put into thee." This translation is not only absurd but also misleading. It should have been actually translated as: "Offspring I bestow on thee, cattle wealth I bestow on thee."

Expressing his disgust at inaccurate, absurd and conjectural translations of the Ṛgveda, M. Winternitz aptly remarks[33]: "The outsider who takes a translation of the Ṛgveda in his hand often wonders that so much in these hymns is unpoetical, indeed unintelligible and senseless. But the reason is frequently only that the translators do not content themselves with translating that which is intelligible, but that they think they *must* translate *every thing*, even that which has up till now not been rightly interpreted."

It is an admitted fact that inspite of important researches conducted during the last hundred and fifty years, the Vedas have not yet been interpreted in their entirety. In this connection Ralph T.H. Griffith rightly observes[34]: "But it must not be supposed that European students and interpreters of the Veda claim anything like infallibility, completeness, or finality for the results to which their researches have led them. All modern scholars will allow that many hymns are dark as the darkest oracle, that, as Professor Max Müller says, there are whole verses which, as yet yield no sense whatever, and words the meaning of which we can only guess." Giving expression to a similar view on this point, A. Barth remarks:[35] "In spite of all our efforts at exegesis, at philology, and at linguistics, the vocabulary has none-the-less remained uncertain and in a floating state for the greater part; and this is the case, not merely with rare and unique words, of words with an obscure derivation, or which have fallen out of use, but with words of very frequent occurrence, of which the etymology is not doubtful and which still continue in the language." M. Winternitz also expresses a similar opinion on this problem:[36] "We must here remember the important fact that the Ṛgveda is as yet by no means fully explained. There are, indeed, a large number of hymns, the explanation of which is as certain as that of any other Indian text. But on the other hand, there are many hymns and very many verses and isolated passages of the Ṛgveda whose right meaning is still in the highest degree doubtful."

An intensive study of the Vedas has made the Western scholars fully aware of the difficulties inherent in Vedic interpretation and also of the shortcomings and limitations of the translations attempted hitherto. H. Oldenberg has very aptly and succinctly summed up such difficulties as follows[37]: "When we cast a retrospective glance on the accumulated mass of the philological labours, described so far above, which had been undertaken for a popular understanding of the Veda, it is certain that in what we have said so far we shall have given expression to an exact estimate of the volume of what is attainable in the Veda. We can never understand in all their details what the Vedic poets had said and had wanted to say. Many of the words in the Vedic vocabulary with their finer shades of meanings and many even according to their approximate sense would remain for us unintelligible. And all these difficulties arise on account of the fact that the authors of these texts have never used the kind of linguistic expressions to which we are accustomed. They can never be overcome and a definite idea of the contents of the texts cannot be had by those who do not know anything about them ; and it is also certain that the Vedic poets wanted to do something which was altogether different in so many ways from what we are used to, viz. propounding of riddles, playing hide-and-seek with the meaning, pleasing themselves and the gods with highly artificial expressions and thoughts. For a translation of the RV. with a rendering of every word which is equally appropriate everywhere and which is capable of reproducing the sense of every verse, is, generally speaking, not to be hoped for.''

In their arrogance some of the Western scholars were biased against Indian interpreters and sought to belittle their contributions to Vedic exegesis. For instance, R. Roth expressed his biased view that a qualified European is more competent to determine the right meaning of the Ṛgveda than a Brāhmaṇa interpreter, for the judgment of the former is unfettered by theological bias and he is equipped with historical outlook, scientific scholarship and a wider intellectual horizon.[38] But there were other Western Sanskritists who thought that an Indian scholar fully conversant with Indian background can interpret the Veda better than a Western scholar. In this connection we may refer to the opinion of Pischel and Geldner that since the Veda is an Indian book a Vedic scholar acquainted with Indian literature, climatic conditions and traditions can better interpret the Veda.[39] Even H. Oldenberg, who generally decries Indian commentators, points as follows to the drawback of those Western interpreters of the Veda who never trod on the Indian soil[40]: "The old generation of the founders of Vedic philosophy, Roth being the pioneer amongst them, had done their best; the freshness of their intellectual power and their initiative began now to slacken. New workers came forward. To almost all of them—this was the case also with their predecessors—one thing was common, that they never had trodden upon the Indian soil. The intellectuals who were working in India, because of the situations which they held, were usually occupied with modern literature. The Veda, therefore, fell to the share of those who remained in Europe, in a preponderant measure to the share of the German and French scholars, and side by side with them also of the American scholars."

It is frankly admitted by several scholars that the distortion of Vedic interpretation has resulted mainly from two factors, viz. first the lack of proper understanding of Vedic milieu and Indian background, and secondly the attempt to read one's preconceived notions into the Veda. The Western scholars who boast of their scientific approach to the Veda have been criticised for such shortcomings. For instance, the eminent French scholar Abel Bergaigne who accuses Roth and other Western scholars of misinterpreting the Veda remarks[41]: "M. Roth will kindly allow me to reply that the translation which he has proposed presents at least in some portions a very clear example of the way how the sense of Vedic expressions, which are absolutely clear and have been preserved perfectly (he does not propose himself any correction for this passage), might be conceived by the European exegesis, when it is under an obsession to remove all bizarre things and to bring the hymns of the ṛṣis in line with their own aesthetic sense, in a word to transform their theosophic lucubrations into small pieces of simple and sane poetry. I have to add that most often it is this same spirit which makes people discover textual corruption in texts which are perfectly free from corruptions, when the other expedients of which a misuse has been made by them even to a greater degree, such as multiplication of the meanings of words and the hypothesis of homonyms, do not suffice to suppress from the Vedic texts something which they do not want to see there."

It follows from the foregoing that the interpretations of the Vedas attempted hitherto both by Indian and Western scholars cannot be regarded as perfect and final and leave much to be desired. Under such circumstances it would be rash to jump to historical conclusions on the basis of available Vedic translations which are in part not only inaccurate but also misleading. However, it is a pity that inspite of such an unsatisfactory state of Vedic interpretations and defective translations many modern historians are inclined to pass judgement on Vedic history and culture on the basis of these translations without ever casting a glance at the original Vedic texts. In this connection the case of Stuart Piggot is worthy of note. Candidly admitting the obvious difficulty in using the Ṛgveda as a source of information on the material culture of the Vedic Aryans, he observes:[42] "In the hymns the transition from the more or less literal to the wholly metaphorical is often sudden, and frequently almost imperceptible. The physical war-chariot of an Aryan chieftain turns, with bewildering rapidity, into the noon-day sun; the boisterous young cattle-raiders are suddenly the four winds of heaven. And the accident of survival of words descriptive of aspects of material culture is really dependent on their adaptability to religious metaphor and their appropriateness to the warrior aristocracy for whom the hymns were composed." Inspite of this observation Mr. Piggot's statements about the history and culture of the Vedic Aryans are based mainly on Griffith's English translation of the Ṛgveda.[43] The case of Sir Leonard Woolley is still far more astounding. Without even going through the Ṛgveda, he has passed the following strictures on this great work on the basis of second-hand information:[44] "The Ṛgveda is the epic of destruction of one of the great cultures of ancient world."

It is entirely due to the wrong and misleading translations of the Ṛgveda that eminent scholars like Sir Leonard Woolley do not hesitate to pass such derogatory remarks about it. Therefore, the problem of Vedic interpretation calls for fresh efforts to tackle it on a historical and scientific basis.

Notes and References

1. Nirukta I, 15 –*Anarthakā hi mantrāḥ*.
2. See my paper entitled "On Anti-Vedic Kautsa quoted in the Nirukta" presented at the Golden Jubilee Session of All-India Oriental Conference held at Poona in 1978 and published in the *Saṃskṛta-Vimarśāḥ*, Vol. IV, Parts I & II, pp. 173ff.
3. Introduction to the Nighaṇṭu and the Nirukta.
4. Cf. Nirukta I, 1-*Audumbarāyaṇa*; I, 2-*Vārṣyāyaṇi*; I, 3.12-*Śākaṭāyana*; I, 3.12-*Gārgya*.
5. Ibid. II, 16; XII, 1-*Aitihāsikas*; VI, 9; VII, 12-*Naidānas*; I, 12; II, 8.14-

16; III, 8.14 etc.--*Nairuktas*; II, 8-*Parivrājakas*; V, 11; VII, 4.23; XI, 29.31; XIII, 9-*Yājñikas*; IX, 5; XIII, 9-*Vaiyākaraṇas*.

6. Ibid. III, 4.5 etc.
7. See *Vedic Index*, *s.v*.
8. Asv. S.S. I, 2, 5; 4, 6; VII, 1, 19.
9. Gobh. G.S. III, 10, 4, *Cf. India of Vedic Kalpa-Sūtras*, pp. 19 and 415.
10. Mbh. I, 53, 6.
11. Ibid. XII, 137, 26.
12. Raghuvaṃśa V, 1.
13. Cf. Mallinātha on the Raghuvaṃśa V, 1; Pāṇini IV, 1, 114, *Kutsa* is mentioned as a Vedic seer in the RV. (see *Vedic Index*, s.v.); AV. IV, 29, 5; P. Br. XIII, 6, 9; Nirukta III, 11; Bṛhad-devatā III, 125; and Kātyāyana's Sarvānukramaṇī. The Ṛgvedic hymns I, 94-115 and IX, 97, 45-48 are ascribed to the seer *Kutsa Āṅgirasa*. The hymns ascribed to *Kutsa* are styled as Kautsa in the Brāhmaṇas and the Vedāṅgas; *Cf.* P. Br. IX, 2, 21 etc.; Kṣudra-Sūkta I, 5 etc.; Ārṣeya-Brāhmaṇa I, 9, 4 etc. The RV. VII, 25, 5 mentions *Kutsas*, the descendants of *Kutsa*; Cf. Pāṇini II, 4, 65.
14. Bhar. S.S. X, 14, 7.
15. Ibid. X, 14, 8.
16. Kat. S.S. VII, 6, 2; Hir. S.S. VII, 1, 72; Vaikh. S.S. XII, 5.
17. Ap. S.S. X, 20, 12.
18. Man S.S. II, 1, 3, 51.
19. See quotations cited from various Smṛtis in Gopīnātha-Bhaṭṭa's commentary on the Hir. S.S. VII, 1, 72; Manu III, 158.180; X. 80; Yaj. I, 165.223.
20. RV. I, 53, 10; II, 14.7; V, 18, 13; VIII, 53, 2.
21. Jaim. Br. III, 199-202; P. Br. XIV, 6, 8.
22. Jaim. Br. III, 199-200.
23. Nirukta I, 16.
24. Cf. Nirukta II, 8.16; IV, 15.18; VI, 28; VII, 22-23; VIII, 6.
25. Ibid. I, 18; Cf. RV. X. 71, 5 cited in Nirukta I, 19.
26. Nirukta I, 15-*athāpīdam antareṇa* mantreṣvartha-pratyayo na vidyate.
27. See in this connection the following observation of F, Max Müller: "But there is throughout the Brāhmaṇas such a complete misunderstanding of the original intention of the Vedic hymns, that we can hardly understand how such an estrangement took place, unless there had been at some time or other a sudden and violent break in the chain of tradition. The authors of the Brāhmaṇas evidently imagined that those ancient hymns were written simply for the sake of their sacrifices, and whatever interpretation they thought fit to assign to those acts, the same, they supposed, had to be borne out by the hymns. This idea has vitiated the whole system of Indian exegesis. Not only was the true nature of the gods, as conceived by the early poets, completely lost sight of, but new gods were actually created out of words

which were never intended as names of divine beings." (op. cit. pp. 392-93).

28. In this connection the following observation of A.A. Macdonell is noteworthy: "On the very threshold of Indian literature more than three thousand years ago, we are confronted with a body of lyrical poetry which, although far older than the literary monuments of any other branch of Indo-European family, is already distinguished by refinement and beauty of thought, as well as by skill in the handling of language and metre (A History of Sanskrit Literature, 5th Edition, p.29).M. Bloomfield has also made a similar observation on this point: "The entire Vedic tradition, the Ṛgveda not excepted, presents rather the conclusion than the beginning of a long period of literary activity. Conventionality of subject-matter, style, form (metre), etc. betray themselves at every step." (SBE., Vol. 42, p. lxiii).
29. Sat. Br. VI, 1, 1, 2-parokṣa-kāmā hi devāḥ; Gopatha-Brāhmaṇa I, 2, 21-parokṣa-priyā iva hi devā bhavanti pratyakṣa-dviṣaḥ; Cf. Ait. Br. III, 33.
30. *The Vedas*, p. 49. Cf. *Ṛgvedānukramaṇī* (edited by C. Kunhan Raja) Part II, p. 80-Jñāteṣvapi padārtheṣu Vākyārtha-parikalpanam, aśakyam ṛkṣu bahvīṣu narairakṛtabuddhibhiḥ.
31. SBE, Vol. 32, preface to the first edition, p. xxxii.
32. SBE., Vol. 29, p. 22.
33. A History of Indian Literature, Vol. I, p. 69.
34. Preface to the First Edition of "The Hymns of the Ṛgveda", p. xviii.
35. Journal des Savants, March 1896.
36. Op. cit., p. 69.
37. *Vedic Research* (English translation by V.G. Paranjpe), pp. 33-34.
38. Cf. Macdonell's "A History of Sanskrit Literature" (5th edition), p. 63.
39. Vedische Studien, Vol. I, p. xxxii.
40. Op. cit., p. 7.
41. *Vedic Religion* (English translation by V G. Paranjpe), Vol. III, p. 329.
42. *Prehistoric India*, Middlesex, 1950, p. 258.
43. Op. cit., p. 244.
44. History of Mankind, Vol. I (Cultural and Scientific Development, Pre History and Beginnings of Civilisation, London, 1963, p. 389).

3

The Yājñika School of Vedic Interpretation

The problem of Vedic interpretation, as we have pointed out above, is not of recent origin, and since very early times scholars have sought to interpret the Vedas in different ways. It shows that, as no uninterrupted reliable tradition of Vedic interpretation was handed down alongwith the Vedic verses, the inheritors of these texts began to advance their own conjectures with regard to the sense of the Vedas. Therefore, in the absence of an authentic tradition of Vedic interpretation the tendency to make surmises and read pre-conceived notions into the Vedas led to the emergence of different schools of Vedic interpretation. Already by the time of Yāska at least the following five schools of Vedic interpretation, namely, those of the Yājñikas, Nairuktas, Aitihāsikas, Parivrājakas, and Naidānas had come into existence (see note 5 of Chapter 2).

As most of the Vedic interpretations attempted by both ancient and modern exegetes fall into these five categories, it is important to trace their history and make a correct appraisal of each of these ancient schools of Vedic interpretation.

It cannot be gainsaid that the Yājñika School of Vedic exegesis which puts ritualistic interpretations on the Vedas is the most ancient and predominant among all the existing schools of Vedic interpretation. It has got a very long and uninterrupted tradition. The earliest attempt to put ritualistic interpretation on the Vedic Mantras is discernible in the compilation of the Yajurveda (literally meaning "the Veda of the Ritualistic Formulas") in which a considerable number of verses from the Ṛgveda had been adapted for sacrificial purposes.

It appears that since very early times there were two distinct traditions of Vedic studies. According to the original tradition, the Vedic verses together with their original meanings were handed down from generation to generation, and the application of reason to the determination of meaning of Vedic stanzas must have been a forte of this tradition as indicated in some ancient texts.[1] In the other tradition the Vedic verses were committed to memory and recited as part of worship performed in various forms. That mere recitation of Vedic verses was also regarded as a form of worship in the time of the Ṛgveda is clearly evident from several Ṛgvedic verses cited in the Asv. G.S.[2] At a very early stage in the development of Vedic religion, the offering of oblations in the fire to the gods was accompanied by the recitation of Vedic verses. When the Vedic ritual developed further, the priests felt the need of a collection of verses and formulas to be recited at the performance of sacrifices; and this necessity led to the compilation of certain Ṛgvedic verses and ritualistic formulas in the form of the Yajurveda. The inclusion of certain Ṛgvedic verses in the Yajurveda did not affect the independent entity of the Ṛgveda, and the priest who recited the selected Ṛgvedic verses at the sacrifices was called *hotṛ*.

Once the texts of the Ṛgveda and the Yajurveda had been finally fixed, it was not possible to make any alterations or additions in them on any ground including the exigencies of the ever-growing ritual. However, the priests were hard pressed to find suitable Vedic Mantras to meet the needs of their growing rituals, for the Vedic people held the belief that a sacrifice which was accompanied by the recitation of Vedic verses yielded desired results. The orthodox Hindus still cherish this belief. The Aitareya-Brāhmana and the Gopatha-Brāhmaṇa refer to this belief in their statement that if a sacrificial act is accompanied by the recitation of a Ṛgvedic verse or a Yajus formula expressing the sense of the concerned act, that harmony (of act and speech) being the perfection of sacrificial performance leads to its success.[3] Yāska in his Nirukta 1, 16 cites this passage of the Gopatha-Brāhmaṇa differently, and elsewhere expresses the same idea in a different way emphasizing that on account of the temporary nature of human knowledge, a Vedic Mantra is the cause of success of a sacrificial act.[4] In keeping with this belief the ritualists strove hard to pick up such Vedic Mantras as could fit into the ritual in hand on the slightest similarity of sound or sense between a ritual act and a Mantra.

After the inclusion of certain Ṛgvedic verses in the Yajurveda, the Brāhmaṇas which were concerned exclusively with the exposition of Vedic sacrifices made further advance in the ritual application of Vedic Mantras and attempted ritualistic interpretation of such Mantras as had originally nothing to do with the ritual, as aptly pointed out by Max Müller in the following words (see note 27 of Chapter 2): "The authors of the Brāhmaṇas evidently imagined that those ancient hymns were written simply for the sake of their sacrifices, and whatever interpretation they thought fit to assign to these acts, the same, they supposed, had to be borne out by the hymns. This idea has vitiated the whole system of Indian exegesis. It might be justified, perhaps, if it had only been applied to the purely sacrificial hymns, particularly to those which are found in the Saṃhitās of the Sāmdveda and Yajurveda. The Ṛgveda too has experienced the same treatment at the hands of Indian commentators, and the stream of tradition, flowing from the fountain-head of the original poets, has, like the waters of the Sarasvatī, disappeared in the sands of a desert."

The tendency to employ Vedic Mantras at the performance of all sorts of rituals unconnected with them reached its culmination in the time of the Kalpa-Sūtras. The authors of these ritualistic treatises invariably prescribe the recitation of a Mantra at the performance of each ritual described in their works irrespective of the fact whether the Mantra in question is actually concerned with that ritual or not. It is hardly necessary to point out here that a large number of rituals described in the Kalpa-Sūtras are a later development and have got no connection whatsoever with the Vedic Mantras. In the absence of any real connection between a Mantra and a ritual, the ritualists prescribe the recitation of a Mantra at the performance of a ritual on the basis of a superficial similarity of a word, or a syllable or even a letter between a Mantra and a ritual. For instance, several Gṛhya-Sūtras prescribe the recitation of the Ṛgvedic verse (IV, 39, 6) beginning with the compound *dadhikrāvṇah* to accompany the ritual of eating curds (*dadhi*) at the performance of Upanayana, Upākarman and wedding rites, on the basis of a mere similarity of sounds between *dadhi* and *dadhikrāvṇah*, although the verse in question has got nothing to do with the eating of curds. Similarly the occurrence of the words *śaṃ naḥ* in the beginning of the Ṛgvedic verse X, 9, 4 suggested to the ritualists a sort of phonetic similarity between *śam naḥ* and *śani* and therefore prompted the author of the Jaimini-Gṛhya-Sūtra to prescribe the recitation of this Mantra at the performance of a ritual intended for the propitiation of *Śani* (the planet Saturn), although the verse in question is in no way connected with *Śani* nor does the word *Śani* occur anywhere in the Vedic literature.

The insistence of the authors of the Kalpa-Sūtras on employing, as far as possible, the Mantras contained in their own Vedic Saṃhitās for the performance of rituals led to a biased and incorrect ritualistic interpretation of the Vedic Mantras. For instance, the Asv. G.S. 1, 20, 8 prescribes the recitation of the Ṛgvedic hemistich (III, 8, 4) *Yuvā suvāsāḥ parivīta āgāt* at the performance of the Upanayana ceremony of a young boy with the obvious purpose of conveying the idea "that a well-dressed young boy has come (for the Upanayana)". However, it is quite clear from the tenor of the hymn (RV. III, 8) that neither there is any reference to the Upanayana ceremony in this hemistich nor does the word *Yuvā* here signify a young boy. The Ait. Br. (II, 2), the Kaus. Br. (X, 2) and the Tait. Br. (III, 6, 1, 3) employ the hymn in question at the ritual of anointing a sacrificial post; and the Ait. Br. in this connection offers the exegetical explanation: "The Youth well clad is the breath, for it is enclosed with the bodily parts." In keeping with the ritual application of the hymn in the above-mentioned Brāhmaṇas and the Asv. S.S. and also Kātyāyana's view in the Sarvānukramaṇī that the hymn is the eulogy of a sacrificial post, Veṅkaṭamādhava and Sāyaṇa followed by most of the modern scholars such as Griffith and Geldner explain the word *Yuvā* of this verse as a strong sacrificial post. It is another question whether the word *Yuvā* here stands for a sacrificial post or not. But there is no doubt that the verse under discussion has got no connection whatever with the Upanayana ceremony and that the word *Yuvā* has been employed in a figurative sense in this verse. Therefore the ritual employment of this hemistich in the Asv. G.S. leads to an entirely incorrect interpretation of the verse.

It is a well-known fact that all the sacrifices and rituals described in the later texts did not exist at the time of the composition of the Ṛgveda. With the gradual development of sacrifices several new rituals were evolved in later times. It was, therefore, a difficult task to find appropriate Mantras which could be recited at the performance of such later rituals. In order to meet this exigency the ritualists arbitrarily employed the Vedic Mantras without caring for their sense and context. As a consequence of the indiscriminate employment of the Mantras at the performance of rituals one and the same Mantra was sometimes prescribed for various opposite rituals. For instance, the Ṛgvedic verse X, 53, 8 (Cf. AV. XII, 2, 26; V.S. 35, 10) is on the one hand prescribed for the performance of a funeral rite[5], and on the other hand the recitation of the same Mantra is enjoined at the performance of a rite connected with wedding.[6] It is worth noticing that the followers of the ritualistic school of Vedic interpretation interpret the same Mantra arbitrarily according to its ritual application. For instance, Haradatta, the commentator of the Mantras employed in the Asv. G.S. for the performance of domestic rituals, offers two entirely different and rather contradictory interpretations of the above-mentioned Ṛgvedic verse in pursuance of its contradictory ritual applications. Justifying its application to a funeral rite, Haradatta explains the verse as follows[7]: "The gods invoked by Agni to a sacrifice address each other: '*Aśmanvatī*, i.e. the unobstructed divine army, should march forward. You should also get ready to go to the sacrifice. Traverse the journey, O friends. In our journey let us avoid uncomfortable paths and adopt the comfortable ones for the sake of sacrificial foods'. On account of the occurrence of the word *aśman* the verse is employed at the performance of this rite. Or else it is connected with the sense of this rite: *Aśmanvatī* (full of stones), i.e. having a stone placed towards the north, this rite *rīyate* proceeds, i.e. concludes. O relatives! you should get ready to traverse the paths leading to your houses. The remaining words of the verse are to be constructed as before."

But Haradatta puts an entirely different, arbitrary and untenable interpretation on the same verse in its application to the ritual, performed at the time of crossing a river by a newly married couple:[8] "In accordance with its ritual application the verse is addressed by the bridegroom to the bride. It is a personally or directly addressed Mantra as indicated by the use of the second person in *saṃrabhadhvam* etc. As the form *aśmanvatī* is not vocative, the construction of the sentence should be completed by supplying the pronominal words *yad* and *tad*: 'You who are *aśmanvatī*, i.e. prosperous with cereals such as rice and barley, should go to my house. Ascend this boat and cross the river, O companion! Let us avoid these riverine perils like whirlpools which are here, and let us cross the river comfortably'." In order to justify his above-quoted arbitrary interpretation Haradatta imposes his own pre-conceived grammatical and semantic notions on the language of the verse. So Haradatta explains the word *aśmanvatī* (full of stones) as "prosperous with cereals", and the present tense form *rīyate* (flows) as "You should go", taking the third person in the sense of the second person and the present tense form in the sense of the imperative. Similarly he arbitrarily interprets the plural form *saṃrabhadhvam*, *tiṣṭhata*, *tarata* and *sakhāyaḥ* in the sense of singular forms. Such interpretations amount to the distortion of the Vedas.

In view of the callous indifference of the ritualists to the original meaning of the Vedas it would not be unsafe to assume that the corrupt readings of the Ṛgvedic verses found in the Yajurveda-Saṃhitās, the Brāhmaṇas and the Kalpa-Sūtras resulted from the ritualists' gross ignorance about the meaning of Vedic words. It appears that the ritualists generally learnt the Vedic verses by rote without paying any heed to their meaning. This lamentable state of Vedic studies is alluded to by Yāska in the following two stanzas quoted in his Nirukta:[9]

1. He is just a blockhead and bearer of burden, who having learnt the Veda does not understand its meaning. He who understands the meaning attains happi-

ness, and reaches heaven after his sins have been purged through knowledge.

2. Whatever is learnt without understanding is mere cramming and it does not illuminate like dry fuel which has not been placed on fire.

In these stanzas Yāska obliquely raps the ritualists who merely crammed the Vedic Mantras for the sole purpose of reciting them at rituals without caring to understand their meaning.

The ritualists' indifference towards the meaning of the Vedas went on increasing and later on things came to such a sorry pass that the ritualists did not understand at all the meaning of the Vedic verses crammed by them, nor did they feel the necessity of understanding their meaning. On the contrary, they ridiculed those who showed any keenness to understand the meaning of the Vedas. Āditya-darśana, an ancient commentator, alludes to such a lamentable state of Vedic studies and to the ritualists' total apathy towards the meaning of the Veda in the following stanzas:[10]

1. Generally all the priests here learn the Veda, but never understand a word of it.
2. Being contented with mere cramming of the Veda, the priests thunder at home in vain like an autumnal cloud.
3. They talk among themselves 'What do we gain by the meaning of the Veda?' and deride those scholars who are devoted to the pursuit of knowing the meaning of the Veda.
4. Without knowing the meaning of the Veda they undertake to perform wrongly such sacrifices as could be rightly performed by scholars only, and thus bring about opposite results.
5. Having somehow acquired a smattering of a Brāhmaṇa-text, others give themselves the airs of a scholar and continuously engage themselves in the performance of sacrifices.

It would be interesting to know that not only the later ritualists, as pointed out above, were regarded as ignorant about the meaning of the Vedic Mantras, the authors of the Kalpa-Sūtras who suggested the ritual application of a large number of the Mantras were also not considered to be fully competent to pass an authoritative judgment on the meaning of Vedic Mantras. In this connection, the following observations made by the Vedic commentator, Veṅkaṭamādhava, are worth noticing:[11]

6. In such Mantras as *sṛṇyeva* (RV. X, 106, 6) the meanings of words as well as sentences are abstruse. Therefore dull persons with a little knowledge should not try to determine the meaning of the Veda.
7. Similarly ritualists determine the meaning of the Veda with the help of the Kalpa-Sūtras and ignore the Mantra or the Brāhmaṇas.
8. On this point my own view-point is that the authors of the Kalpa-Sūtras are not fully conversant with the entire Vedic lore as is inferred from Āpastamba's statement (Ap. D.S. I, 4, 12, 10): 'All the precepts were (originally) taught in the Brāhmaṇas, but their texts have been lost. Their former existence is now inferred from usage.'
9. Even though the texts have been lost, *Smārta* and *Śrauta Dharmas* are now inferred from usage.
10. The position is that the authors of the Kalpa-Sūtras who have not seen all the *Śākhās* of the Vedas determine the meaning of the Vedas with the help of their own Śākhās only.

Pāraskara[12] takes note of a practice prevalent in his time, according to which a student who intended to adopt the profession of a priest could be allowed to discontinue his studies after studying only the ritual texts without completing the study of the Veda along with its six auxiliary treatises. It clearly shows that in the time of the Sūtras also the ritualists' knowledge of the Vedas was as shallow as in later times.

How the later Yājñikas spread misleading notions about the Veda through their arbitrary interpretations has been amply demonstrated by Haradatta's wilful interpretation briefly quoted above (see notes 7 and 8). If the readers desire to see one more instance of the same type, they should see it on pages 53-54 of his *Āśvalāyana-Gṛhya-Mantra-Vyākhyā* where attempting an alternative explanation of the famous Gāyatrī Mantra (RV. III, 62, 10) Haradatta interprets the word *bhargas* as "sacrificial oblation" or "water", and the word *dhīmahi* as "we sacrifice" or "we drink". No rational student of Sanskrit can countenance such arbitrary and capricious interpretations of these words. This tendency is also met with in the other Yājñika interpretations of the Vedic Mantras. For instance, Jayarāma and Gadādhara, the commentators of the Pāraskara-Gṛhya-Sūtra, betray their utter ignorance of the Vedic idiom in several places. Explaining the Ṛgvedic Mantra (X, 85, 33) in the description of wedding, Jayarāma wrongly splits *datvāyāthāstam* as *datvā yātha astam* being ignorant of the correct padapāṭha (*datvāya atha astam*), and consequently attempts a patently wrong and absurd interpretation.[13] Gadādhara follows suit. Such examples demonstrate the undependability of the Vedic interpretations attempted by the ritualists. But unfortunately the ritualistic interpretations of the Vedas gradually supplanted the other systems of Vedic interpretations, for the sacrificial employment of the Vedic Mantras came to be regarded as their main utility in the period of the Kalpa-Sūtras and later on. This is why almost all the ancient extant commentaries on the RV. are predominantly ritualistic in their approach. The famous commentator Sāyaṇa in the introduction to his commentary on the Ṛgveda asserts that since the Yajurveda is useful mainly for the performance of sacrifices, he has first explained that Veda and has later on taken up the Ṛgveda for explanation.

The ritualistic interpretations occupy a predominant position not only in the commentaries of Sāyaṇa, Uvaṭa and Mahīdhara on the Yajurveda as expected but also in the commentaries of Skandasvāmin, Udgītha, Veṅkaṭamādhava and Sāyaṇa on the RV., and also in the commentaries on the SV. and the AV. The dominant tradition of ritual application of Vedic Mantras and the tremendous influence exercised by the ritualistic texts like the Brāhmaṇas, Kalpa-Sūtras and Paddhatis on the Vedic students seem to account for the preponderance of ritualistic interpretation of the Vedas. Therefore the ancient Indian commentators attempting the ritualistic interpretation of the Vedas refer in the first place to those passages of the Brāhmaṇa and the Kalpa-Sūtras which prescribe the ritual application of the hymn or the verse concerned, and then they try to interpret it in accordance with its ritual application. For instance, Sāyaṇa in the beginning of his commentary on each hymn of the Ṛgveda refers to its ritual application according to the Asv. S.S./the Ait. Br. and gives due importance to its ritual application in his interpretation. Along with the ritualistic interpretation the views of other school of Vedic interpretation such as the etymologists, mythologists, and mystics are also recorded in the commentaries of Skandasvāmin, Veṅkaṭamādhava and Sāyaṇa on the RV. However, the pride of place in their commentaries, as pointed out above, belongs to the ritualistic interpretation.

Now let us briefly examine the ritualistic interpretations of the enigmatic Ṛgvedic verse (IV, 58, 3) referred to above in Chapter II. The earliest ritualistic interpretation of this verse is met with in the Gopatha-Brāhmaṇa I, 2, 16 which records an incorrect reading *śṛṅgāḥ* instead of *śṛṅgā* (most probably due to the mistake of the scribe) and offers the following explanation : "The four Vedas are termed his four horns. His three feet are the three daily libations of Soma. The sacrificial ceremonies called *Brahmaudana* and *Pravargya* symbolize his two heads. Seven metres represent his seven hands. *Mantra*, *Kalpa* and *Brāhmana* represent the three bonds with which he is bound. The recitation of invocatory verses taken from all the four Vedas at the sacrifices symbolizes the roaring of the mighty (*Vṛṣabha*). The sacrifice is the mighty deity that has entered mortals."

The above explanation has been adapted in the Nirukta with a few alterations.[14] In the Nirukta *Brahmaudana* and *Pravargya* are replaced by *Prāyaṇīya* and *Udayanīya*. The Gopatha-Brāhmaṇa explains the roaring of the mighty as the recitation of the invocatory verses taken from all the four Vedas at the sacrifices, while the Nirukta omits to mention the verses of the Atharvaveda and explains that they invoke him with Ṛk-verses, sacrifice with Yajus-formulas, and praise with Soma-chants.

Sāyaṇa in his Ṛgveda-bhāṣya prefaces his explanations of

this verse with the remarks that although this Mantra may be explained in five different ways in accordance with the characteristics of each of the five deities (fire, sun, etc.) of the hymn, in pursuance of the method explained in the Nirukta etc. the verse is explained as alluding to the sun as well as to Agni representing sacrifice on account of their illuminating nature. In this respect Sāyaṇa seems to follow the view expressed in the Bṛhaddevatā that, as mentioned in a Brāhmaṇa, this hymn appears to be addressed either to the sun or to Agni.[15] About the deities of the hymn the Bṛhaddevatā refers also to the view of the other scholars who speak of this verse as praise of either Waters or Ghee, or as addressed to Cows or to the Sun[16]. Summarising the views expressed in the Nirukta and the Bṛhaddevatā, Kātyāyana in his Sarvānukramaṇī states that any one of the five, namely Agni, Sūrya, Waters, Bull (Go) and Ghee, is the deity of the hymn. Sāyaṇa quotes Kātyāyana's view in the beginning of his commentary on this hymn.

In keeping with his stand-point referred to above, Sāyaṇa explains the verse in question as applicable to Agni representing sacrifice and to the Sun. In the case of its ritualistic interpretation Sāyaṇa mainly follows the Gopatha-Brāhmaṇa excepting the part where he follows the Nirukta (see note 14) in omitting the recitation at the sacrifices of Ātharvaṇic verses along with those from the other three Vedas. It is important to note that the commentary ascribed to Sāyaṇa on the same verse occurring in the V.S. (Kāṇva) XIX, 5 contains two different ritualistic interpretations: first of them is almost identical with the one attempted by Uvaṭa on the V.S. (Mādhyandina) XVII, 91, while the second agrees more with the Nirukta (see note 14) than with his own commentary in the Ṛgveda-bhāṣya. It shows that the author of the Sāyaṇa-bhāṣya on the V.S. (Kāṇva) is different from the author of the Ṛgveda-bhāṣya ascribed to Sāyaṇa. This problem will be discussed further in Chapter 7. As pointed out above, Uvaṭa's commentary on this Mantra is almost identical with one of its two explanations contained in the Sāyaṇa-bhāṣya on the V.S. (Kāṇva). In contradistinction to the other ritualistic interpretations mentioned above, the Uvaṭa-bhāṣya regards the four principal priests (*Brahman*, *Udgātṛ*, *Hotṛ* and *Adhvaryu*) as the four horns of the bull symbolizing sacrifice, the three Vedas (*Ṛgveda, Yajurveda* and *Sāmaveda* as his three feet, *Havirdhāna* and *Pravargya* as his two heads, seven sacrificial priests (*saptahotāraḥ*) or seven metres as his seven hands, and the three (morning, mid-day and afternoon) Soma libations as his three bonds. Mahīdhara in his first ritualistic interpretation of this verse follows Uvaṭa, but in his alternative ritualistic interpretation he secms to follow the Nirukta.

It is obvious from a perusal of the various ritualistic interpretations referred to above that they are all arbitrary. For instance, in the opinion of some commentators the four Vedas symbolize the four horns of an allegorical bull representing sacrifice, while the others believe that the four principal priests represent its four horns. According to one interpretation, the allegorical bull is bound with Mantra, Brāhmaṇa and Kalpa. This interpretation would lead to the absurd inference that the Brāhmaṇas and the Kalpa-Sūtras had been composed prior to the composition of the Ṛgveda Therefore, all the ritualistic interpretations of the Vedic verses cannot be blindly accepted and each case must be examined on merit.

The first criterion about the correctness of a ritualistic interpretation is to determine whether the Mantra in question was originally intended to be recited at a ritual in the same manner in which its recitation is prescribed by the later ritual texts. The second criterion is to ascertain whether the form and details of the ritual to which the Mantra is applied were at the time of composition of the concerned Mantra the same as contained in the later treatises prescribing the ritual application of the Mantra. As the Yajus-formulas are mainly concerned with the performance of sacrifices, it may be presumed that they were originally intended to be recited at the performance of sacrifices; and to that extent their ritualistic interpretation seems to accord with the original intention of the Ṛṣis. However, all the Mantras compiled in the Yajurveda are not ritualistic in their content and substance. It would, therefore, not be correct to put ritualistic interpretation on all the Mantras of the Yajurveda.

As regards the Mantras contained in the Ṛgveda, the position is very much different. There is no doubt that the bulk of the Mantras enshrined in this Veda is not directly connected with the performance of any ritual. Nevertheless, some of the Mantras which are later prescribed to be recited at such popular Gṛhya rites as marriage and funeral might have been since the time of their composition intended for the performance of these rites as is attested by their subject-matter. In my previous work entitled *India of Vedic Kalpa-Sūtras* I have examined the various views on the relationship between the Gṛhya rites and the Vedic Mantras to be recited at their performance. For the convenience of our readers the relevant portion from my said work is reproduced below[17] :

"The Gṛhya sūtras, however, employ many Mantras borrowed from the Saṃhitās on the occasion of the performance of the Gṛhya ritual. Some of these Mantras clearly indicate the antiquity of the Gṛhya ceremonies as far back as the early Vedic age. The Ṛgvedic hymn X, 85, which contains the Mantras to be employed at the time of wedding, shows that a number of wedding rites described in the Gṛhyāsūtras were prevalent among the Indo-Aryans already in the days of the Ṛgveda. Some traces of the funeral ritual set out in the Gṛhyāsūtras can no doubt be found in certain hymns of Ṛgveda, i.e. in the fourteenth, fifteenth and sixteenth hymns of its tenth Maṇḍala. Regarding the position of the Gṛhya ritual in the age of the Ṛgveda, Prof. Oldenberg observes, 'We may assume that the acts of the Gṛhya worship, being more limited in extent and simpler in their ritual construction than the great Soma offerings, were not yet at that time, so far as they existed at all, decked out with the reciting of the poetic texts, which we find later on connected with them, and which in the case of the Soma offerings came early to be used. Probably they were celebrated in simple unadorned fashion; what the person making the offering had to say was doubtless limited to short, possibly prose formulas, so that these ceremonies remained free from the poetry of the above-mentioned families (Vasiṣṭhas and Viśvāmitras etc.) of priests.' The same scholar further remarks: 'We think that the character of the verses given in the Gṛhyasūtras, which had to be repeated at the performance of the different ceremonies, justifies us in making these conjectures. Some of these verses indeed are old Vedic verses, but we have no proof that they were composed for the purpose of the Gṛhya ceremonies, and the connection in which we find them in the Ṛgveda proves rather the contrary. Another portion of these verses and songs proves to have been composed indeed for the very Gṛhya ceremonies for which they are prescribed in the texts of the ritual, but these verses are more recent than the old parts of the Ṛgveda. Parts of them are found in the Ṛgveda in a position which speaks for their more recent origin, others are not contained in the Ṛgveda at all. Many of these verses are found in the more recent Vedic Saṃhitās, especially in the Atharvaveda, a Saṃhitā which may be regarded in the main as a treasure of Gṛhya verses; others finally have not as yet been traced to any Vedic Saṃhitā, and we know them from the Gṛhyasūtras only. We may infer that, during the latter part of the Ṛgveda period, ceremonies such as marriage and burial began to be decked out with poetry as had long been the case with the Soma offering.' In order to justify the view that Gṛhya ceremonies, such as marriage and burial, came to be decked out with poetry during the latter part of the Ṛgvedic period, Prof. Oldenberg advances two main arguments: firstly, that 'the principal collection of marriage sentences and the sentences for burial of the dead are found in the Tenth Maṇḍala of the Ṛgveda', and secondly that these Ṛgvedic verses relating to the Gṛhya ceremonies are composed in the Anuṣṭubh metre which, according to him, exhibits a stage of later metrical development But this view of Prof. Oldenberg has been refuted by Prof. Winternitz who says, 'I confess I am not convinced by Prof. Oldenberg's argumentation of the comparatively late origin of the Gṛhya Mantras. It seems to me highly improbable that the marriage rites and burial ceremonies should have been performed without any prayers, until they began to be decked out with poetry after the analogy of the Soma sacrifice. In fact, many of the Gṛhya 'rites' consist merely in invocations addressed to popular deities, or in the recitation of magic formulas, while other are no 'rites' at all unless they are accompanied by prayers or formulas. And it has not yet been proved that the elaborate Soma sacrifice can claim a higher antiquity than the simple Gṛhya offerings (Cf. Knauer 'Festgruss an R. Roth', p. 64). I am rather inclined to think that the artificial poetry of the Brāhmaṇas, as represented by the hymns of the Ṛgveda, and the popular poetry connected with Atharvan practices and Gṛhya rites, as represented by the Atharvaveda Saṃhitā, and the Gṛhya Mantras, are two parallel streams running in different channels, approaching each other at times, and diverging widely at other times. The peculiarities of the Anuṣṭubh pointed out by Prof. Oldenberg may just as well be due to the fact that these Mantras were popular poetry, and as such followed different rules of metrics from those followed by the authors of the Vedic hymns. Besides, a glance at our Mantrapāṭha will show that the metrical laws are disregarded in these Gṛhya Mantras quite as much as the rules of grammar. See, e.g. MP. I, I, 9; II, 16; 1, 1, 3 etc. I doubt whether, with such a state of things, it would be safe to draw any conclusion as to chronology from metrical usage of Gṛhya Mantras. See, Bloomfield, SBE Vol. XLII, p. 296.' "

Even if we accept Prof. Oldenberg's view that the Ṛgvedic verses to be employed at the Gṛhya rites, such as marriage and burial, are later than the older parts of the Ṛgveda, it does not necessarily imply that no Mantras of similar nature were composed in earlier times and that prior to the composition of these Mantras the Gṛhya ceremonies were not accompanied by the recitation of any verses. It is not improbable that the verses which were then recited on the occasion of performing the Gṛhya rites were so common and popular that it was not felt necessary to include them in the Saṃhitā of the Ṛgveda, a collection of rare and uncommon hymns; a few of the best hymns dealing with marriage and funeral rites were included in the Tenth Maṇḍala which, in view of its contents, might be termed as a bundle of miscellanies. Anyway, the verses of the Ṛgveda, pertaining to the marriage and funeral rites, tell us something about the way how these ceremonies were performed in those days.

Ritualistic interpretation of certain Mantras is of course justifiable in view of the long and uninterrupted tradition of their ritual application conforming to their context and subject-matter. But when the ritual application of a Vedic Mantra is purely arbitrary based on a superficial similarity of any sounds or words, its ritualistic interpretation is bound to be erroneous and misleading. Therefore, it is imperative to determine the propriety of ritual application of a Vedic Mantra before passing a judgment on its ritualistic interpretations attempted by ancient Indian commentators. There is no doubt that the tradition of ritual application of Vedic Mantras has proved both a boon and a bane of Vedic studies. On the one hand, it has contributed a good deal to the preservation of the Vedic texts. But on the other, it has, to a certain extent, proved a hindrance in the correct and unbiased interpretation of the Vedas.

Notes and References

1. Cf. Nirukta XIII, 12 wherein it is stated that when the Ṛṣis were ascending to the heaven men asked the gods "Who will be our Ṛṣi?" The gods granted them this reasoning (*Nirukta* according to the commentator) employed in deducing the sense of the Vedic Mantras as their Ṛṣi. Therefore, whatever is deduced by reasoning by a scholar versed in the Vedas pertains to a Ṛṣi. In the introduction to his commentary on the seventh Adhyāya of the eighth Aṣṭaka of the Ṛgveda Veṇkaṭamādhava ascribes the above passage contained in the Nirukta to a Brāhmaṇa.
2. Cf. RV. VI, 16, 47; VIII, 19, 5; 24, 20. Asv. G.S. I, 1, 4-5; Sat. Br. VII, 4, 1, 30.
3. Gopatha-Brāhmaṇa II, 2, 6; Ait. Br. I, 4, 9 etc. which omits Yajus; Cf. Kaush. Br. X, 2.
4. Nirukta I, 2.
5. Sat. Br. XIII, 8, 4, 3; Kat. S.S. XXI, 4, 21; Tait. Ar. VI, 3, 2; Asv. G.S. IV, 6, 13.
6. Asv. G.S. I, 8, 2-3; Sankh. G.S. I, 15, 18; and Kath. G.S. 26, 12 prescribe the recitation of this Mantra when the newly married couple crosses a river in a boat; Cf. *India of Vedic Kalpa-Sūtras*, p. 241.
7. Áśmanvatī rīyate sáṃ rabhadhvam
   úttiṣṭhata prá tarata sakhāyaḥ
   Átrā jahāma yé ásannáśevāḥ
   śivā́n vayám út taremābhí vā́jān. (RV. X, 53, 8).
   See on this verse the Āśvalāyana-Gṛhya-Mantra-Vyākhyā, Chapter 4, p. 248.
8. Op. cit., pp. 14-15.
9. Nirukta I, 18. Patañjali in the Paspaśāhnika of the Mahābhāṣya quotes the second stanza but reads *adhītam* instead of *gṛhītam* of the Nirukta.
10. See Introduction to the Laugākṣi-Gṛhya-Sūtra, Vol. I, pp. 7-8.
11. Introductory verses (6-10) of Veṅkaṭamādhava's commentary on the

3rd Adhyāya of the 8th Aṣṭaka of the RV. (p. 3591 of Vishva Bandhu's edition).

12. Par. G.S. II, 6, 8.
13. See Jayarāma's commentary on the Par. G.S. I, 8, 9.
14. Nirukta XIII, 7. Cf. Śabara-bhāṣya on Mīmāṃsā I, 2, 46 and Kumārila's Tantriavārtika on the same sūtra.
15. Bṛhaddevatā V, 11. The Brāhmaṇa referred to here is obviously the Ait. Br. V, 16, 6; Cf. Asv. S.S. VIII, 9.2. According to the Nirukta VII, 16-17, either Agni or the Sun is the deity of this hymn.
16. Ibid., V, 11.
17. India of Vedic Kalpa-Sūtras, pp. 14-16.

4

The Aitihāsika School of Vedic Interpretation

Yāska in his Nirukta mentions the Aitihāsikas[1], besides *Yājñikas, Nairuktas, Parivrājakas* and *Naidānas*, who follow their respective traditions of Vedic interpretation (see note 5 of Chapter II). The followers of the Aitihāsika school of Vedic interpretation believe each Vedic hymn or a group of Vedic Mantras to be related to an Itihāsa, i.e. a traditional account of ancient events, and interpret the concerned hymn or Mantras accordingly. For instance, before entering upon the interpretation of the 5th, 6th and 10th verses of the 33rd hymn of the Third Maṇḍala of the RV., Yāska relates an Itihāsa connected with the hymn as follows[2]: "In this connection they relate the Itihāsa. The seer Viśvāmitra was the family priest of Sudās, son of Pijavana. Having obtained wealth, he (Viśvāmitra) arrived at the confluence of the rivers Beas and Sutlej. Others followed him. Viśvāmitra praised the rivers and implored them to be fordable. In his praise he addressed them in the dual as well as in the plural number."

We come across in the Vedic and post-Vedic literature nearly fifty legends forming the basis of the Aitihāsika interpretation of certain hymns of the RV. Among them the legends relating to Indra-Vṛtra, Agastya-Lopāmudrā, Viśvāmitra-Śakti, Yama-Yamī, Saramā-Paṇi, Urvaśī-Purūravas, Nāhuṣa-Sarasvatī, Devāpi-Śantanu, Prajāpati-duhitṛ, Sudās Paijavana, and Apālā are prominent and well known.

The earliest specimens of the Aitihāsika interpretation of Vedic Mantras are met with in the Brāhmaṇas. Several legends concerning the legendary interpretation of Vedic Mantras are found in the Brāhmaṇa portions of the Kṛṣṇa-Yajurveda, Tait. Br., Sat. Br., Ait. Br.. Jaim. Br. and P. Br. For instance, the Brāhmaṇa portion of the M.S. contains the legends relating to Manu's inheritance (1, 5, 8), Urvaśī-Purūravas (I, 6, 12; III, 9, 5), clipping of mountain wings (I, 10, 13), Indra-Viśvarūpa (II, 4, 1), Prajāpati and his daughter (III, 6, 5; IV, 2, 12), Manu's wife (IV, 8, 1) etc. The legends of Urvaśī-Purūravas (8, 10), Indra-Viśvarūpa (12, 10), Śunaḥśepa (19, 22), Indra-Yati, Indra-dānavī etc., find mention in the K.S. also. The following legends are alluded to in the Tait. S. :—Indra-Vṛtra (II, 1, 4, 5-6; VI, 5, 9, 1), Indra-Tvaṣṭṛ (II, 4, 12; 5, 2), Indra-Viśvarūpa (II, 5, 1), Agni's disappearance (II, 6, 6, 1; VI, 2, 8, 4-5), Manu (II, 6, 7, 1), Manu's inheritance (III, 1, 9), Vasiṣṭha (III, 5, 2,1; VII, 4, 7, 1), Urvaśī (IV, 4, 3, 2), Śunaḥśepa) (V, 2, 1, 3), Kadrū Suparṇī (VI, 1, 6, 1-2), Gandharva-Viśvāvasu (VI, 1, 6, 5-6), destruction of Asura-city (VI, 2, 3, 1-2), Indra-hyena (VI, 2, 4, 4) Indra-Yati (VI, 2, 7, 5), Aditi's sons (VI, 5, 6, 1-2), Devabhāga and Sṛñjayas (VI, 6, 2, 2), Manu's sacrifice (VI, 6, 6, 1), etc. Similarly the Sat. Br., Jaim. Br. and Ait. Br. also refer to several legends relating to Vedic Mantras.

It is important to point out that apart from the extant Brāhmaṇas there were some other Brāhmaṇas which contained legends connected with Vedic Mantras. Among such extinct Brāhmaṇas, the *Śāṭyāyna-Brāhmaṇa* was very prominent, which finds frequent mention in several Vedāñgas, such as Asv. S.S., Ap. S.S., Lat. S.S., Hir. S.S., Bhar. G.S., etc., under the name of *Ṣāṭyāyani-Brāhmaṇa* or *Śāṭyāyanaka.* Did this Brāhmaṇa belong to the *Śāṭyāyanī* Śākhā of the Kṛṣṇa-Yajurveda as indicated by the Charaṇa-Vyūha, or to the Sāmaveda as suggested by the several Śrauta-Sūtras? The followers of this Śākhā as well as the students of the Śāṭyāyana Brāhmaṇa were called *Śatyāyaninaḥ* as alluded to in several ancient works such as Drah. S.S., Lat. S.S., Nidāna-Sūtra, etc. Referring to the legends connected with numerous Vedic Mantras, ancient commentators including Skandasvāmin, Veṇkaṭamādhava and Sāyaṇa quote passages from the Śaṭyāyana-Brāhmaṇa. Did these commentators take these quotations direct from the original Śāṭyāyana-Brāhmaṇa or from some secondary source ? If this text actually existed in the time of Sāyaṇa, its total loss within a short span of a few centuries is really a matter of surprise. Dr. C. Kunhan Raja stated in his preface (p. xxvi) to the Ṛgvedānukramaṇī of Mādhavabhaṭṭa that his colleague Mr. T.R. Chintamani discovered a manuscript bearing the title Śāṭyāyana-Brāhmaṇa, and further observed: "The manuscript is being examined and we have not been able to ascertain if it is really that work." As nearly half a century has elapsed since then (1932) and no tangible result has come to light, the inference is obvious.

It is not possible to state with any amount of certainty whether there were independent works on *Itihāsa* in the Vedic times or *Itihāsa* merely formed part of the works dealing with various subjects. However, repeated references to *Itihāsa* in the Vedic literature leads us to the conclusion that the literary genre named *Itihāsa* occupied an important place in the literature of the Vedic times, whatever might have been its form and content. The earliest occurrence of the word *Itihāsa* is met with in the AV[3]., where the literary genre named *Itihāsa* along with the other categories of literature, namely, the Ṛgveda, Sāmaveda, Yajurveda, Atharvaveda, Purāṇa, Gāthās and Nārāśaṃsīs, is said to follow the divine Vrātya. The Brāhmaṇas, Āraṇyakas, Upaniṣads and Vedāṅgas variously speak of *Itihāsa.* For instance, the Sat. Br. extols the study of *Itihāsa-Purāṇa* like that of the R.V., S.V. and Yajurveda.[4] Further on, the same Brāhmaṇa classes *Itihāsa* as a Veda like Ṛgveda etc. and associates it with fish and fishermen.[5] Similarly the Gopatha Brāhmaṇa, Sankh. S.S., Asv. S.S., Vaikh. G.S., Kauṭilya's Arthaśāstra, etc. speak of an *Itihāsa-Veda.*[6] Extolling the study of Itihāsa along with that of the RV. etc. (Cf. note 4) the Tait. Ar. uses the word *Itihāsa* in the plural number.[7] Does the use of this plural form of the word *Itihāsa* imply that either several works on *Itihāsa* or several recensions of *Itihāsa* were in existence at that time ?

In this connection it is worthy of note that in the abovementioned ancient works, such as the AV., Sat. Br., Gop. Br., etc. the word *Purāṇa* occurs immediately after the word *Itihāsa.*[8] It shows that there was a constant and unbreakable nexus between *Itihāsa* and *Purāṇa*, and consequently both these words are found coupled together in ancient works. On account of such an intimate connection the words *Itihāsa* and *Purāṇa* were used as members of a copulative compound.[9] The Chh. Up. declares the *Itihāsa-Purāṇa* to be the fifth Veda.[10] Separate as well as joint mention of *Itihāsa* and *Purāna* in ancient works poses the problem of determining their distinguishing features and also the basis for their copulative compound. According to Śaṅkara's commentary on the Bṛh. Up., a Brāhmaṇa-portion in the form of a dialogue etc. such as one between Urvaśī and Purūravas (Cf. Sat. Br. XI, 5, 1, 1) is *Itihāsa*, and a Brāhmaṇa-portion dealing with creation, such as "It was all unmanifest in the beginning" (Cf. Sat. Br. VI, 1, 1, 1) etc., is *Purāṇa.* In the opinion of *Durgāchārya,*[12] *Itihāsa* is that narrative which mainly traces the origin and causes of any important event. Sāyaṇa has suggested several definitions of *Itihāsa* and *Purāṇa.* Their two alternative definitions have been proposed in Sāyaṇa's commentary on the Tait. Ar.[13]: (1) the works such as the Mahābhārata etc. are *Itihāsas,* and the *Brahmāṇḍa* etc. are *Purāṇas*; or (2) the narratives of battles between the gods and the demons are *Itihāsas,* and the descriptions of creation of Universe are Purāṇas. The definitions of *Itihāsa* aad *Purāṇa* given in Sāyaṇa's introduction to his commentary on the RV. are similar to the alternative ones mentioned above :— narratives such as 'there was a conflict between the gods and the demons' (Cf, Tait. S. V, 3, 11, 1) etc. are *Itihāsas,* and the description of creation of Universe such as 'there was nothing in the beginning' (Tait. Br. II, 2, 9, 1) etc. is Purāṇa.[14] Further on in the same introduction (see pages 29-30 of the Poona edition). Sāyaṇa speaks of the utility of *Itihāsa* and *Purāṇa* for the understanding of the Vedas and remarks : "Yājñavalkya (I, 3) refers to the utility of the *Purāṇas* etc., like the six auxiliary branches of knowledge (ṣaḍaṅgavat), for the understanding of the Vedas. It has been observed elsewhere also (see note 23) : 'One should augment the Veda with *Itihāsa* and *Purāṇa.* The Veda is afraid of a person of little knowledge lest he should harm the Veda'."

The definitions of *Itihāsa* and *Purāṇa* contained in Sāyaṇa's commentary on the Sat. Br. are contrary to those contained in Śaṅkara's commentary on the Bṛh. Up. (see note 11) : the description of creation of Universe is *Itihāsa,* and the narration of events connected with ancient personages is *Purāṇa.*[15]

Haradatta, Kullūka, Vijñāneśvara, etc., the commentators of the later Dharmaśāstras, regard *Itihāsa* as denoting the Mahābhārata etc. and *Purāṇa* as signifying later Purāṇas such as Viṣṇu, Brāhma, etc.[16] However, the words *Itihāsa* and *Purāṇa* occurring in the Vedic literature have not been obviously used in these later senses. According to a very wide and loose definition of *Itihāsa* attempted in the Kauṭilīya Arthaśāstra, *Itihāsa*, includes within its scope various categories of literature, namely *Purāṇa, Itivṛtta, Ākhyāyikā, Udāharaṇa, Dharmaśāstra* and *Arthaśāstra*.[17] It can be said without any fear of contradiction that the word *Itihāsa* employed in the Vedic literature is not so comprehensive in its connotation, though there is a close nexus between *Itihāsa* and *Purāṇa*. There is no doubt that a close affinity of subject-matter between *Itihāsa* and *Purāṇa* led to the popular usage of *Itihāsa-Purāṇa* as a copulative compound in the Vedic language and to their designation as the fifth Veda in the Chh. Up. In keeping with this trend the Mahābhārata is designated as the fifth Veda and is often called *Itihāsa* but sometimes *Purāṇa* also.[18] Besides, the Mahābhārata is several times termed as *Ākhyānā* also.[19] The use of the terms *Itihāsa, Ākhyāna* and *Purāṇa* for the same work Mahābhārata apparently suggests their synonymity. But in fact it is not so. An analysis of these three words employed in the Mahābhārata shows that the Epic has preserved, as we shall see below, the distinguishing meaning of each word. The reason for assigning each of the three epithets—*Itihāsa, Ākhyāna* and *Purāṇa*—to the Mahābhārata is that it possesses the qualities of each of them. In other words, in addition to being the best *Itihāsa* the Mahābhārata is also an *Ākhyāna* as well as a *Purāṇa*. With a view to emphasizing its religious content, the Mahābhārata is also called *Dharmaśāstra*. The *Itihāsa-Purāṇa* mentioned in the Chh. Up. (see note 10) might have combined, like the Mahābhārata, the qualities of both *Itihāsa* and *Purāṇa*. Is the Mahābhārata intended by the *Itihāsa-Purāṇa* of the Chh. Up. or does it allude to the existence of a similar work earlier than the Mahābhārata?

In this connection several modern scholars including Geldner and Sieg conjecture that even prior to the Mahābhārata there existed a single work called *Itihāsa-Purāṇa* which might have been a collection of all sorts of old heroic, cosmogonic and genealogical legends.[20] According to this viewpoint, the subject-matter of such *Itihāsa-Purāṇa* was old like the Vedic Mantras, but due to its popularity and bulk neither the form of that work could be fixed nor could it be fully preserved like the Mantras. Nevertheless, the entire subject-matter of such a work, according to the proponents of this point of view, might have been fixed to a certain extent and compiled in a big collection; otherwise it could not have merited the title of the *fifth Veda.* The authors of this thesis hold that the subject-matter of the *Arthavādas* narrated in the form of myths and legends in the Brāhmaṇas might have been derived from that ancient common stock called the *fifth Veda*, and that the authors of the later *Itihāsas* and *Purāṇas* also drew upon that source. In this connection Sieg further puts forward the view[21] that in ancient India there were such *śrotriya Aitihāsikas* (students and knowers of Itihāsa)[22] who studied the *Itihāsa-Veda* as the fifth Veda alongwith any of the four Vedas, and who might have interpreted the old Mantras according to the *Aitihāsika* point of view Thus there arose a new school of scholars called *Aitihāsikas* who interpreted the Veda according to the ancient *Aitihāsika* standpoint. According to Sieg, among the Vedic scholars there was another category of Aitihāsikas who were also linguists at the same time, and the following Śloka was the motto of this Aitihāsika school :

itihāsapurāṇābhyām vedam samupavṛmhayet,
bibhety alpaśrutād vedo mām ayam prahared iti.[23]

Sieg further observes that as numerous subjects of the ancient Itihāsa-Purāṇa have been preserved in the Brāhmaṇas as well as in the later epic and Purāṇa-literature, so the scholarly Vedic tradition has preserved a number of legends alongwith the exegetical suggestions and theories of the *Aitihāsikas.*

Several modern scholars including Macdonell, Keith and Winternitz do not accept the above-mentioned view that a single work styled as "*Itihāsa-Purāṇa*" actually existed in the Vedic times.[24] As we have pointed out above, on account of the close relationship between *Itihāsa* and *Purāṇa*, these words were combined in a copulative compound and perhaps there was also an intermixture of their subject-matter. The *Itihāsa-Purāṇa* termed as the fifth Veda in the Chh. Up. etc. might have been such a work. Since the Mahābhārata finds mention in the Vedic works including the Asv. G.S.,[25] it would not be unreasonable to assume that the above-mentioned '*Itihāsa-Purāṇa*' might have been an earlier version of the present Mahābhārata. Internal evidence from this great Epic lends support to this view (see note 20).

On account of intermixture of *Itihāsa*, *Purāṇa* and *Ākhyāna* in the Mahābhārata their real nature was confused, and some people began to regard them as synonymous.[25a] However, an analysis of their Vedic usages clearly brings out their distinguishing features. It may be pointed out that excepting the only example occurring in the AV. (see note 3) the Vedic Saṃhitās do not mention such literary genres as *Itihāsa*, *Purāṇa* and *Ākhyāna* which find mention mainly in the later works such as the Brāhmaṇas, Āraṇyakas, Upaniṣads and Vedāṅgas. It shows that these literary genres developed mainly in the Brāhmaṇa-period, and on account of their popularity they were later incorporated into the Mahābhārata. The pre-Mahābhārata literature contains ample evidence testifying to the separate existence of *Itihāsa*, *Purāṇa* and *Ākhyāna*.

Apart from the occurrence of *Itihāsa*, *Itihāsa-Veda*, *Purāṇa* and *Purāṇa-Veda* in the above-mentioned Vedic works (see notes 3-10), their mention in the Nirukta, Bṛhaddevatā, Mahābhārata, etc. is worthy of note. This fact must be particularly noticed that while introducing a legend connected with any Vedic hymn the Nirukta and the Bṛhaddevatā employ the term *Itihāsa* or *Ākhyāna*, and the term *Purāṇa* has never been used in them for any such legend. Therefore Yāska in his Nirukta uses the term *Itihāsa* six times for such legends[26] and thrice alludes to the *Aitihāsikas* who base their Vedic interpretations on such *Itihāsa*.[27] Similarly the Bṛhaddevatā employs the term *Itihāsa* seven times in this particular sense.[28] It is quite clear from a perusal of the Nirukta and the Bṛhaddevatā that the words *Ākhyāna* and *Itihāsa*, differ in their connotation. Therefore, *Pavitrākhyāna* is one of the several categories of the Mantras, e.g. *Stuti*, *Nindā*, *Paridevanā*, etc. enumerated in the

Bṛhad. (I, 36); further on in I, 53 the first verse of the *Urvaśi-Purūravas*-hymn (RV. X, 95) has been designated as *Ākhyāna*; and elsewhere the Bṛhad. states that the narrative (*Ākhyāna*) with regard to their (Urvaśī's and Purūravas's) mutual call (Āhvāna) is termed as *Saṃvāda* (dialogue) by Yāska but *Itihāsa* by Śaunaka[29]. It is Yāska's style to preface the explanation of a Mantra conforming to an *Itihāsa* with the remarks (see note 26) : "In this connection they relate *Itihāsa* (*tatretihāsam āchakṣate*)" and then he narrates the *Itihāsa* concerned. However, when Yāska has to refer to an alternative explanation of a Mantra according to the *Ākhyāna* school of Vedic interpretation, he generally offers such an explanation as the last one ending with the remarks "*such is the Ākhyāna*" (*ityākhyānam*).[30] The passages of the Nirukta referred to in note 30 clearly point to the fact that there is a marked difference between the Vedic interpretations of the Nairuktas and those of the followers of the *Ākhyāna* School.

The Nirukta twice employs the expression "*Prītiḥ...Ākhyāna-Samyuktā*" and the commentator Durgāchārya who is not sure about its meaning offers two explanations.[31] Durga's first explanation which is corroborated by an analogous expression used in the Bṛhad. appears to be nearer the mark.[32] At the end of Śunaḥśepa legend the Ait. Br. VII, 18 terms it as *Śaunaḥśepa Ākhyāna* (Cf. Asv. S.S. IX, 3, 13; Sankh., S.S. Ap. S.S., etc.), and elsewhere (III, 25) alludes to the opinion of *Ākhyānavids* (experts in legends) who call as *Sauparṇa* (*Ā*khyāna) the legend relating to the bringing from heaven of Soma by metres in the guise of birds. The Sat. Br. speaks of a revolving legend called *Pāriplava Ākhyāna*,[33] which during the one-year freedom period of the sacrificial horse of Aśvamedha is repeated in thirty-six cycles of ten days each. In the course of a ten-day cycle the *Hotṛ*-priest instructs the subjects (men, Pitṛs, Gandharvas, Apsaras etc.) of ten kings (Manu Vaivasvata, Yama, Varuṇa, Soma Vaiṣṇava etc.) in their respective Vedas (Ṛgveda, Yajur-veda, Atharva-veda, Āṅgiro-veda, Sarpa-Vidyā-veda, Devajana-Vidyā-veda, Māyā-veda, Itihāsa-veda, Purāṇa-veda, Sāma-veda) on the 1st, 2nd, 3rd, 4th, 5th, 6th, 7th, 8th, 9th and 10th day respectively. And at the end of the *Hotṛ*-priest's above-mention-ed instruction on each of the ten days the lute-players sing in musical chorus the praises of the king (who performs the sacrifice) along with the glories of the righteous kings of yore.

In view of the inter-mixture of prose and verse in the above-mentioned *Śaunaḥśepa Ākhyāna* of the Ait. Br., some scholars have advanced the conjecture that a legend composed in prose mixed with verse is called *Ākhyāna*. Pushing further this conjecture, certain other scholars have propounded the thesis that the so-called *Ākhyāna*-hymns of the RV. represent the earliest form of an Indian drama, in which prose was originally mixed with verse or might have been mixed according to the necessity of acting.[34] Such a theory about the Ṛgvedic hymns has been proved to be untenable by Hertel, Keith and others (see note 34). In this connection Sieg advances the conjecture that though *Ākhyāna* generally denotes only a story, e.g. *Pāriplavam Ākhyānam*, and can be therefore identical with individual *Itihāsa* or *Purāṇa*, or can, in other words, be borrowed from *Itihāsa-Purāṇa*; while *Itihāsa* and *Purāṇa* refer to the subject-matter of the stories, *Ākhyāna, Ākhyāyikā* and *Kathā* are rather concerned with the form and external arrangement of the same.[35]

The post-Vedic works such as the Mahābhārata, the Mahābhāṣya, and other grammatical commentaries yield some information on the distinguishing features and titles of *Itihāsa, Purāṇa, Ākhyāna* and *Ākhyāyikā*. For instance, while explaining the Vārtika *Ākhyānākhyāyiketihāsapurāṇebhyaścha thag vaktavyaḥ*, the Mahābhāṣya besides exemplifying *Aitihāsika* "a specialist in Itihāsa" and Paurāṇika "a specialist in Purāṇa", cites the following examples relating to the secondary formations concerning *Ākhyāna* and *Ākhyāyika*[36]:

Ākhyāna · *Yāvakrītikaḥ, Praiyaṅgavikaḥ, Yāyātikaḥ* ;
Ākhyāyikā : *Vāsavadattikaḥ, Saumanottarikaḥ*.

The later commentators such as Kaiyyaṭa and Bhaṭṭojidīkṣita explain the above-cited secondary formations as follows[37]:

Yāvakrītikaḥ : an *Ākhyāna* relating to the famous personage *Yavakrīta* is metaphorically termed as *Yāvakrīta* (Kaiyyaṭa) and one who specialises in it is called *Yāvakrītikaḥ*.

Praiyaṅgavikaḥ : One who specialises in the *Ākhyāna* of a famous beauty named *Priyaṅgu* is termed as *Praiyaṅgavikaḥ*. According to V.S. Agrawal (Pāṇinikālīna Bhāratavarṣa, p. 299), *Priyaṅgu* was the wife of Śauri Vasudeva.

Yāyātikaḥ : One who specialises in the *Ākhyāna* of Yayāti is termed as *Yāyātikaḥ*.

Vāsavadattikaḥ : One who specialises in the *Ākhyāyikā* of the famous queen Vāsavadattā is termed as *Vāsavadattikaḥ*.

Saumanottarikaḥ : One who specialises in the *Ākhyāyikā* relating to a famous lady named *Sumanottarā* is termed *Saumanattarikaḥ*. According to V.S. Agrawal (op. cit., p. 300), the story of Sumanottarā finds mention in the Buddhist literature.

Vāmana explaining the Pāṇinian Sūtra VI, 2,103 cites the following instances of *Ākhyānas* qualified by a word expressing direction or time: *Pūrvādhirāmam*, *Pūrva-Yayātam*, *Apara-Yāyātam*. Vāmana further explains *Ādhirāmam* as a *grantha* (treatise or literary production) relating to *Adhirāma* and similarly *Yāyātam*. But Nāgeśa (Cf. Laghuśabdenduśekhara on the same Sūtra) clearly explains *Yāyātam* as an *Ākhyāna* relating to Yayāti.

Among the *Ākhyānas* referred to above those relating to *Yayakrīta* and *Yayāti* are found in the Mahābhārata.[38] It must be noted that besides *Itihāsa*, *Purāṇa* and *Ākhyāna* the terms *Upākhyāna*, *Ākhyāyikā* and *Kathā* are also employed in the Mahābhārata. According to Sieg's estimate, the Mahābhārata uses the term *Itihāsa* 176 times, *Ākhyāna* 77 times and *Ākhyāyikā* twice; but in a footnote (op. cit.) he himself expres es doubt about the authenticity of the above figures. It may be pointed out that in the Mahābhārata the term *Itihāsa* is often qualified with such adjectives as *Purāṇa*, *Purāvṛtta* and *Purātana*. As pointed out above (see note 18), the Mahābhārata is often styled as *Itihāsa*. Besides, it is several times described as *Jayo nametihasoyam*. In I, 1, 19; 1, 2, 41 etc., the Epic describes itself as "*Bhārata* Itihāsa." According to Mahābhārata I, 1, 50, *Itihāsas* with explanations and various *Śrutis* have been enumerated in the Epic. In several places the Mahābhārata prefaces the narration of an ancient story with such introductory remarks[39] as *atrāpyudāharantīmamitihāsam purātanam* or *atraivodāharantīmamitihāsam purātanam.* The Epic usage shows that the term *Itihāsa* is not confined to the main story of the Mahābhārata but is also employed for other ancient stories embodied in the Epic. However, no distinguishing features of *Itihāsa* are spelt out in the Epic.

Just like *Itihāsa* the term *Ākhyāna* is also employed in the Epic several times for the Mahābhārata and the adjectives *Purāṇa*, *Purātana* and *Purāvṛtta* are used to qualify it. Moreover, the term *Ākhyāna* is used in the Epic to designate the secondary stories connected with the principal narrative of the Mbh.; e.g. *Āstīka Ākhyāna* (I, 13, 4, etc.) *Surabhīndrākhyāna* (III, 9, 6, etc.), *Sāvitryākhyāna* (III, 299, 17, etc.), etc. It appears that the word *Itihāsa* originally denoted the narrative of an ancient event, whereas *Ākhyāna* denoted a story in general. In the Mahābhārata both *Ākhyāna* and *Kathā* came to be employed in the general sense of a story. The term *Upākhyāna* is often used in the Epic to denote a subsidiary story which has no direct connection with the principal narrative but has been appended to it on some pretext, e.g. *Rāmopākhyāna*, *Nalopākhyāna*, etc. In a few places the word *Ākhyāna* is also used in this sense. Pointing to the supplementary nature of *Upākhyānas*, the Mahābhārata (I, 1, 101-102) records the fact that the Epic coupled with its *Upākhyānas* consists of a hundred thousand verses, but divested of the *Upākhyānas* it contains only 24,000 verses.

Unlike *Ākhyāna* the word *Purāṇa* is not employed in the Epic to denote a story in general, but it is used there in the sense of a particular literary genre. If the word *Purāṇa* appearing to be an appellation of the Epic in a few passages[40] may be construed as an adjective qualifying *Itihāsa* or *Ākhyāna*, it would greatly facilitate our task of solving the problem of use of *Purāṇa* in the Mahābhārata. Besides mentioning *Purāṇa* and *Paurāṇika* a number of times, the Epic alludes to the subject-matter of *Purāṇa* and names certain *Purāṇas*. Sauti Ugraśravas, son of the Sūta Lomaharṣana, is described as Paurāṇika, an expert in *Purāṇa*[41]. In the dialogue between Śaunaka and Sauti the former asks the latter whether he is conversant with the entire *Purāṇa* studied by his (latter's) father which contains divine stories and the genealogies of the wise, and then expresses his desire to hear the genealogy of Bhṛgu.[42] In reply Sauti promises to narrate the genealogy of Bhṛgu as embodied in the *Purāṇa* (see note 42). Further on when Śaunaka says to Sauti that the former wants to hear from the latter the account of Garuḍa's birth if it is contained in the *Purāṇa*, in reply Sauti affirms that it is the subject-matter of the *Purāṇa*.[43] According to Sauti, the priests told King Janamejaya that the snake-sacrifice is described in detail in the *Purāṇa* (Mbh. I, 51, 6). The Epic describes *Harivamśa* as a *Purāṇa* designated as a supplement.[44] Besides, the *Purāṇas* ascribed to *Mārkaṇḍeya, Matsya* and *Vāyu* are also mentioned in the Epic.[45]

It follows from the foregoing discussion that the genealogical literature was then known by the name of *Purāṇa*, and a person versed in a *Purāṇa* was called *Paurāṇika* or *Purāṇa-vid. Itihāsa* was the principal theme of the Mahābhārata to which the accretion of *Paurāṇika* stories seems to have been made in course of time. From the standpoint of Vedic interpretation the *Paurāṇika* stories do not occupy the same importance as the *Aitihāsika* ones, though the well-known verse quoted above (see note 23) assigns equal importance to both *Itihāsa* and *Purāṇa* in this respect. Just as there was a mixture of *Aitihāsika* and *Paurāṇika* stories in the Mahābhārata, similarly there was a commingling of both types of such stories in the later Purāṇas; and consequently it became difficult to differentiate one type of story from the other. However, it is important to notice that the term *Purāṇa* is seldom used in the ancient Vedic commentaries to describe any of the legends quoted therein for exegetical purposes, while the terms *Itihāsa, Aitihāsikī Kathā* or *Ākhyāna* are often employed by Sāyaṇa and the other commentators to describe such legends.[46]

Does the absence of the term Purāṇa for a story cited in connection with Vedic interpretation, unlike the use of *Itihāsa, Ākhyāna* and *Kathā*, not indicate that it was not usual to employ for a single story the term *Purāṇa* which was normally used either for a literary genre or for a collection of such stories, whereas the terms *Itihāsa* and *Ākhyāna* could be freely used for any story representing its class? As we have pointed out above, the Nirukta and the Bṛhaddevatā often employ the terms *Itihāsa* and *Ākhyāna* in this connection. Discussing the Ṛgvedic verse I,105,8, Yāska (IV, 6) remarks that this hymn manifested itself to Trita fallen in a well, and that in the said hymn *Brahman* (Veda) is mixed with *Itihāsa* (see below details of Trita-story). The Bṛhaddevatā mentions an *Itihāsa-Sūkta.*[17]

It is still a moot point whether the Vedic Mantras actually contain the *Itihāsas* which the later *Aitihāsikas* seek to read into them. It would therefore amount to begging the question to express any opinion on the matter without its thorough investigation. However, it is necessary to specify the important works which record, to some extent, the attempts made by the Aitihāsika school of Vedic interpretation. In addition to the Saṃhitās of the Kṛṣṇa-Yajurveda and the Brāhmaṇas mentioned above, the Nirukta, the Bṛhaddevatā and the Sarvānukramaṇī contain Aitihāsika legends purporting to be connected with certain Mantras of the Ṛgveda. A very small number of *Aitihāsika* legends—nearly a dozen—are found very succinctly and partly narrated in the Nirukta.[18] However, the Bṛhaddevatā is a veritable repertory of *Aitihāsika* legends, as it contains nearly fifty such legends and records of various viewpoints of several ancient authorities on the subject.[19] The Bṛhaddevatā may be regarded as a real representative of the Aitihāsika school of Vedic interpretation, There is no gainsaying the fact that the Brhad. mentions Yāska and draws upon his Nirukta. The Sarvānukramaṇī of Kātyāyana which is undoubtedly later than the Nirukta and the Brhad. is indebted to both of them. So following the Brhad., the Sarvānukrmaṇī briefly alludes to several Aitihāsika legends.[50] It is, however, to be noted that all the legends recorded in the Brhad. have not been referred to in the Sarvā.; and on the contrary certain legends or parts thereof not narrated in the former have been mentioned in the latter. For instance, the Brhad. merely refers to the number of four Śārṅga Ṛṣis connected with Ṛgvedic hymn X,142, whereas the Sarvā. mentions the names of the four Ṛṣis.[51] It seems that the Sarvā. did not depend entirely on the Brhad. and tapped the other available sources also. For instance, the Sarvā. refers to the views of the *Śāṭyāyana-Brāhmaṇa* and the *Tāṇḍaka-Brāhmaṇa* in connection with an Aitihāsika legend relating to the

RV. VII,32.[52] Elsewhere, too, the Sarvā. refers to diverse viewpoints.[53] Does Kātyāyana's reluctance to mention in his Sarvā. each and every legend recorded in the Bṛhad. lead to the inference that he doubted the authenticity of the legends omitted in his work? It may be noticed that Ṣaḍguruśiṣya in his commentary (Vedārthadīpikā) has quoted several Aitihāsika legends not found in the Bṛhad. and the Sarvā.

Apart from the Bṛhad., the Mahābhārata is an important storehouse of the Aitihāsika legends connected with the Vedic themes. Most of the legends narrated in the former are found in the latter which besides contains several legends found in the Brāhmaṇas and the other Vedic works. Thus the Epic has preserved a good deal of important matter useful for the Aitihāsika school of Vedic interpretation. On the basis of material derived from the Bṛhad. and other ancient works Dyā Dviveda. the author of the Nītimañjarī composed in the 15th century A.D., has narrated a number of Vedic legends and has attempted the didactic interpretation of certain Ṛgvedic verses in accordance with these legends. In his Vedic interpretation Dyā Dviveda generally follows Sāyaṇa, but strikes an independent path in a few places (see Chapter 7).

In the introduction to the *Mādhavānukramaṇī* which has appeared as Appendix IV to the Ṛgvedānukramaṇī edited by C. Kunhan Raja (Madras, 1932) Mādhava asserts that he has composed twelve *Anukramaṇikās* and the eleventh among them is *Itihāsānukramaṇikā*. He further observes that unless the concerned Itihāsa is known the meaning of the Vedic Mantras does not become clear. Although no *Itihāsānukramaṇikā* is now available, it is evident from Mādhava's above statement that some positive efforts were made in this direction in ancient times, and traditional Aitihāsika legends were regarded as useful for interpreting the Vedas. This is why ancient commentators such as Skandasvāmin, Veṇkaṭamādhava and Sāyaṇa cite such Aitihāsika legends in their commentaries in several places and interpret the Mantras accordingly.

Stressing the importance of *Nidāna*[54] (a story explaining the primary cause of composition of a Vedic hymn) for Vedic exegesis, Durgāchārya in the commentary on the Nirukta I,5 (embodying the story of Agastya and Indra connected with

RV. I,170,1) observes: "Desirous of explaining the example (of an expletive employed in a Vedic verse) Yāska here presents a *Nidāna—'Agastya Indrāva'* etc. In the interpretation of Mantras having a *Nidāna*, the *Nidāna* must be presented first of all, because with its help the subject of exposition becomes abundantly clear. Then individual words, then the meaning (of the whole sentence) and finally the derivation of each word through analysis must be explained. This is indeed the order of explanation."

Dr. Emil Sieg in his scholarly work[56] has made a deep and thorough study of the tradition of *Vedic Itihāsa* and has thrown a good deal of welcome light on various aspects of *Itihāsa* connected with the following: (1) *Śārṅgāḥ*, (2) *Śyāvāśva Ātreya*, (3) *Vṛṣā Jāna*, (4) *Vāmadeva Gautama*, (5) *Agastya*, and (6) *Devāpi* and *Śantanu*. However, it is a matter of deep regret that the learned scholar could not complete his important project of investigating *Vedic Itihāsa*.

Following in the footsteps of ancient commentators such as Yāska, Skandasvāmin, Veṅkaṭamādhava and Sāyaṇa, several modern scholars including Oldenberg, Griffith, Grassmann, Geldner and Sieg interpret many Vedic hymns in accordance with the ancient Aitihāsika legends supposed to be connected with them. With a view to illustrating the Aitihāsika approach to Vedic interpretation we are presenting below the various versions of *Trita* legend which has been adopted as a basis by the ancient and modern scholars for interpreting the RV. I,105.

The Bṛhad. III, 132-37 contains the following version of Trita legend: "Having thrown into a well *Trita* who was tending his cows, the cruel sons of a she-wolf (*Sālāvṛkī*) carried off all his cows. Then Trita who had a very good knowledge of Mantras pressed Soma in the well and invoked all the gods. Bṛhaspati heard his invocation. On having seen the gods coming to him, Trita reproached them as follows: 'Where does the all-seeing power of Varuṇa and Aryaman abide? My limbs were bruised by the bricks of the well. Having seen all the gods, I praise them, though none of them sees me.' At the instance of Bṛhaspati all the gods went to that sacrifice of *Trita* and partook of their shares together. As a Ṛṣi Bṛhaspati declared this knowledge and discernment of Trita by means of the last triplet (I,105.16-18) of the hymn." It is worth noting that the Sarvā. does not mention *Trita* legend in connection with this hymn.

In the beginning of his commentary on this hymn, Sāyaṇa presents the following version of this *Itihāsa*, according to the followers of Śāṭyāyana: "Here the followers of Śāṭyāyana narrate the Itihāsa. In olden times there were three seers named *Ekata, Dvita* and *Trita.* Once being tormented by thirst in a jungle in the desert they found a well. Trita entered the well to drink water. Having drunk water, he brought water from the well for the other two. After drinking water they threw Trita into the well and covered it with a chariot-wheel. Having robbed him of all his wealth, they went away. Being unable to come out of the well, Trita thought in his mind—'May all the gods rescue me.' Then he saw this hymn in praise of the gods. Seeing the rays of the moon in the well at night, he wails."

However, the following version of the same legend ascribed by Veṅkaṭamādhava to the *Śāṭyāyana Brāhmaṇa* and cited in the beginning of his commentary on RV. I,105 is different from the above version quoted by Sāyaṇa: "Now the *Śāṭyāyana-Brāhmaṇa* in this connection. Travelling with wealth (*Sātena Yataḥ*[56]) in the forest *Āptyas* (see note 60) became thirsty. They found a well in the desert. *Dvita* and *Ekata* were unable to climb down in the well. *Trita* climbed down in it. When the other two had drunk water and become refreshed, they went away with the cows after having covered him with a chariot-wheel (in the well). He desired: 'I may get out from here (*ud itaḥ iyām*[57]) and find a patron'. Fallen in the well he saw at night the rays of the moon." The Nītimañjarī of Dyā Dviveda also contains this version of Trita legend. However, at the end of his commentary of this hymn Venk. quotes six verses, the first three of which relating to Trita legend have been obviously derived from the Brhad. III, 132-136. But we do not know the source of the last three verses in which the question concerning the seer of the hymn (*Kutsa* or *Trita*) is debated together with that of the reading *mā* and *sakṛt* (RV. I,105,18) as two words (in pursuance of Śākalya's view) or as a single word in keeping with Yāska's opinion (N.V, 21).

The following version of Trita legend contained in the Jaim. Br. I,184 agrees in part with the above-cited Śāṭyāyana-Brāhmaṇa version, but is much more elaborate and interspersed with the glorification of various Sāmans: "Travelling with wealth (see note 56) in the forest Āptyas became thirsty. They found a well in the desert. Ekata and Dvita were unable to climb down in the well. Trita climbed down in it. When the other two had drunk water and become refreshed, they went away with the cows after having covered him with a chariot-wheel (in the well). He desired: 'I may get out from here and find a patron.' He saw this Sāman. He praised with it. He reached the *Nidhana* (the concluding passage of a Sāman '*Sam indubhiḥ*'). By means of heavy rain Parjanya flushed him up and washed away the chariot-wheel with which he was covered. He followed (them) on foot. Having seen him, one of the two became a bear and the other a monkey; and they leaped into the forest. He turned them into a bear and a monkey who had incurred his hostility. He turned them into animals."

The version of Trita legend contained in the Mahābhārata IX,36 is very different from those given above. Trita legend as narrated in the Epic is briefly as follows:

"In ancient times there were three sages named *Ekata*, *Dvita* and *Trita*. Their father Gautama was highly respected by all the kings, and after his death his three sons were also held in high esteem. Among the three sons, *Trita* was the best and most respected like his father. Once the three brothers got a lot of cattle-wealth by performing sacrifices for their rich patrons. When they were proceeding towards the east with the herd of cattle, Trita was moving in front and the other two were at the rear. Having surveyed the vast herd of cattle, the two brothers at the rear conferred together: 'How can both of us appropriate all these cows? Since Trita is an adept in sacrifices and learned in the Vedas, he will be able to earn many more cows. So let us decamp with the cows.' In the course of their journey at night a wolf suddenly appeared in their way. Having seen the wolf standing in his way, Trita ran away in panic and fell into a deep well not far away from the bank of the river Sarasvatī. There he loudly cried for help within the hearing of his two brothers. They did hear his cries, but went away leaving him there to his fate on account of the wolf's fear and their greed for cows. Deserted by his borthers in a dry and dusty well, Trita apprehended death without having performed a Soma sacrifice, and thought: 'How shall I drink Soma here?' Thinking thus he per chance sighted a creeper there. Envisioning there himself as sacrificial priests in the presence of sacrificial fires, the creeper as Soma, pebbles as Soma-pressing stones, water as Ājya, and thinking of the relevant verses belonging to the RV., YV. and SV., Trita mentally performed a Soma sacrifice and raised a loud voice which reached heaven and perturbed the gods. Bṛhaspati heard his voice and said to the gods: 'Trita's sacrifice is going on. Let us all go there; otherwise he may forsake us in anger.' On arrival there all the gods partook of Trita's offerings and granted him boons. Trita asked for the boons that they should rescue him from there and that any one who performs ablutions in that well may attain the same heavenly reward as the performer of a Soma sacrifice. The river Sarasvatī came there with a strong current and flushed him out of the well. Reaching home, Trita cursed his two brothers: 'On account of your greed for cattle you deserted me. Therefore due to my curse both of you shall become ferocious, fanged and wandering animals assuming the forms of wolves, and your progeny shall become langurs, bears and monkeys.' As soon as he pronounced his curse, both of them became so."

The *Itihāsa* cited by Skandasvāmin in the beginning of his commentary on the RV. I,105 follows to a large extent the above-quoted version of the Mahābhārata: "With regard to this hymn they narrate an *Itihāsa*. The seer Āptya had three sons named Ekata, Dvita and Trita. In order to perform sacrifices they begged their sacrificial patrons for cows. Having received the cows, when they were going along the bank of the river Sarasvatī, they saw at night a wolf sitting on the opposite bank. The wolf stood up and frightened them by swimming towards them across the river. In the course of their flight Trita fell into a deep, dry, and dusty well covered with creepers and blades of grass; and then Ekata and Dvita reached home with the cows. Lying in the well, he thought: 'It is not auspicious to die without performing a Soma sacrifice. How can I drink Soma here?' Thinking so he per chance sighted a creeper dangling there. He imagined that creeper to be Soma and pebbles to be Soma-pressing stones and the rest of the means such as fires etc. required for the performance of a sacrifice. Thus mentally performing a sacrifice he invoked the gods who being unable to know the cause of invocation became perturbed. Then Bṛhaspati heard that invocation and said to the gods: 'Trita's sacrifice is going on. Let us go there.' All the gods went there. Desirous of getting out of the well Trita successively praised the gods present there with '*Chandramāḥ* (RV. I.105,1) etc."

In order to explain the derivation of the word *māṣa* Yāska (N.IV,6) cites the RV. I,105,8, and after explaining this Mantra he refers to the Itihāsa that this hymn revealed itself to Trita fallen in a well.

The ancient commentators such as Skand., Venk., and Sāyaṇa explain the RV. I,105 in accordance with the *Itihāsa* discussed above, and Yāska (IV,6) also follows the Aitihāsika school of Vedic interpretation with regard to RV. I,105,8. Among the modern scholars, Wilson and Geldner following Sāyaṇa accept the Aitihāsika interpretation of this hymn, and Geldner has also discussed in detail the Trita legend.[58] In his translation Griffith mainly follows the Aitihāsika interpretation of the hymn, though he occasionally refers to Ludwig's difference of opinion on the subject.

Since very ancient times doubts were expressed about the prevalent Aitihāsika interpretation of the hymn in question. Therefore ancient scholars were not sure about the author of the hymn, and advanced the conjecture that either *Trita* or *Kutsa* was its seer.[59] Venk. in the beginning of his commentary on this hymn presents diverse views on the variants of Āptya,[60] and at the end records difference of opinion about the authorship of the hymn as pointed out above. Although Yāska (IV,6) briefly refers to the Itihāsa connected with this hymn, yet later rejecting Śākalya's padapāṭha (*mā+sakṛt*) he takes *māsakṛt* as a single adjectival form qualifying *Vṛka* which he interprets as the moon.[61] And thus the Nairukta interpretation suggested by Yāska does not agree with the Aitihāsika interpretation attempted by the other commentators, although Sāyaṇa tries to reconcile them.[62] Moreover, elsewhere[63] Yāska explains *Trita* as a name of Indra and not the name of a person figuring in the legend discussed above.

It is obvious from the preceding that if the word *Trita* is used in the RV. as one of the epithets of Indra the Aitihāsika interpretation of RV.I,105 and I,52,5 on the basis of the legendary explanation of the word *Trita* is open to doubt.

Besides, an analysis of the use of the word *Trita* in the various Vedic passages[64] also leads us to the conclusion that at least in the RV. *Trita* is not the name of any legendary person but that of a god, as Macdonell observes[65]: "The above evidence may perhaps justify the conclusion that Trita was a god of lightning, the third or aerial form of fire, originally the middle member of the triad Agni, Vāyu or Indra, Sūrya." On the basis of Vedic evidence Macdonell and Keith have come to the conclusion that Trita is clearly a god in Vedic literature.[66]

It is evident from the foregoing discussion that since the Aitihāsika interpretation of the above-mentioned Vedic Mantras attempted in accordance with the *Trita* legend is not wholly tenable and needs to be re-examined, similar interpretations based on ancient Itihāsas cannot be considered as authentic and final. The upshot of the whole discussion is that the Aitihāsika school of Vedic interpretation has not made such an impeccable contribution to Vedic exegesis as may be emulated with profit. On the contrary, if the Aitihāsika interpretation of the Mantras is blindly followed it is likely to deflect an interpreter from making an independent, unbiased and correct approach to the Vedas. It is worth noting that even in ancient times all the *Itihāsas* were not given full credence, as the Sat. Br. rightly observes[67] that everything narrated in *Anvākhyāna* and *Itihāsa* is not a gospel truth. Even the Brhad., the principal exponent of Aitihāsika school of Vedic interpretation, does not blindly accept all the Aitihāsika interpretations, and expresses its reservations in this respect. For instance, the Brhad. does not fully subscribe to the Aitihāsika interpretation of RV. X,58 and gives vent to the doubt that either the hymn narrates the revival of Subandhu (mentioned in Subandhu legend supposed to be narrated in RV.X, 57-59) who had lost consciousness, or the hymn is in praise of mind.[68] It is obvious that the Bṛhad. does not regard the Aitihāsika interpretation of the hymn as final and indisputable.

It must be noted in this connection that many a legend supposed to be narrated in the Vedas owes its origin to the misinterpretation of allegories underlying the Mantras. For instance, the legend of Prajāpati and his daughter, which several modern scholars including Geldner[69] believe to be alluded to in the RV.I, 71,5, is an allegory according to such ancient authorities as the MS., Ait. Br., P.Br., and Sat. Br. The MS. and the P.Br. hold the view that *Uṣas* (Dawn) is Prajāpati's daughter in this legend.[70] According to the Ait. Br. and the Sat. Br., either Heaven or Dawn is Prajāpati's daughter in the said legend.[71] Similarly the *Urvaśī-Purūravas* legend which is taken as a basis for the Aitihāsika interpretation of the RV. X,95 is also explained as an allegory in some ancient works. For instance, the MS. explains *Urvaśī* as speech and *Purūravas* as vital breath.[72] With regard to the allegory underlying the *Saramā-Paṇi* legend supposed to be connected with the RV.X,108, the MS. IV, 6, 4 explains *Saramā* as speech.

The above-mentioned examples clearly show that since very ancient times the legends relating to the Vedic Mantras were not taken in their literal sense by several Vedic authorities who endeavoured to explain their allegorical meaning. In modern times also some Vedic scholars have attempted to unravel the allegories underlying Vedic legends. See in this connection the Vedic Bibliographies of Renou and Dandekar (Chapter 8). The entire discussion leads us to the conclusion that a modern interpreter should not content himself with merely a literal translation of the Mantras to narrate a legend but should delve deep to find out if any allegory lies hidden therein.

Notes and References

1. Nirukta II, 16; XII, 1; XII, 10.
2. Ibid., II, 24; Cf. Bṛhaddevatā IV, 106-109 and Sarvānukramaṇī. Sāyaṇa prefaces his interpretation of the Hymn with this very *Itihāsa*.
3. AV. XV, 6, 8-12.
4. Sat. Br. XI, 5, 6, 8; 7, 9.

5. Ibid., XII, 4, 3, 12.
6. Gop. Br. I, 1, 10; Sankh. S.S. XVI. 2, 24; Asv. S.S. X, 7, 9; Vaikh. G S. I, 2; Kauṭilya's Arthaśāstra I, 3, 2.
7. Tait. Ar. II, 9, 1; 10, 1; 11, 1.
8. See notes 3, 4, 5, 6 and 7 above.
9. *Cf. Itihāsa-puraṇam* used in Sat. Br. XI, 5, 6, 8; Gop. Br. I, 1, 21; Sankh. Ar. 8, 11; Chh. Up. III, 4, 1; Sankh. G.S. I, 24; Baudh. D.S. IV, 3, 4 etc.; and *Itihāsa-purāṇāni* in Asv. G.S. III, 3, 1-3; IV, 6, 6; Agni. G.S. II, 6, 3; Baudh. D S. II, 5, 27 etc.; and see Baudh. G.S. Bhar. G.S. Vas. D.S., etc.
10. Chh. Up. VII, 1, 2.4—*Itihāsa-purāṇaḥ pañchamo vedānāṃ vedaḥ*.
11. Śaṅkara's commentary on Brh. Up. II, 4, 10.
12. Durgāchārya's commentary on Nirukta II, 10; II, 24; IX 23; X, 26 etc.
13. Sāyaṇa's commentary on Tait. Ar. II, 9, 1. Cf. Sat. Br. XI, 1, 6, 9 and its commentary for the second definition of *Itihāsa* (see note 67 below).
14. Sāyaṇa's Ṛgveda-bhāṣyabhūmikā, p 17 of Poona edition.
15. Sāyaṇa-bhāṣya on Sat. Br. XI, 5, 6, 8; Cf. SBE., vol. 44 p. 98, f.n. 4.
16. Haradatta-bhāṣya on Gaut. D.S. 8, 6; Kullūka-bhāṣya on Manu III, 232; Mitākṣarā on Yaj. I, 45.
17. Kaut. Arth. I, 5, 14.
18. Cf. Mbh. I, 63, 89; I, 1, 54; I, 1, 19; I, 1, 268; I, 2, 36; I, 1, 17; I, 62, 20; I, 62, 16; I, 13, 6. See note 40 below.
19. Ibid., I, 1, 18; I, 59, 5.
20. Geldner's Vedische Studien, Vol. I, pp. 290 ff.; E. Sieg, Die Sagenstoffe des Ṛgveda, pp. 33 ff. See note 55 below.
21. Op. cit., p. 35.
22 Cf. Pāṇini IV, 2, 59-60 and the *bhāṣya-vārtika* on it and *Kāśikā*.
23. Sāyaṇa in his Ṛgveda-bhāṣya-bhūmikā reads "*prahared iti*" (see note 14 above), whereas the Mbh. I, 1, 267 and Vas. D.S. 27, 6 read "*prahariṣyati*" instead. The B.O.R.I. edition of the Epic (I, 1, 204) reads *pratariṣyati*.
24. Vedic Index, I, pp. 76-77; A History of Indian Literature Vol. I, pp. 313 and 518.
25. *See* 'India of Vedic Kalpa-Sūtras', pp. 329-330.
25a. Cf. Macdonell's History of Sanskrit Literature (5th edition), p. 281.
26. Nirukta II, 10 (RV. X, 98—Devāpi-Śantanu legend); II, 24 (RV. III, 33—Viśvāmitra and rivers); IX, 23 (RV. X, 102—Mudgala-Bhārmyaśva legend); X, 26 (RV. X, 81—Viśvakarmā Bhauvanaḥ); XII, 10 (RV. X, 17, 1-2—Saraṇyū legend ; IV, 6 (RV. X, 105—Trita legend).
27. Ibid., II, 16; XII, 1; XII, 10.
28. Brhad. III, 156; IV. 46; VI, 107.109; VII, 7.153; VIII, 11.
29. Brhad. VII, 153. Cf. Macdonell's translation for difference of opinion about *ākhyāna* and *pratyākhyāna*.
30. Nirukta V, 21; XI, 19.25.24; XII, 41.
31. Ibid., X, 10.46.

32. Durga's first explanation: *Ṛṣerdṛṣṭārthasya anubbūtendramaitrasya* Indra-vyasyasya Gṛtsamadasya Indram prati "prītiḥ" tuṣṭiḥ (stutiḥ) bhavati "ākhyānasaṃyuktā" ākhyāna-sambandhāt. Ataścha darśayati mantrāṇām aitihāsiko 'pi artha upekṣitavyo' sāvapi teṣām viṣaya iti. Cf. Brhad. VII, 84—Sūktam ākhyāna-saṃyuktaṃ Vaktukāmasya me śṛṇu.
33. Sat. Br. XIII, 4, 3, 2.15. Cf. Asv. S.S. X, 6, 10; Sankh. S S. XVI, 1, 22; 2, 36; Ap. S.S. XX, 6, 7; Lat. S.S. IX, 9, 10; Hir. S.S. 14, 2; Vait. S.S. 36, 22.24.
34. Cf. Vedic Index, I, pp. 77-78; Keith's Sanskrit Drama, pp. 13 ff.
35. Op. cit., pp. 34-35.
36. Mahābhāṣya on Pāṇini IV, 2, 60. Regarding the secondary formations based on this Vārtika, the later commentators including Jayāditya and Kaiyyaṭa observe that the words *Ākhyāna* and *Ākhyāyikā* refer to the titles comprehended within these categories, whereas the words *Itihāsa* and *Purāṇa* here refer to their own individual forms.
37. The Siddhānta-Kaumudī on Pāṇini reads *Yayakrītam* instead of *Yāyakrītam* of Kaiyyaṭa.
38. Mbh. I, 75-93 (Yayāti-story); III, 135-38 (Yavakrīta-story).
39. Ibid., II, 68, 65; III, 28, 1; 30, 21; 217, 6; 259, 35; V, 33, 103; 35, 5; 36, 1; 97, 11; 106, 7; 133, 1; VII, 52, 20 etc.
40. See references given in note 18 and particularly the following passages: I, 1, 17—*Dvaipāyanena yat proktam purāṇam paramarṣiṇā*; I, 13, 6—*Itihāsam imam viprāḥ purāṇam parichakṣate*; I, 62, 16—*Purāṇam ṛṣisaṃstutam*. It is possible to supply *Ākhyāna* as a substantive qualified by the adjective *Purāṇa* in such passages.
41. Cf. Mbh. I, 4, 1—*Sautiḥ Paurāṇikaḥ*; 2—*Paurāṇikaḥ Purāṇe Kṛtaśramaḥ*.
42. See particularly ibid. I, 5, 1-7.
43. Ibid., I, 31, 3-4.
44. Ibid., I, 2, 82—*Harivaṃśastataḥ parva Purāṇam Khilasañjitam*.
45. Ibid., I, 2, 193 (*Mārkaṇḍeya-Purāṇa*). Cf. III, 182-200; III, 187, 57 (*Matsya-Purāṇa*); III, 191, 16 (*Vāyu-Purāṇa*).
46. According to Sieg (op. cit. p. 25), Sāyaṇa in his Ṛgvedabhāṣya employs the following terms for the legends quoted in his explanations: *Itihāsa* 33 times, *Aitihāsikī Kathā* 3 times, *Ākhyāna* 17 times, *Ākhyāyikā* 14 times, *Upākhyāna* 5 times, *Kathā* 6 times.
47. Brhad. VIII, 11—
Pretitihāsa-sūktam tu manyate Śākaṭāyanaḥ.
Yāsko Draughaṇam aindram vā Vaiśvadevam tu Śaunakaḥ.
These views have been offered with regard to the RV. X, 102 beginning with the words "*Pra te*."
48. Nirukta I, 5 (*Indra-Agastya*); II, 10 (*Devāpi-Śantanu*); II, 24 (Viśvāmitra and the rivers); IV, 6 (*Trita*); V, 13 (*Urvaśī-Mitravaruṇa*); V, 21 (*Uṣas-Aśvinas*); VI, 22 (*Kuruṅga*); X, 26 (*Viśvakarmā Bhauvana*);

XI, 25 (*Saramā* and *Paṇis*); XI, 34 (*Yama-Yamī*); XII, 10 (*Saraṇyū-Āditya*).

49. The following teachers and Vedic schools find mention in the Bṛhad:—*Āśvalāyana*, *Aitara*, *Aitareyaka*, *Aupamanyava*, *Aurṇavābha*, *Kātthakya*, *Kauṣītaki*, *Krauṣṭuki*, *Gārgya Gālava*, *Bhāguri*, *Māṭhara*, *Yāska*, *Rathītara*, *Lāmakāyana*, *Śākaṭāyana*, *Śākapūṇi*, *Śāṇḍilya*, *Śaunaka*, *Śvetaketu*; *Ādhāvaryavaḥ*, *Chhandogāḥ*, *Nairuktāḥ*, *Bāṣkalāḥ*.

50. Cf. Brhad. IV, 130—Sarvā. on RV. IV, 15; Brhad. VI, 35-41—Sarvā. on RV. VIII, 1; Brhad. VI, 154—Sarvā. on RV. X, 10 (Nirukta XI, 34); Brhad. VII, 35-36—Sarvā. on RV. X, 33; Brhad. VII, 49-56—Sarvā. on RV. X, 47; Brhad VII, 84-10.—Sarvā. on RV. X, 56-60; etc.

51. Brhad. VIII, 54; Sarvā. on RV. X, 142. See on this point my article "Vedic Sources of the Śārṅgaka Legend of the Mahābhārata", on pp 397-401 of *Umesh Mishra Commemoration Volume*.

52. Sarva. on RV. VII, 32—*taṃ putroktam Vasiṣṭhaḥ Samāpayateti Śāṭyayanakaṃ*, *Vasiṣṭhasyaiva hataputrasya ārṣam iti Tāṇḍakam*.

53. Cf. Sarvā. on RV. III, 38; V, 27; VIII, 4; VIII, 67; IX, 5; IX, 104; X, 30; X, 105; X, 116; etc.

54. Durgāchārya explains *Itihāsa* as based on *Nidāna* (a story explaining the primary cause of composition of a Vedic hymn). Cf. Durga on N. II, 10—"*Nidānabhūta iti haivam āsīditi ya uchyate sa itihāsaḥ*"; Ibid. on II, 24—"*tatra imam Nidānabhūtam Itihāsam āchakṣate iti āchāryāḥ*", Ibid. on X, 26—"*Yaḥ kaśchid ādhyātmika ādhidaivika ādhibhautiko vārtha ākhyāyate diṣṭyuditārthavabhāsanārtham sa Itihāsa ityuchyate*". Ṣaḍguruśiṣya on the Sarvā. observes: "*Itihāso hetubhūtaḥ*".

55. Die Sagenstoffe des Ṛgveda und die indische Itihāsa-tradition I, Stuttgart, 1902.

56. There are variant readings of this portion, e.g. "*Sāteyena yataḥ*" in Kunhan Raja's edition, "*sātaṃ nayataḥ*" in Vishva Bandhu's edition, "*sāte ye nayataḥ*" in the Adyar MSS., and "*sāte nayataḥ*" in the Jaim. Br. I, 184. If the initial *na* of *nayataḥ* of the last-mentioned variant is read by combining it with the preceding *sāte*, it would give the reading "*sātena yataḥ*" which appears to be more sensible and logical in keeping with the context.

57. In place of *imām* given in the Vishva Bandhu edition the Lakshman Sarup edition and the Jaim. Br. I, 184 record the reading *iyām* which is definitely more sensible and logical.

58. Cf. Vedische Studien, III, pp. 168 ff.

59. See the introductory part of Skand. bhāṣya on RV. I, 105—"*Tritena Kutsena* vaitat dṛṣṭam ityarthaḥ"; Sāyaṇa-bhāṣya on the same: "*Apām putrasya Tritasya Kūpe patitasya Kutsasya vā ārṣam*"; and Sarvā. on it.

60. *Āptya* is an epithet of *Trita* in the RV., and here Trita and his two companions (*Ekata* and *Dvita*) are called *Āptyas*. According to N. XI, 20, *Āptyas* are Ṛṣis who, in the opinion of Durga, are so named

on account of their association with Indra. Venk. in the beginning of his commentary on RV. I, 105 says that the Kaṭha school reads *Āpeya* instead of *Āptya* and the Brāhmaṇa (Tait. Br. III, 2,8,11) records the reading *Āpya*. Cf. Sāyaṇa's view on *Āpya* in the beginning of his bhāṣya on RV. I, 105.

61. N. V, 20-21.
62. Sāyaṇa on RV, 1, 105, 18 : *atra māsakṛt iti Yāska ekam padam manyate Śākalyastu padadvayam*—...etc.
63. N. IX, 25—*Tritas tristhāna Indraḥ.*
64. Cf. RV. VIII, 7, 24; X, 8, 8; X, 99, 6; II, 11, 19; V, 9, 5; TS. I. 8, 10, 2: etc.
65. Vedic Mythology, p. 69.
66. Cf. Vedic Index, I, p. 329.
67. Sat. Br. XI, 1, 6, 9—*Tasmād āhur na etad asti yad daivāsuraṃ yad idam anvākhyāne tvad udyate Itihāse tvat.*
68. Brhad. VII, 85 - *Jīvāvṛttiḥ Subandhor vā yadi vā manasaḥ stavaḥ.*
69. See footnote on Geldner's German translation of RV. I, 71, 5 (HOS, Vol. 32, p. 93).
70. MS. III, 6, 5; P. Br. VIII, 2, 10.
71. Ait. Br. III, 33; Sat. Br. I, 7, 4, 1.
72. M.S. III, 9, 5. Monier Williams (A Sanskrit-English Dictionary, *s.v.*) explains *Urvaśī* as the Dawn personified as a heavenly nymph, and *Purūravas* as the Sun. Cf. Sat. Br. XI, 5, 1; Kālidāsa's play *Vikramorvaśīyam.*

5

The Nairukta School of Vedic Interpretation

The first systematic attempt to interpret the Vedas was made by the Nairuktas, the proponents of the science of etymology (Nirukta), who sought to interpret Vedic words on the basis of their derivative connotation. So it may be termed as etymological or Nairukta method of Vedic interpretation. The origin of this method may be traced to the Brāhmaṇas which attempt the derivation of a number of Vedic words.[1] And Yāska in his Nirukta has quoted some of the etymologies attempted in the Brāhmaṇas.

It may be pointed out that the development of etymological method of Vedic interpretation is closely connected with the progress of grammatical and lexicographical studies in India. Therefore Yāska in his Nirukta declares the science of etymology to be complementary to grammar.[2] Several generations of grammarians, lexicographers and etymologists must have elapsed between the amateurish etymologies of the Brāhmaṇas and the systematic exposition of etymological interpretation embodied in Yāska's Nirukta which is, of course, the last and the best representative of the Nairukta school of Vedic interpretation. Yāska refers by name to about a dozen authorities on Nirukta, the science of etymology, viz., *Aupamanyava, Śākapūṇi, Gālava. Maudgalya, Āgrāyaṇa, Kātthakya, Krauṣṭuki, Aurṇāvabha, Audumbarāyāṇa, Gārgya,* and *Śākaṭāyana*. Besides, he also refers to the etymologists in general as *Nairuktāh*. The works of all the predecessors of Yāska seem to have been irretrievably lost, and we do not know anything about them excepting stray references to their names. However, it would not be correct to assume that all the authorities referred to in Yāska's Nirukta must be only etymologists. In fact, etymology was not an independent and isolated branch of study (see note 2) but was only one of the several branches of the linguistic study of the Vedas. The Padapāṭha and the Prātiśākhyas were the other two important branches of the Vedic linguistic study which, being anterior to the Nirukta, are explicitly mentioned by Yāska in his work, and which undoubtedly contributed to the development of the science of etymology. The Prātiśākhyas are referred to by Yāska (I. 17) as *Pārṣadāni*, while Śākalya, the author of the Padapāṭha of the Ṛgveda is mentioned by name and his analysis of the Vedic text is questioned in the Nirukta (VI, 28). It is not improbable that *Gārgya*, mentioned in the Nirukta (I, 3) is the author of the Padapāṭha of the Sāmaveda. Similarly other authorities such as Śākaṭāyana and Gālava mentioned by Yāska were eminent grammarians. In order to understand the development of Nirukta in proper perspective it is essential to have an idea of the Saṃhitāpāṭha and padapāṭha of the RV. and the other Vedas.

Padapāṭhas

There is no doubt that the Saṃhitā-text and the Pada-text of the RV. represent an advanced stage of grammatical studies in ancient India. Most modern scholars are inclined to hold the view that the Saṃhitā-text was constituted by its grammarian-editors at a later date through the strict applications of the rules of euphonic combinations (*Sandhis*) in disregard of the metrical laws of the original composition. It is no doubt true that some of the euphonic combinations affect the required number of syllables in the Vedic metres which can be restored by removing such combinations. But one wonders whether any orthodox reciter or scholar of the Veda could have dared to introduce any type of alteration into the sacred Vedic text to make it conform to the grammatical notions of his own time.

It is certain that Vedic students were finding it difficult to analyse the Saṃhitā-text into separate words and needed help for this purpose. In order to meet this demand of Vedic students Śākalya composed the Padapāṭha of the RV., which is not only a thorough grammatical analysis of the Saṃhitā-text but also an important aid to its understanding and preservation. The Padapāṭha guarantees the authenticity of the Vedic text as it existed at the time of preparing its Padapāṭha. The six verses of the RV. (VII, 59, 12; X, 20, 1; 121, 10; 190, 1-3) which are contained in the Padapāṭha in the Saṃhitā-form without analysis were not recognized by Śākalya as fully authentic, while the supplementary hymns, called *Khilas*, appended to the RV., were not included in the Padapāṭha in any form. It shows that the Vedic hymns analysed in the Padapāṭha were acknowledged by Śākalya to be fully authentic, while the six verses given in the Saṃhitā form in the Padapāṭha might have been recognized by some teachers, but Khilas, which were not recognized as canonical by any authority, were completely left out.

It is important to note that the various Pāṭhas, such as *Kramapāṭha*, *Jaṭā-Pāṭha*, *Ghanapāṭha*, etc., which were invented by the ancient Indian scholars to guard the Vedic text against any change or interpolation, are all based on the Padapāṭha. Moreover, the Prātiśākhyas which contain rules for pronunciation, euphonic combinations, accent and conversion of the Saṃhitā-text into Padapāṭha and vice versa proceed on the basis of the Padapāṭha.[3]

Although Śākalya's Padapāṭha is an important landmark in the annals of Vedic exegesis and no student of the Veda can afford to ignore it, yet it has got its limitations. Śākalya has not analysed those compounds or combinations which appeared to be doubtful to him. For instance, Śākalya does not analyse certain seemingly compound forms which have been variously interpreted by ancient and modern scholars.[4] Besides, the analysis of certain combinations attempted by Śākalya has been questioned by the ancient and modern commentators of the RV. For instance, Śākalya's analysis of *vayo* into two words *va* and *yáh* (RV. X, 29, 1) has been challenged by Yāska who takes *vāyaḥ* as a single word derived from *vi* "bird" and rejects Śākalya's analysis on two grounds : (1) if *yáḥ* had been a nominative singular of the relative pronoun *yad*, the following finite verb *Adhāyi*, should have been accented on account of it; and (2) if *vā* and *yā́ḥ* are taken as two separate words here the meaning of the sentence remains incomplete.[5] However, the Bṛhaddevatā (II, 114) criticises Yāska for misunderstanding the accent of the finite verb *adhāyi* in this connection, and thus supports Śākalya. Udgīthāchārya attempts two explanations of this verse—one favouring Śākalya and another Yāska. Veṅkaṭāmadhava explains it in accordance with Yāska's analysis, while Sāyaṇa copies verbatim Durga's explanation of this verse in his commentary on the Nirukta.[6] Among the modern scholars Grassmann, Geldner and Vishva Bandhu[7] uphold Śākalya's analysis, but Wilson, Griffith, etc. follow Sāyaṇa in this respect.

Similarly rejecting Śākalya's analysis of mā + sakṛt (RV. I, 105, 18) into two words, Yāska (V, 21) takes the combination as a single word *Māsakṛt* qualifying the following word *vṛkah* which means "moon" according to him. Brhad. II, 112 supports Śākalya and rejects Yāska's analysis without assigning any reason. Skanda and Veṅkaṭa accept Śākalya's analysis in their explanations, whereas Sāyaṇa offers one explanation according to Śākalya's analysis and another according to Yāska's without showing preference for either. Most of the modern scholars including Grassmann, Geldner and Vishva Bandhu accept Śākalya's analysis and do not favour Yāska's.

However, some modern scholars question Śākalya's analysis in several places and suggest their own to obviate the difficulty of explanation faced by them. For instance, a number of modern Vedic scholars find it difficult to explain the locative singular form *mā́nuṣe* of RV. III, 23, 4c in accordance with Śākalya's analysis and suggest a different analysis. So Grassmann in his dictionary and German translation of the RV. takes it as a nominative singular form *mā́nuṣah* and Vishva Bandhu is also inclined to suggest its emendation to a genetive singular form. I have elsewhere fully discussed all these suggestions and explanations of this word and come to the conclusion that Śākalya's analysis *mā́nuṣe* is quite correct.[8] Doubts have been expressed about Śākalya's analysis of other euphonic combinations also.[9]

Pāṇini in his grammar refers four times to Śākalya's views; and the Sankh. G.S., Vaj. Pr., A. Pr., Kātyāyana (Vārtikakāra) and Patañjali also speak of Śākalya. The R. Pr. not only mentions Śākalya but is also based on his Padapāṭha. Similarly the other Prātiśākhyas also formulate their rules on the basis of the Padapāṭha as pointed out above (see note 3). Gārgya is the Padakāra of Sāmaveda, and Ātreya is credited with the Padapāṭha of the T.S. Although the Padapāṭhas of the AV. and the Vaj. S. are also available, the question of their authorship is still open.

It may be mentioned here that Padapāṭha which requires a good knowledge of grammar gave an impetus to the linguistic study of the Vedas and laid the foundation of Nirukta. Although the Saṃhitā-text of the Veda was fixed in accordance with the grammatical principles of Sandhi, the composition of Padapāṭha entails a more minute grammatical analysis which requires a thorough knowledge of not only Sandhi but also of accent, compounds, prepositions, certain suffixes, *Pragṛhya*, *Riphita Visarjanīya*, nominal stem, root, cases, etc. The real purpose of the sign of separation called *avagraha* in Padapāṭha is to indicate the constituents of a word; and this is also the main object of grammar called *Vyākaraṇa* which literally means "analysis". Thus the aim of both is the same, but their scope is different. The scope of grammar is very vast indeed embracing the formation of all types of words and their mutual relationship, whereas Padapāṭha confines itself mainly to the separation of euphonic combinations (*Samhitā*) and a broad indication of the important constituents of various types of compounds and case-endings. Despite its limited scope and shortcomings Padapāṭha marks an important stage in the linguistic study of the Veda.

Nighaṇṭu

After Padapāṭha, the Nighaṇṭu occupies an important place in the annals of linguistic study of the Veda and may be termed as the first lexicographical attempt in the world. The Nighaṇṭu seems to be a Prākṛta term signifying a collection of important words. The Nighaṇṭu, or *Samāmnāya* as it is called in the beginning of the Nirukta, is divided into five chapters and is therefore also called *pañchādhyāyī*. The first three chapters contain classified groups of synonyms. For instance, the synonyms of earth are listed in the first section of the first chapter and those of atmosphere and heaven in the third and the fourth sections respectively. In the opinion of Dr. L. Sarup, there is some sort of a principle discernible in the arrangement of synonyms in the first three chapters. So the first chapter deals with physical objects and natural phenomena such as earth, air, water, clouds. dawn, day and night. The synonyms collected in the second chapter relate to man, his limbs, qualities, actions and aehievements. The synonymous words collected in the third chapter deal with abstract qualities such as heaviness, lightness etc., according to Dr. L. Sarup. But there are so many exceptions also. The first three chapters containing Vedic synonyms are regarded to constitute the *Naighaṇṭuka Kāṇḍa.* The fourth chapter which is styled as *Naigama Kāṇḍa* contains a list of such Vedic words whose meaning is not easy to understand and needs to be explained. The fifth chapter called *Daivata Kāṇḍa* is a glossary of the names of Vedic deities.

As regards the authorship of the Nighaṇṭu, there is no definite evidence on this point. It is certain beyond any shadow of doubt that Yāska is not the compiler of the Nighaṇṭu, for at the outset of his Nirukta, he clearly states that the *Samāmnāya*, Nighaṇṭu, which had been already compiled, needs to be explained. Moreover, in I,20 Yāska attributes the compilation of the Nighaṇṭu to a later generation of sages who lacking direct perception of Dharma (Veda) resorted to the compilation of this work and the Vedāṅgas for the sake of convenience.

With regard to the authorship of the Nighaṇṭu, I am inclined to agree with Dr. L. Sarup who holds the view that the Nighaṇṭu is probably not the production of a single individual, but the result of the united efforts of a whole generation, or perhaps of several generations.[10]

The Nirukta

The word *Nirukta* literally means 'explanation' or 'etymological interpretation of a word'. So Yāska's work entitled *Nirukta* which is an explanation of the Vedic words listed in the Nighaṇṭu, is a commentary on the Nighaṇṭu as admitted by him in the very beginning of the Nirukta. Since it is the only work of its kind available at present, the title *Nirukta* now means the Vedic commentary composed by Yāska. The Nirukta which consists of twelve chapters and an appendix is the earliest systematic commentary on selected words, passages and deities of the RV. The first chapter which is introductory in nature deals with the scope and importance of Nirukta; and in the course of discussion Yāska brings in several linguistic questions of a general nature and presents a systematic debate on them. For instance, the following controversial issues are debated by Yāska in the first chapter:

(a) Whether speech exists in the speech organs only;
(b) whether the prepositions have any independent meanings of their own;
(c) whether all the nouns have been derived from verbs; and
(d) whether the Vedic words have any meanings. The views expressed by Yāska on such controversial issues are rational and reflect his vast learning.

In the beginning of the second chapter, Yāska enunciates the principles of etymology. First of all, he lays down the general principle that one should derive a word in conformity with its regular accent, grammatical form and radical modification. However, when the accent, grammatical form, and radical modification of a word are irregular, its derivation becomes difficult. In such a situation Yāska's advice is that one should etymologize in accordance with the meaning of the word on the basis of a similarity of common usage or of even a syllable or a letter but one must never give up the attempt to etymologize. In this connection Yāska cautions an etymologist against placing undue reliance on grammar, for the usages of words are obscure. Therefore, one should interpret grammatical affixes in keeping with the sense of words. Yāska advises an etymologist to take due notice of important phonetic phenomena, such as syncope, metathesis, anaptyxis, haplology, assimilation, etc., at the time of derivation. The most important principle of etymology enunciated by Yāska is that words should be derived in accordance with their meaning, and that no attempt should be made to derive single words, i.e., words torn out of context.

Commencing from the fifth section of the second chapter upto the end of the third chapter, Yāska takes up a systematic derivation of some selected synonyms listed in the first three chapters of the Nighaṇṭu. First of all, he mentions the exact number of synonyms listed in a particular section of the Nighaṇṭu and then gives the derivation of a few important words of the section. In order to illustrate the Vedic usage of the words under discussion, he cites a Vedic passage and paraphrases it explaining the meaning of difficult words occurring in it. The obscure Vedic words compiled in the fourth chapter of the Nighaṇṭu have been systematically explained by Yāska in the fourth, fifth and sixth chapters of his work in the manner explained above. Chapters seven to twelve of the Nirukta have been devoted to the discussion of various aspects of the Vedic deities listed in the fifth chapter of the Nighaṇṭu. In the beginning of the seventh chapter of the Nirukta Yāska attempts the definition of a deity (*devatā*), enumerates various types of ṚK-verses according to their subject-matter, and presents different view-points on the question of ascertaining the deity of those Mantras where no deity has been specifically mentioned. Then Yāska discusses the nature, number, form, and place of operation and mutual relationship of Vedic deities. From the fourteenth section of the seventh chapter up to the end of the twelfth chapter, Yāska takes up for discussion the place of operation, nature and etymology of Vedic deities in the same order in which their names are listed in the fifth chapter of the Nighaṇṭu. In order to illustrate his view-point he cites verses from the RV. and explains the verses and obscure words occurring in them in the manner described above. The thirteenth chapter of the Nirukta which is called *Pariśiṣṭa*, appendix, is not Yāska's composition, because it contains the words "*namo Yāskāya*" at the end. Besides, the style of explanation and the contents of the 13th chapter also distinguish it from the preceding twelve chapters. Moreover, since Yāska's commentary on the Nighaṇṭu concludes with the 12th chapter, there is no *raison d'etre* for the 13th chapter. It is thus obvious that the 13th chapter which is found in some MSS. divided into two chapters was appended to the Nirukta at a later date.

In the twelve chapters of the Nirukta Yāska explains nearly 600 verses of the RV. and suggests the etymology of about 1300 words. Yāska's explanation of the Vedic verses is rational and free from supernatural elements, because following in the footsteps of the Nairuktas he endeavours to explain the natural phenomena underlying the names occurring in the Veda and thus offers naturalistic interpretation of Vedic gods. For instance, with regard to the interpretation of *Vṛtra* Yāska (II, 16) quotes with approbation the view of the Nairuktas that *Vṛtra* is a cloud, and elucidates the same with the remarks that the phenomenon of rain is produced by the combination of water and light, and that the Vedic descriptions of fights between Indra and Vṛtra are metaphorical. Similarly the Nirukta (II,8) interprets the RV. I,164,32 as description of rain. Although Yāska is a follower of the Nairukta school of interpretation, yet he does not hesitate to cite the views of the other schools of Vedic interpretation such as Yājñikas, Parivrājakas, Aitihāsikas, and Naidānas, while discussing various interpretations. It shows his vast learning and catholicity of outlook. He draws a distinction between the Vedic and post-Vedic usages of certain indeclinable words (I, 5-11) and secondary derivatives (II, 5). He alludes to the use of metaphorical expressions in the Veda (II, 16). Yāska's following remarks in regard to the nature of Vedic deities (VII, 4) are illuminating and useful for the correct interpretation of the Veda: "On account of the pre-eminence of the deity One Soul (i.e. the All-prevading Soul) is praised in various ways. Other (manifest) gods are (like) the limbs of One Soul. The Specialists in this branch of study observe that the seers praise beings according to the plurality and universality of their intrinsic nature. The gods are (figuratively described in the Veda as) born from each other (e.g., RV.X, 72, 4-5 makes the paradoxical statement that *Dakṣa* is born from *Aditi* who is his daughter). The gods are the primary source of each other. They owe their birth, i.e., coming into existence to their specific functions as well as to the (Universal) Soul. Soul alone is their chariot, horse, weapon and arrows".

Yāska's interpretation may be regarded as systematic and scientific to some extent. No other interpreter of ancient India has displayed so much rationality in his approach to the problem of Vedic interpretation. Complimenting Yāska, Dr. L. Sarup observes that his method is scientific and, notwithstanding his remote antiquity, surprisingly modern.

As regards the quality of Yāska's etymologies, divergent opinions ranging from downright condemnation to high encomium have been expressed by modern scholars. In the opinion of Prof. V.K. Rajavade, the derivations given by Yāska have nothing to do with sound-laws,[11] and the Nirukta is not a science but a travesty of science.[12] On the other hand, Dr. L. Sarup is of opinion that Yāska is the first to claim the scientific foundation and also the first to formulate the general principles for etymology.[13] H. Skold in his treatise on the Nirukta also compliments Yāska as follows[14]: "Many etymologies seem nonsensical but we ought rather to be astonished because the Nirukta contains so many good and true etymologies as it does." The same scholar observes in the preface of the same treatise: "In the first period of etymological studies in Western Europe the European scholars profited, to a great extent, by the work of Niruktakāra, and it is quite certain, that it has not yet yielded all it might be able to yield." In the opinion of Dr. Siddheshwar Varma, Yāska was a remarkable etymologist far in advance of his times, whose etymologies have a sound scientific basis, and who has evinced a considerable grasp of phonological principles which formed the background of the Vedic language.[15] On a complete, critical and systematic examination of Yāska's etymologies in the light of comparative philology Dr. Varma has made the assessment that out of 1298 etymologies attempted by Yāska 849 are more or less primitive, 224 would be entirely acceptable to comparative philology and 225 are obscure.[16]

It cannot be gainsaid that Yāska's insistence on the derivation of each and every word shows his excessive and irrational zeal for etymologization and leads to preposterous etymologies in certain cases. However, this circumstance does not detract from the intrinsic merit of the etymological method of interpretation. The Vedic language is highly developed and the seers choose their words very carefully to express their thoughts in a poetic style marked with metaphors and play upon words. The correct etymology of a word often provides a clue to its real meaning intended by the seer. For instance, the Vedic seers employ the word *jāra* in the following phrases in a poetical style to denote the Sun : *jāraḥ kanīnām, svasur jārah*, *Jāra uṣasām*, and *apām jārah*, which if literally translated according to the popular sense of the word *jāra* would mean —"the paramour of maidens", "the paramour of his sister", "the paramour of downs", and "the paramour of waters" respectively. But if the word *jāra* in these contexts is etymologically interpreted as "consumer", *jarayitā*, in keeping with Yāska's derivation,[17] from the root Jṛ, the meaning would be rational and linguistically sound, because several verbal forms derived from the same root are found used in the RV. in this very sense. Thus the main advantage of the etymological method of interpretation is that it helps us to distinguish the original radical meaning of a word from its conventional meaning in those cases in which the seers deliberately employ a word capable of yielding two such meanings. It is evident from an analysis of Vedic usages that the seers are fond of using *double entendre* in order to show off their poetical skill. Alluding to this tendency of the Vedic language the Brahmaṇas observe that the gods love recondite speech and abhor direct statements (see note 29 of Chapter 2). In several Vedic passages the Ṛsis lay special stress upon the radical nature of the name of a particular deity by using verbal and other derivative forms of the same root in conjunction with the radical name of the deity. For instance, we often come across in the RV. the verbal and derivative forms of the root *sū* 'to impel' with the name of the god *Savitṛ* which is evidently derived from the same root; and similarly the verbal and derivative forms of *bhaj* "to distribute" are found employed in the Veda with the name of the god *Bhaga* formed from it.[18] In such cases the etymological method of interpretation is definitely very helpful.

Post-Yāska Etymologies

Although no systematic treatise on etymologies was composed after Yāska, the trail blazed by Yāska has continued to guide the successive generations of scholars. In addition to explaining the formation of words occurring in the Vedic and post-Vedic language, Pānini has explained the redical base of a large number of Sanskrit words in his detailed treatment of the primary (*kṛt*) suffixes, and has made pointed references to such Vedic words as are peculiar in their formation. Besides, he has specifically mentioned the meanings expressed by certain derivative words[19] However, Pāṇini's attempts in explaining the derivation of certain Vedic words are not wholly acceptable. For instance, Pāṇini's attempt to explain the Vedic words *Napāt, Nāsatyā, Nakṣatra, Nāka* etc. as negative compounds having the negative paricle *na* as their first member is not sustainable in the light of modern researches.[0] There is no doubt that the Pāṇinian grammar embodies a part of the then existing knowledge of Vedic exegesis and linguistic studies, but it cannot be considered to be complete and comprehensive with regard to the treatment of the Vedic language. There is therefore no solid basis for the claim to interpret the Veda according to the Pāṇinian system of interpretation,[21] because Pāṇini has made no direct contribution to the realm of Vedic exegesis and etymologies, although his grammar is very useful for a proper understanding of the Vedic and Classical Sanskrit.

Although Kātyāyana has appended a number of Vārtikas to the Sūtras of Pāṇini to notice certain peculiarities of the Vedic language, the number of Vārtikas dealing with the derivation of Vedic words is very small.[22] Patañjali in his Mahābhāsya has explained with necessary illustrations the Sūtras and Vārtikas dealing with the peculiarities of the Vedic language. From this point of view, Patañjali's contribution to the study of the Vedic language is valuable. It is important to point out here that unlike Yāska Pāṇini, Kātyāyana and Patañjali do not subscribe to the view that all nouns are derived from verbs, and hold the view that such nouns as do not indicate a clear-cut radical base should be regarded as *avyutpanna* "having no clear etymology". For attempting the derivation of nouns of doubtful etymology Pāṇini (III, 3,1) refers his readers to the *Uṇādi* Sūtras of Śākaṭāyana. Kātyāyana and Patañjali also refer to the view that one should resort to the *Uṇādi* Sūtras of Śākaṭāyana to attempt the derivation of *naigama* (Vedic) words and such traditional words as are apparently not derivable according to the standard grammatical norms.[23] There are nearly 750 *Uṇādi* Sūtras ascribed to

Śākaṭāyana which suggest the etymology of Sanskrit words including some important Vedic vocables. Although all the etymologies attempted by the *Uṇādi* Sūtras do not stand the test of modern philology, yet they record the attempts of ancient Indian etymologists to decipher certain difficult and obscure words. In the derivation of Vedic words Śākaṭāyana has postulated some such suffixes as are not met with in Pāṇini's grammar.[24] The *Uṇādi* Sūtras supplement the Nirukta and the Pāṇinian grammar.

We discern a tendency in ancient Indian works—right from the Brāhmaṇas to the Epics, Purāṇas and Classical Sanskrit poets—to make free use of the etymological method of interpretation to attribute any meaning of one's choice to any word. Many such etymologies are met with in the Mahābhārata.[25] Kālidāsa derives the word *rājan*[26] from the root *ranj* "to delight" which is obviously wrong as is well known to all students of Sanskrit. Perhaps it was regarded as a proof of ingenuity to suggest a novel etymology.

The later commentators including Sāyaṇa have suggested a number of new etymologies of Vedic words besides citing those attempted by Yāska. It is difficult to pass judgment on all such etymologies. However, it would not be irrelevant to point out that the etymologies based on roots, linguistic tendencies and ideas current in the later language only cannot be considered to be sound and helpful for Vedic exegesis. For instance, taking a cue from Yāska's interpretation of *bekanāṭas* as usurers (VI, 26), Sāyaṇa in his commentary on the RV. VIII, 66, 10 derives the word *bekanāṭa* from a heterogeneous conglomeration of the Apabhraṃśa *be* "two"+Skt. *eka* "one" + causative of *naṭ* "to dramatize". Any one acquainted with the history and nature of the Vedic language will simply laugh at this preposterous etymology.

Recognizing the importance of etyomologies conforming to the Vedic usage, modern scholars also endeavour to suggest the probable etymologies of Vedic vocables in their lexicons.[27] It is interesting to note that to resort to some sort of a conjectural etymology in order to decipher the meaning of an obscure Vedic word is not the weakness of Yāska alone who regards all nouns as derived from verbs, but later commentators including Sāyaṇa and modern scholars such as Roth, Grassmann, Monier-Williams etc. also take recourse to this method in case of difficulty of interpretation. For instance, the Vedic word *alātṛṇá*, which has not been analysed by Śākalya on account of its doubtful meaning, has been derived by Yāska (VI, 2) from *alam+ā+tṛd* (*alam ā tardanaḥ meghaḥ*). Veṅkaṭa simply follows Yāska, but Sāyaṇa suggests different etymologies. In his commentary on the RV. III, 30, 10, he first explains the word according to Yāska's etymology but later derives it from *alam+tṛh* in its etymological explanation. However, in his commentary on the RV. I, 166, 7 Sāyaṇa suggests the following three etymologies of *alātṛṇà* : (i)*ana+tṛd* (nakārasya sthāne lakāraḥ. *ānātṛṇāsaḥ ātardanarahitāḥ*); (ii) *alam + ā + tṛd*; (iii) *alam atyaśtham dātāraḥ phalānām*. Roth derives the word from *a* + *lā* =*rā* "to give"+suffix *tṛṇā*, meaning "not granting any thing, miserly". Grassmann and Monier-Williams follow Roth with regard to the meaning *alātṛṇa*. A careful examination will show that Roth's etymology is as conjectural as Sāyaṇa's and seems to be a mere negative of Sāyaṇa's third (last) etymology mentioned above. Max Müller does not accept Roth's derivation of this word and suggests an entirely new etymology : *a+lātra=rātra* meaning "not barking", i. e. "not reviling" from the root *rai* or *rā* "to bark" which in his opinion explains the Latin *lātrare*, to bark.[28] Griffith follows Max Müller's explanation of this word in his English translation of RV. III, 30, 10 but accepts Wilson's explanation "devoid of malevolence" in the translation of RV. I, 166, 7. Langlois translates the same word as "Leureux de nos louanges" in RV. I, 166.7 and as "qui laissait fleterir les plantes", while Geldner translates it in these passages as "die nicht zurūckzuforden (?)" and "ohne zurūckzufordern (?)" respectively. It is clear from a perusal of the different interpretations of *alātṛṇa* suggested by modern scholars that its meaning is even at present as obscure as it was in the time of Śākalya who left it unanalysed. This study leads us to the conclusion that the etymological method of interpretation can render some help to a limited extent only when the usage of various forms of the concerned root can be attested in the Vedic language. In the absence of certainty of the root forming the word under consideration, etymologization generally degenerates into a game of guessing *ad infinitum*, as Yāska offers as many as 14 derivations for Indra (X, 8), 6 for Jātavedas (VII, 19) and 5 for Agni (VII, 14) in pursuance of his well-known dictum (II, 1) that one should endeavour to derive each and every word on the basis of the slightest similarity of even a single syllable or letter. In this connection it must be noted that it is not safe to suggest the etymology of an obscure word on the basis of a faint phonetic similarity between such a word and a root. It is not improbable that either some of the obscure Vedic words like *Kuṇāru* and *bekanā́ṭa* might have been borrowed from another language, or all signs indicating the origin of such words have been obliterated in course of time. It cannot be gainsaid that the etymological method of interpretation will prove utterly futile if either obscure words of foreign origin are traced to Sanskrit roots or the obscure words of unknown origin are derived from non-Vedic roots in accordance with the notions of later times. An etymologist must observe due restraint in the fascinating task of etymologisation.

Notes and References

1. See, for instance, the etymologies of *Yama, Vṛtra, Śara, Yūpa, Pṛthivī, Aśva*, etc. in the Brahmaṇa-portion of the Tait. S.
2. Nirukta I, 15...*tadidam vidyāsthānam vyākaraṇasya kārtsnyam svārtha-sādhakaṃ cha.*
3. Cf. Nirukta I, 17...*Padaprakṛtīni Sarvacharaṇānām Pārṣadāni.*
4. See, e.g. *ṛśā́das, ā́śuśukṣaṇi, alātṛṇā́, anūpa, ā́ghṛṇi, āṅgūṣa, ādaghná, āhanās, duroṇá, pṛtanā́j, pramaganda, prá́skaṇva, vātāpya,* śirimbiṭha.
5. Nirukta VI, 28.
6. It is to be noted that Veṅkaṭa following Yāska explains *Vāyaḥ* as *pakṣi* (as a nominative singular form), whereas Durga followed by Sāyaṇa explains the same as *Vāyam ātmīyam putram* (as an accusative singular) which is not in keeping with even Yāska's analysis. It may be mentioned here that Durga's explanation of RV X, 30, 11 has also been copied verbatim by Sāyaṇa in his commentary and duly acknowledged with the remarks that the explanation of this verse has been taken from the commentary on the Nirukta.

7. In fact Vishva Bandhu in his Vai. P. (*s.v.*) suggests the emendation *vām* in place of *vā*, which is far-fetched and uncalled for.
8. See my paper "A New Interpretation of the Vedic Word Mānuṣa" published in the Journal of the Ganganatha Jha Research Institute Vol. XVII, parts 3-4, pp. 193-202.
9. See my "Vaidika-Vyākaraṇa" Part I, pp. 189-90. Besides, Patañjali in his commentary on p. III, 1, 109; VI, 1, 207 and VIII, 2, 16 does not accept the authority of the Padakāras and asserts that grammar should not follow the Padakāras but should be followed by them and that word-analysis should be made in accordance with the rules of grammar.
10. Introduction to the Nighantu and the Nirukta p. 14.
11. Yāska's Nirukta Vol. I, p. xlii.
12. Ibid., p. xli.
13. Op. cit., p. 64.
14. The Nirukta, p. 181.
15. The Etymologies of Yāska, preface p. XI.
16. Ibid., p. XII.
17. Nirukta III, 16; V, 12; X, 21; Cf. Vārtika 4 on Pāṇini III, 3, 20.
18. Cf. RV. IV, 54, 2-6; VII, 41, 2; V, 46, 6. It may be noted that the etymological basis of the words *mātariśvan*, *jāta-vedas* and *purohita* is clearly alluded to by the seers in the Ṛgvedic passages III, 29, 11; VI, 15, 13 and VI, 70-4-5 (Cf. VII, 53, 1) respectively. *See* Bergaigne's "Vedic Religion" (English translation) Vol. I, pp. 53, 120, 121; and Vol. III, p. 342.
19. Cf. Pāṇini III, 1, 103, 105, 115-117, 129; 3, 68-71 etc.
20. Cf. "The Etymologies of Yāska", pp. 136-137. See the Tait. S. V, 3, 7, 1; S. Br. VIII, 4, 1, 24; P. Br. XXI, 8, 4 and the Nirukta II, 14 for a similar etymology of the word *Nāka*.
21. Cf. S.S. Bhawe : "The Soma Hymns of the Ṛgveda", M.S. University, Baroda, 1957, 1960, etc; D.P. Patanjal : "*A Critical Study of the Ṛgveda*", New Delhi, 1963, about which Renou remarked : "the tentative and hazardous view that Pāṇini is helpful for interpretation of RV. pushed to the extreme".
22. Nearly 450 Vārtikas deal with the peculiarities of the Vedic Language. The peculiarities of the Vedic language noticed by Kātyāyana are at least as important as those recorded by Pāṇini. It shows that Kātyāyana found Pāṇini's treatment of the Vedic language very inadequate and therefore appended such a large number of Vārtikas on it. As regards the Vārtikas suggesting the derivation of the Vedic words, the following instances are particularly worthy of note : (a) the Vārtikas on P. III, 2, 135 dealing with the derivation of *hotṛ*, *potṛ*, *udgātṛ*, *neṣṭṛ*, *tvaṣṭṛ*, *kṣatṛ*, *saṃgrahītṛ*; (b) Vārtika 4 on P. III, 2, 139 for *daṅkṣṇu;* (c) Vārtika 2 on P. III, 2, 171 for *sedi* and *nemi;* (d) Vārtika 3 on P. III, 2, 178 for *didyut*, *jagat* and *juhū*; and Vārtika 4 on the same sūtra for *dhī*; (e) Vārtika 4 on P. III, 3, 20 for *dāra* and

java; (f) Vārtika 3 on P. III, 3, 36 for *udgrābha* and *nigrābha*; (g) Vārtika 4 on P. III, 3, 56 for *java* and *sava*.

23. See Kāśikā and Mahābhāṣyavārtikas on P. III, 3, 1; and Mahābhāṣya on P. VII, 1, 2, and VII, 2, 8—*Uṇādayo avyutpannāni prātipadikāni*.

24. See my "Vaidika Vyākarṇa" Vol. II, p. 792; and also pp. 796-812.

25. Cf. the etymology of Jaratkāru in 1, 40, 2-4. Can the first member *Jarat* be derived from the root *jṛ* "to praise"? Its popular etymology is from the root *jṛ* "to decay".

26. Raghuvaṃśa IV, 12., in 11, 53 a new etymology of the word *kṣatra* is suggested.

27. See, e.g., the lexicons of Roth, Grassmann, Neisser, aud Monier-Williams and Vishva Bandhu's Vai. P.

28. SBE., Vol. 32 pp. 227-228.

6

The Other Ancient Schools of Vedic Interpretation

In addition to the three major schools of Vedic interpretation discussed in the preceding chapters, some other systems of Vedic interpretation also existed in ancient India. Among such minor schools of Vedic interpretation, the *Parivrājaka* school of Vedic interpretation, which may be called the Mystic School of Vedic interpretation, figures prominently because it has got a long history and a traditional base. Besides, grammarians (*Vaiyākaraṇas*), Jurists and *Naidānas* attempted in their own way the interpretation of certain Vedic Mantras as attested by the Nirukta, the Mahābhāṣya, the Baudh. D.S., etc.

The Parivrājaka (Mystic) School of Vedic Interpretation

The Parivrājaka school of Vedic interpretation referred to by Yāska (II, 8) may be regarded as representing those scholars who attempt a mystic interpretation of the Vedas. According to this school of exegesis, not only those Vedic Mantras which are considered to be of philosophical import both by ancient and modern scholars,[1] but also the other Vedic Mantras can be interpreted to conform to their mystic ideas.

The earliest specimens of mystic interpretation of the Vedas are met with in the Brāhmaṇas as well as in the Āraṇyakas and the Upaniṣads embodied in them. For instance, the Śatapatha Brāhmaṇa XIV, 4, 2, 21-22 (Bṛhadāraṇyaka Upaniṣad I, 4, 10) connects the RV.IV, 26, 1 with the following philosophical exposition: "*Brahman* indeed was this in the beginning. It knew itself only as 'I am Brahman'. Therefore it became. Whoever among the gods became awakened to this, indeed became that. It is the same in the case of seers, same in the case of men. Seeing this, indeed, the seer Vāmadeva knew: 'I was Manu and the sun too' (RV.IV, 26, 1). This is so even now. Whoever knows thus, 'I am *Brahman*', becomes this all." The question of determining the subject-matter of the Ṛgvedic hymn under reference (especially its first three verses) has been agitating the minds of the Vedic exegetes since long. According to Kātyāyana's Sarvānukramaṇī, either the seer of the hymn has praised himself as the god Indra, or Indra is praising himself.[2]

The followers of this school of Vedic exegesis attempt the mystic interpretation of Vedic deities and sacrifices also. Several instances of such interpretations are found in the Brāhmaṇas, the Āraṇyakas and the Upaniṣads. For instance, *Mitra* and *Varuṇa* are interpreted as inhalation (*Prāṇa*) and exhalation (*Apāna*) respectively in the prose portion of the Tait. S. and in many Brāhmaṇas.[3] But such mystic explanations offered in the Brāhmaṇas suffer from inconsistency, as one and the same Vedic deity has been variously interpreted in them. For instance, the god *Indra* has been interpreted in the Brāhmaṇas as *speech*,[4] *inhalation*[5] (*Prāṇa*), *mind*,[6] *the Sun*,[7] *wind*[8] (*Vāyu*), *etc*. Yāska (VII, 24) refers to this tendency of the Brāhmaṇas.

Among the mystic explanations of Vedic sacrifices, that of *Aśvamedha* is worth noticing, for the TS., the S. Br., and the B. Up. interpret the sacrificial horse as a cosmic force identical with the world through an allegory.[9] Accordingly, the Dawn is the head of the sacrificial horse, the Sun its eye, the Wind its breath, Agni Vaiśvānara its open mouth, the Moon its ear, quarters its feet, the sky its back, the air its belly, the earth under-part of its belly, the intermediate quarters its ribs, the seasons its limbs, the months and half-months its joints, the day and night its winking, the stars its bones, the clouds its flesh, the sand its intestinal food, the rivers its bowels, the mountains its liver and lungs, the herbs and trees its hair, the rising sun its forepart, the setting sun its hind part, the lightning its yawning, the thundering its whinning, and speech is its voice. The Brāhmaṇas emphasize that a wise man who meditates upon the real nature of the sacrificial horse identical with the cosmic force understands the real *Aśvamedha*.[10]

We witness in the Āraṇyakas and the Upaniṣads an upsurge of the tendency of attempting a mystic interpretation of Vedic sacrifices, which in its turn led to the mystic interpretation of Vedic verses. For instance, the Fifth Prapāṭhaka of the TA. suggests the mystic explanation of the oblation given in the fire in the first Pravargya ceremony introductory to the Soma sacrifice. The TA. asserts that in fact *Agni* (fire) here stands for inhalation (*Prāṇa*[11]). In the Nārāyaṇa Upaniṣad comprised in the TA. some important sacrifices, their constituent ceremonies and materials have been symbolically and mystically interpreted for a knower of truth who has renounced the world.[12] For such a person his own self is the sacrificer, faith (*śraddhā*) his wife, body the sacrificial fuel, chest the altar, hair the sacrificial grass, heart the sacrificial post, desire clarified butter, anger the sacrificial animal, and austerity is the sacrificial fire. Self-control is the slayer of the sacrificial animal. Speech is his sacrificial fee. Inhalation (*Prāṇa*) is his Udgātṛ priest, eye his Adhvaryu priest, mind his Brahman priest, and ear is his Agnīdh priest. His whole life is an act of sacrificial consecration. His food is the sacrificial oblation, and his drink is the sacrificial Soma—draught. Day and night are his full-moon and new-moon sacrifices. Half-months and months are his *chāturmāsya* sacrifices. Seasons are his animal sacrifices. Years are the series of his sacrificial days (*aharganāh*). His life is a great Soma sacrifice called *Sarva-Vedasa* in which entire property is given away; and his death is the final sacrificial bath called *Avabhṛtha*. This is a symbolical *Agnihotra* sacrifice lasting throughout life.

The tenth chapter of the Sankh. Ar. also contains a symbolical and spiritual interpretation of the Agnihotra sacrifice. Similarly the Chh. Up. III, 16-17 symbolically describes a person's entire life as a sacrifice. Following the Āraṇyakas and the Upaniṣads, the Bhagavadgītā IV, 23-33, too, offers a symbolical and spiritual explanation of Vedic sacrifices.

In pursuance of the mystic interpretation of Vedic verses and sacrifices some Āraṇyakas and Upaniṣads regard breath, speech, etc., as the subject-matter of certain Vedic verses. For instance, the Ait. Ar. and the J. Up. Br. regard *Prāṃa* as the deity of the RV.I,164,31 and accordingly offer its mystic interpretation.[13] Similarly the Ṛgvedic verses I,164,38 and X,114,4 are also interpreted by the Ait. Ar. as connected with the description of breath, while the other scholars suggest an entirely different explanation of these verses.[14] According to the J. Up.Br., the Ṛgvedic verses X,177,1-2 relate to *Prāṇa*.[15] In the supplementary portion (Chapters XIII and XIV) of the Nirukta the mystic interpretation of nearly twenty Vedic verses[16] has been suggested, and most of the later commentators and scholars also favour their mystic interpretation.

The ancient scholars who suggested the mystic interpretation of Vedic verses were called *Ātmavids*,[17] *Ātmavādins*,[18] or *Ātmapravādas*.[19] As already pointed out above, *Parivrājakas* mentioned by Yāska are included in this category of Vedic interpreters.[20]

The Āraṇyaka tradition of suggesting the mystic interpretation of Vedic sacrifices and verses has continued in the later works also. So laying down the duties and code of conduct of a *Samnyāsin* or *Parivrājaka*, the Dharmasūtras and the other allied works offer a mystic explanation of the Vedic verses and sacrifices. For instance, the Baudh. D.S. suggests a mystic interpretation of several Vedic Mantras and sacrifices in the course of prescribing the procedure of adopting Saṃnyāsa and a code of conduct for a Saṃnyāsin.[21] In the Bh. G. portion of the Mahābhārata the mystic interpretation of Vedic sacrifices has been highlighted.[22] According to a viewpoint presented in the Mahābhārata, the word *aja* does not mean a goat but a kind of seed in the context of Vedic sacrifices, and therefore a goat should not be sacrificed at a sacrifice.[23] Further on, the Epic propounds the view that in ancient times the pious sacrificers used to offer at sacrifices an animal made of rice, i.e., of rice flour.[24] In the Āśvamedhika Parvan of the Epic the symbolical mystic explanation of sacrifices has been suggested.[25] In this explanation ten senses symbolize ten priests; the subjects of senses represent the sacrificial oblations; and directions, wind, the Sun, the Moon, earth, fire, Viṣṇu, Indra, Prajāpati and Mitra stand for ten sacrificial fires. Elsewhere in the Mahābhārata the five senses together with the mind and intellect are symbolically interpreted as seven priests[26] (*hotāraḥ*); and similarly the five *Prāṇas* as five priests.[27] In the course of propounding the Sāṃkhya system of philosophy, the Great

Epic[28] interprets the Vedic god Mitra as *Puruṣa* (spirit), and Varuṇa as *Prakṛti* (matter).

The ancient Indian Vedic commentators such as Venk. and Sāyaṇa suggest the mystic interpretation of several verses along with the other types of interpretation. For instance, a commentator who is identified by some scholars with Sāyaṇa in his commentary on the supplement of the TA.[29] suggests a mystic interpretation of the above-cited (supra, p. 13) famous enigmatic Mantra (RV. IV,58,3). But it is important to note that the above-mentioned mystic interpretation of this verse does not figure among its several alternative interpretations contained in Sāyaṇa's commentary on the RV., although its solar interpretation finds a place among the various explanations suggested there. This fact raises doubts about the identification of the said commentator of the supplement of the TA. with Sāyaṇa, the commentator of the RV.

As we shall discuss in chapter 7, the exponent of the Dvaita school of Vedānta has suggested a mystic interpretation of 40 hymns of the RV. to refer to the Supreme Being under the name of Viṣṇu or Nārāyaṇa. His various followers such as Jayatīrtha and Rāghavendra have written commentaries on Ānandatīrtha's Vedic commentary to explain further his system of mystic interpretation. Similarly Ātmānanda in his commentary on the *Asyavāmīya* hymn has avowedly attempted a mystic interpretation on the basis of ideas derived from the *Viṣṇu-dharmottara*.

In modern times both Svāmī Dayānanda Sarasvatī and Shri Arvinda Ghosh have in their own way attempted the mystic interpretation of the Vedas as we shall discuss later.

It cannot be gainsaid that the spiritual interpretation of certain Vedic hymns reflects the real intention of the seers, and most of the ancient and modern scholars are inclined to agree on the tenor of such hymns, though they may differ about minute details. However, it must be pointed out that if any type of interpretation, spiritual or otherwise, is forced on the Vedic verses in utter disregard of context and the rules of Vedic grammar and usage, it will not carry conviction with the competent authorities on the subject, though it may be exploited to mislead the ignorant people. There is still ample scope for the spiritual interpretation of the Vedas in a wider perspective.

Vaiyākaraṇa School of Vedic Interpretation

Discussing the various etymologies of the word *maṇḍūka*, Yāska refers to the view of grammarians.[30] The grammatical interpretation of a number of Vedic verses is met with in ancient works. The supplement of the Nirukta (XIII, 9) mentions *inter alia* the following grammatical interpretation of the RV.I,164,45 (see note 32): "Noun, verb, prepositions and particles (are the four measured divisions of speech) according to grammarians." Patañjali in the *Paspaśā Āhnika*, the introductory portion of the Mahābhāṣya, offers the grammatical explanation of as many as five important verses of the RV. He attempts the following grammatical interpretation of the most enigmatic Ṛgvedic verse IV,58,3 discussed in the preceding chapters of this work: "Noun, verb, prepositions and particles (Nipātas) symbolize the four horns (of the allegorical bull). Three tenses past, present and future represent its three feet; the two forms of word —permanent and temporary— represent its two heads; and the seven cases (*vibhaktavaḥ*) stand for its seven hands. It is bound at three places, i.e., at chest, throat and head. Being called Vṛṣabha on account of its act of showering (the fulfilment of desires), it roars, i.e., produces sound. The Great God, word, has entered mortals. We should study grammar so that we may identify ourselves with the Great God."

It may be noted that Sāyaṇa in his commentary on the RV. clearly alludes to the grammatical interpretation of this verse with the remarks[31]: "The grammarians explain this verse as referring to *śabda-brahman*: the four categories of words are noun, verb, prepositions and particles, etc."

Similarly Patañjali attempts a grammatical interpretation of another enigmatic Ṛgvedic verse I,164,45 which has been variously interpreted in the supplement of the Nirukta and in Sāyaṇa's commentary.[32] The grammatical interpretations of RV.X,71,2 and 4 suggested by Patañjali find an echo in the commentaries of several ancient commentators and cannot be considered to be entirely novel and ingenious. However, Patañjali's grammatical interpretation of RV.VIII, 69,12 is absolutely original which has not been suggested by any other ancient commentator, although the ancient commentators offer the grammatical interpretation of some other Vedic verses. For instance, Sāyaṇa in the alternative interpretation of RV.I,164,41 records the views of some scholars who interpret this verse as a description of speech which, according to them, is single (lit. one-footed) in the crude form only; double (lit. two-footed) through declension and conjugation; fourfold (lit. four-footed) through its fourfold division into nouns, verbs, prepositions and particles; eightfold (lit. eight-footed) through eight cases including the vocative; and ninefold (lit. nine-footed) as the same with the addition of indeclinables; or it may be in diversified form as produced from nine parts of the body, chest, throat, etc.; and the ethereal element of the heart in this interpretation symbolizes the highest heaven.[33]

It has to be admitted that most of the grammatical interpretations of the Vedic verses are fanciful and arbitrary having little relevance to the context and Vedic usage.

Legal Interpretations

A few ancient Indian scholars have suggested the legal interpretation of some Vedic verses. For instance, in the beginning of the third chapter of the Nirukta (III, 1-6) Yāska presents the legal interpretation of half a dozen Vedic verses. Among such verses the RV. III, 4, 7-8 are interpreted to represent Vasiṣṭha's opinion on the question of adoption according to which one should not even think of adopting as one's son another's offspring, because howsoever good an adopted son may be he will ultimately return to his natural parents. Further Yāska (III, 3) observes that certain authorities cite the RV. III, 31, 1 to support a daughter's right to inherit paternal property, while others interpret it to limit the right of inheriting paternal property to sons only. So the verse in question is interpreted by Yāska (III, 4) to prove that the daughter of a sonless father would inherit his property and that the son born of such a daughter would be his grandson if her marriage is contracted on this clear understanding with his son-in-law.[34] According to the legal interpretation of another

Ṛgvedic verse (I, 124, 7) cited in the Nirukta, a brotherless woman even after her marriage continues the extension of her father's family and a sonless widow (in accordance with a practice prevalent in the South) inherits her husband's property after she has performed the ritual of ascending the dais meant for dice in a gambling-house and has been pelted there with dice by gamblers.

According to the Nirukta III, 5, some legal authorities rely on the RV. III, 31, 2 to deny share to a sister in paternal property, while others intrepret this verse to allow the largest share of paternal property to the eldest daughter who was brotherless at the time of her marriage but her brothers were born later. Yāska (III,6) adopts the former interpretation of this Ṛk : a son does not give his sister a share of paternal property and he has made her the receptacle of her husband's progeny; if the parents procreate progeny of both sexes, the son continues the family line and is entitled to inheritance, while the daughter is brought up and given away in marriage.

Following Yāska's interpretation of the RV. III, 31, 1-2, the author of the Bṛhaddevatā describes the subject-matter of these verses as follows :[35] "How one makes one's daughter a *putrikā* or thus impregnates her is told in the stanza (III, 31, 1) beginning with *śāsat*, and in the next stanza (III, 31, 2) beginning with *na* the giving of inheritance to a daughter is forbidden and her younger brother is declared to be treated like the eldest son." The later commentators, such as Veṅkaṭa and Sāyaṇa generally follow Yāska's interpretation of these two stanzas.[36] According to the Baudhāyana Dharmasūtra II,6,11,9-23, some scholars interpret the TS. verse V,7,2,5 ('Four paths leading to the world of the gods go severally from earth to heaven. All the gods place us on that amongst them which will gain us undecaying prosperity') as referring to the four *Āśramas* (stages) of life, while others express the view that the Vedic text 'Four paths' etc. refers to the fourfold division of sacrifices, viz. *Iṣṭis*, animal sacrifices, Soma sacrifices, and Darvi-homas. Several other Vedic verses have also been subjected to legal interpretation in later times. But no interpretation can be regarded as valid unless it conforms to the context and Vedic usage.

Naidāna School of Vedic Interpretation

Yāska refers to the views of the *Naidānas* with regard to the etymologies of the words *Syāla* (VI,9) and *Sāman* (VII,12). In his commentary on the Nirukta VI,9 Durgāchārya explains *Naidānāḥ* as *Nidānavidaḥ*, i.e. those who are expert in *Nidāna*. Elsewhere in his commentary Durgāchārya employs the term *Nidāna* in the sense of primary cause of Vedic verses to explain *Itihāsa* and thus makes *Nidāna* as the basis of Itihāsa.[37] Therefore in the opinion of Durgāchārya the meaning of the word *Naidāna* is very near to that of *Aitihāsika* but is not identical because Yāska's separate and distinct mention of *Naidānāḥ* and Aitihāsikāḥ points to the difference in their meanings. It leads us to the inference that the Naidāna system of Vedic interpretation was definitely distinct from that of the Aitihāsikas, whatever may be the points of subtle difference and similarities between the two.

It appears that a work entitled *Nidāna*, which embodied ancient legends explaining the primary cause of composition of Vedic verses, existed in the age of the Sūtras, because the Bṛhaddevatā V,23 refers to such a work in the following verse after narrating the legend connected with the RV. V,2: "This couplet (V,2,2.9) is mentioned in the Brāhmaṇa of the Bhāllavins; such is the Vedic passage cited in the work entitled *Nidāna* belonging to the Sāmavedins." It shows that the Sāmavedins had a work named *Nidāna* which contained legends relating to the origin of Vedic verses. This view is also corroborated by the following statement of the Vāsiṣṭha Dharma-Sūtra I,14: "Now the Bhāllavins also quote the (following) Gāthā in the *Nidāna*." Durgāchārya also lends his support to the view that a work entitled *Nidāna* existed in ancient times. So explaining the word *Naidāna* used in the Nirukta VII,12 Durgāchārya opines that those who know the work named *Nidāna* are called *Nidānaḥ*.[38] It must be noted that the work now known as *Nidānā-Sūtra* cannot be the Nidāna mentioned by the Brhad. Vas. D. S. and Durgāchārya, because this Sūtra work does not contain any legend connected with the Vedic hymns. It seems that the work *Nidāna* mentioned in ancient literature has been irretrievably lost. Therefore the *Naidāna* system of Vedic interpretation is known in name only, and we do not find any definite specimen of this system of interpretation.

Notes and References

1. Cf. RV. X, 72. 82. 90. 121. 129 etc., AV. XIII and XV, etc., VS. XXXI; XXXII, 1-12; XXXIV, 1-6; XL, etc.
2. Sarvā. on RV. IV, 26, 1 "ahaṃ manuḥ saptādyābhis tisṛbhir Indram iva ātmānam ṛṣis tuṣṭāva Indro vā ātmānam." Bṛhad. IV, 135 observes: "IV, 26 is self-praise in a triplet; for there is praise (in it) as if of him (Indra)." Explaining the first verse of this hymn, Venk. says that this is the speech of either Indra or Vāmadeva. Following the traditional interpretation recorded in Sāyaṇa's commentary on this verse, Wilson observes: "This and the two following verses are attributed either to *Indra* or to *Vāmadeva*: in the latter case it is said the sage uttered them while yet in the womb, knowledge of truth being generated in him, and enabling him to identify himself with universal existence: through the eye of supreme truth I am everything. . . .; we have here, therefore, the basis of the pantheistic *Vedānta*." In this connection Griffith remarks: "The deity of the first three stanzas is said to be either Indra or *Paramātmā* (the Supreme Spirit or Soul of the Universe) . . . Indra is the speaker of the first three verses, although it is not clear what he means by saying that he is *Kakṣīvān* and *Uśanā*, unless he intends to identify himself with all existence." However, some modern scholars including Geldner and Sieg consider these three verses to be self-praise of Indra. Cf. Vedische Studien, III, p. 160; HOS. Vol. 33, pp. 453-54; Sagenstoffe des Ṛgveda, pp. 87 and 95 f.n. 3.
3. Tait. S. V, 3, 4, 2; Tait. Br. III, 3, 6, 9; P. Br. VI, 10, 5; IX, 8, 16; S. Br. VIII, 4, 2, 6; etc.
4. Cf. S. Br. VIII, 7, 2, 6; I, 4, 5, 4; XI, 1, 6, 18; K. Br. II, 7; XIII, 5; J. Up. Br. I, 33, 2.
5. Cf. S. Br. VI, 1, 1, 2; XII, 9, 1, 14; XIV, 4, 3, 19.
6. Cf. S. Br. XII, 9, 1, 13; G. Br. II, 4, 11.
7. Cf. S. Br. IV, 5, 5, 7; II, 3, 4, 12; J. Up. Br. I, 28, 2; I, 32, 5.
8. Cf. S. Br. IV, 1, 3, 19; XIV, 2, 2, 6.
9. TS. VII, 5, 25; S. Br. X, 6, 4; B. Up. I, 1; Cf. TBr. III, 9, 28,
10. S. Br. X, 6, 5, 7; B. Up. I, 2, 7; TS. VII, 5, 25, 1; etc.

11. TA. V, 8, 12 *Indratame' gnau iti āha* (Cf. TA. IV, 10, 5). *Prāṇo vā indratamo' gniḥ*. Cf. Bhagavadgītā IV, 29-30.
12. TA. X, 64.
13. Ait. Ar. II, 1, 6; J. Up. Br. III, 6, 9, 2—5. But TA. V, 6, 4 and S. Br. XIV, 1, 4, 9-10 regard the Sun as the deity of this verse. Venk., Uvaṭa and Mahīdhara follow the TA. in the interpretation of this verse. But Sāyaṇa in his commentary on the RV. I, 164, 31 cites the above-referred passage of the Ait. Ar. to support his solar interpretation of the verse, while in his commentary on the above-referred passage of the Ait. Ar. he interprets the same verse as pertaining to *Prāṇa*. Several modern scholars accept the solar interpretation of the verse. But Geldner puts forward the view that the verse is concerned with the description of breath. Cf. AV. X, 2, 7.
14. (a) See Ait. Ar. II, 1, 8 for the interpretation of RV. I, 164, 38. According to one of the interpretations suggested in the Nirukta XIV, 23, the Sun is the deity of this verse, while another interpretation regards *soul* as its deity. Venk., Sāyaṇa, and Roth aceept the second interpretation, and Griffith is in favour of the first. But Geldner follows the Ait. Ar. in this respect.

(b) See Ait. Ar. III, 1, 6 for the interpretation of RV. X, 114, 4— "*Vāg vai mātā prāṇaḥ putraḥ. tad api etad ṛṣiṇā uktam...'ekaḥ suparṇaḥ'*." Venk. suggests the solar interpretation of the verse, which is accepted by several modern scholars including Ludwig, Griffith and Geldner. Sāyaṇa suggests its three interpretations—one relating to wind, another to breath and the third to the Universal Soul. According to Durga's commentary on Nirukta X, 46, wind is the deity (subject-matter) of this verse.
15. (a) J. Up. Br. III, 35, 1-8...*Pataṅgam aktam*' iti (RV. X, 177, 1) *Prāṇo vai Pataṅgaḥ*. But Venk. aud Sāyaṇa (on TA. III, 11, 10) construe this verse as pertaining to the Universal Soul, whereas Sāyaṇa in his commentary on the RV. offers two explanations—one relating to the Sun and the other to the Universal Soul.

(b) See J. Up. Br. III, 36, 1-5 for the interpretation of RV. X, 177, 2. Venk. and Sāyaṇa (on TA. III, 11, 11) interpret the word *Pataṅga* of this verse as the Sun, but Sāyaṇa in his Ṛgvedic commentary explains it as the Sun or the Universal Soul. Most of the modern scholars including Griffith and Grassmann accept its interpretation as the Sun. But in the opinion of Geldner the word *Pataṅga* of this hymn, which literally means a bird, symbolically signifies the inner light of prophetic knowledge and enlightenment in heart. Cf. RV. VI, 9, 4-5.
16. RV. I, 164, 39, 31; X, 82, 7; IX, 96, 6; IX, 97, 34.40.41; X, 55, 5; I, 164, 15.16.36.37.38; X, 120.1; I, 84, 16-18; I, 164, 20; IV, 40, 5; I, 84, 20.
17. S. Br. XIV, 6, 7, 4, Sāmavedānukramaṇikā I, 20; Atharvapariśiṣṭa I,

39, 4; Chh. Up., B. Up., Mahābhārata, Durgāchārya, and Sāyaṇa on RV. VI, 9, 2 etc.

18. Bṛhad. VII, 71; Atharvaśāntikalpa I, 39, 4.
19. Nirukta XIII, 9. 11; Śuklayajuḥsarvānukramaṇikā II, 428.
20. Nirukta II, 8 mentions a special interpretation of RV. I, 164, 32 suggested by *Parivrājakas*.
21. Baudh. D.S. II, 10, 17-18; III, 1, 1; 2, 2.
22. Mahābhārata VI, 28, 23-30 (Bh. G. IV, 23-30); Cf. S. Br. XI, 2, 6, 13-14.
23. Mahābhārata XII, 337, 4...

    Bījair yajñeṣu yaṣṭvyam iti vai vaidikī śrutiḥ,
    Ajasamjñāni bījāni chhāgaṃ no hantum arhathaḥ.

    Cf. Pañchatantra after III, 106..."ete' pi ye yājñikā yajñakarmaṇi paśūn vyāpādayanti te mūrkhāḥ paramārtham śruter na jānanti. Tatra kila etad uktam ajair yaṣṭvyam. Ajā vrīhayaḥ tāvat saptavārṣikāḥ kathyante no punaḥ paśu-viśeṣāḥ."
24. Mahābhārata XIII, 115, 49...

    Śrūyate hi purā kalpe nṛṇām vrīhimayaḥ paśuḥ,
    Yenāyajanta yajvānaḥ puṇya-lokaparāyaṇāḥ.
25. Ibid. XIV. 21, 1-8.
26. Ibid. XIV, 22, 1-7.
27. Ibid. XIV. 23, 1-3: Cf. XIV, 25, 1-17.
28. Ibid. XII, 318, 39.
29. TA. (Pariśiṣṭa) X, 12, 2 (Nārāyaṇopaniṣad 12, 2). In this interpretation the sound *om* is construed to symbolize Brahman.
30. Nirukta IX, 5 maṇḍayateriti vaiyākaraṇāḥ, Cf. Uṇādisūtra IV, 42.
31. It is important to note that the grammatical interpretation of the same verse contained in Sāyana's commentary on the Kāṇva recension of the VS. IX, 5 differs from that of the Mahābhāṣya in respect of the following details: "First person, second person and third person symbolize the three feet of speech. Noun and verb represent its two heads. It is bound in three ways by singular, dual and plural numbers." Here Sāyaṇa's commentary agrees verbatim with that of Uvaṭa. Mahīdhara also follows Uvaṭa but adds a few alternative explanations. For instance, he opines that either three persons or three tenses stand for the three feet of speech.
32. In the supplement of the Nirukta (XIII, 9) three different interpretations of the verse have been suggested—one of them is attributed to the grammarians and another to the *Nairuktas*. Sāyaṇa's commentary records as many as six different interpretations of the verse including those of the grammarians, ritualists, mythologists, spiritualists and etymologists. Geldner (HOS. 33, p. 236) refers to several ancient texts to explain this verse; Cf. S. Br. IV, 1, 3, 16; T. Br. II, 8, 8, 5; KS. 2, p. 79, 9; MS. 3, p. 70, 16.
33. According to the Nirukta XI, 40, this verse describes the sound produced by the thundering of a raincloud It may be noted that Sāyaṇa's

interpretation of the same verse in his commentary on the T. Br. II, 4, 6, 11 is entirely different where he construes *Gaurī* as pure speech in its diverse forms, i.e. in the entire range of Vedic and post-Vedic literature comprising successively *Praṇava; Vyāhṛi* and *Sāvitrī;* the four Vedas; the six Vedāṅgas, Purāṇa, and Dharmaśāstra; and finally Mīmāṃsā, Nyāya, Sāṃkhya, Yoga, Pāñcharātra, Pāśupata, Āyurveda, Dhanur-Veda and Gāndharva-Veda. Sāyaṇa in his commentary on the TA. I, 9, 4 offers an entirely different interpretation of the same verse though he considers all-white Sarasvatī, the goddess of speech, to be its theme. It shows that the authors of the above-mentioned commentaries ascribed to Sāyaṇa are different persons.

34. Although most of the ancient Indian commentators follow Yāska's interpretation of this verse, some Western scholars such as Ludwig and Bergaigne read into it an incest intended by the father Heaven with his daughter Dawn, and Oldenberg subscribes to this view. But Geldner rejects the idea of an intended incest and regards it as an allegorical description of a sacrificial act in which the father is the sacrificial priest who begets the fire as his son and the *Ghṛtāchī* as his daughter, and *Iḍā* is the daughter of Ghṛtāchī. Thus Agni who is Ghṛtāchī's brother does not give her hereditary wealth, i.e. the offering.
35. Bṛhad. IV, 110-112; Cf. India of Vedic Kalpa-Sūtras, pp. 196 ff. for the definition of a *putrikā*, a daughter given in marriage on condition that a son born of her will belong to her father, i.e. he will continue his maternal grandfather's family line.
36. But Western scholars such as Grassmann, Geldner, Oldenberg and Bergaigne do not accept Yāska's interpretation of these verses and regard their subject-matter as the figurative description of Fire which is said to be the deity of this hymn.
37. See note 54 of Chapter IV. In his commentary on VS. XIV, 9 and 28 Mahīdhara cites legends connected with the Vedic verses under the term *Nidāna: atra śrutyuktam nidānam; atra nidānam·*
38. Durgāchārya on N. VII, 12—Nidānam iti *granthaḥ. Tadvido naidānāḥ.*

7

The Ancient and Mediaevel Bhāsyakāras

A full account of various types of Vedic interpretations attempted in the Brāhmaṇas, Āraṇyakas, Upaniṣads, Kalpa-Sūtras, Nirukta etc. has been given above in the preceding Chapters. However, none of these works excepting the Nirukta can be termed as a Bhāṣya, and the Nirukta also, which attempts the explanation of certain Vedic verses by way of illustration of Vedic usage, is not a regular commentary on any definite portion of the Ṛgveda. Therefore, we are naturally faced with the question as to when the tradition of writing regular and systematic Veda-Bhāṣyas came into existence. None of the extant Veda-Bhāṣyas is earlier than the beginning of the Christian era, although the term *Bhāṣya* occurs in several ancient works. For instance, the V. Pr. refers to the use of the word *atha* in the *Bhāṣyas.* In the description of tarpaṇa. ceremony the Asv. G. S. and the Kaus. G. S. mention the *Bhāṣyas* alongwith the Sūtras, the Bhārata and the Mahābhārata, whereas the Sankh. G. S. mentions the Sūtras and the Bhāṣyas but omits the Bhārata and the Mahābhārata.[2] The Mbh. speaks of *Bhāṣyas* and *Bhāṣya-vids* several times.[3] However, we know nothing about the authorship, nature and scope of the earliest *Bhāṣyas* mentioned in these works. So we have to confine our discussion to the following *Bhāṣyakāras* who are all posterior to the Mbh.

Skandasvāmin

Among the extant Bhāṣyas *of the RV. Skandasvāmin's Bhāṣya* is regarded as the oldest. But it is a matter of deep regret that this commentary is incomplete, and up till now his Bhāṣya on RV. I,1,1 to 1, 56, 1; I,62,1 to I,121, 15; V,57,1 to V, 61, 19 and VI, 29, 1 to VI, 75, 6 only has come to light. That Skandasvāmin wrote his *Bhāṣya* on the entire RV. is confirmed by his reference to his *Bhāṣya* on the tenth Maṇḍala in his commentary on RV. I, 72, 2. In his *Bhāṣya* which is called *Ṛgarthāgamasaṃhṛti* Skandasvāmin gives very exhaustive explanations of the Mantras citing various authorities such as the Ait. Br., the Nighaṇṭu, the Nirukta, the Bṛhaddevatā, etc. Although he does not ignore the ritualistic interpretation of Mantras, yet he does not stress it to the extent to which it is done by Sāyaṇa. It was on account of diffuse and discursive nature of Skandasvamin's Bhāṣya that an abridged version of his Bhāṣya was attempted by an unknown scholar. Such an abridged edition of the first two Adhyāyas of the first Aṣṭaka was published by Dr. C. Kunhan Raja from Madras in 1935 on the basis of two palm-leaf manuscripts in his edition of the first Aṣṭaka of the Bhāṣya.

Devarāja Yajvan in his commentary on the Nighaṇṭu, Ātmānanda in his Bhāṣya on the Asya-Vāmīya Hymn, and Keśavasvāmin in his *Nānārthārṇva-saṃkṣepa* refer to Skandasvāmin.[4] Sāyaṇa also in his Bhāṣya on the RV. refers to the views of Skandasvāmin several times.[5] Veṇkaṭamādhava, another important Bhāṣyakāra of the RV., informs us through a Śloka contained in his Bhāṣya that Skandasvāmin in collaboration with Nārāyaṇa and Udgītha wrote a *Rg-Bhāṣya.*[6] Since Udgītha's Bhāṣya is now available on a part of the tenth Maṇḍala of the RV. and there is a similarity between their styles of interpretation, some scholars are inclined to hold the view that Skandasvāmin might have assigned to Udgītha the Bhāṣya of this Maṇḍala.

In a verse given at the end of his Bhāṣya on RV. I, 80, 16 Skandasvāmin informs us that his native place was *Valabhī* and the name of his father was Bhartṛdhruva. Most of the scholars identify Valabhī with a town of this name in North Gujarat, though K. Sambasiva Sastri in the Introduction to his edition of this Bhāṣya has advanced the conjecture that if it could be identified with a village named *Valapaṭṭaṇa* in

Kerala, then Skandasvāmin was a native of Kerala on account of the similarity of his name with such names as Bhavasvāmin and Nāgasvāmin. Harisvāmin in the introductory verses of his commentary on the Sat. Br. declares himself to be a disciple of Skandasvāmin; and in the colophon it is said that he (Harisvāmin) wrote his commentary in the Kali year 3740 which according to the calculation of several authorities corresponds to 639 A.D., though Dr. L. Sarup[7] believes that this date corresponds to 538 A.D. It indicates that Skandasvāmin flourished in the beginning of the seventh century A.D.

A commentary on Yāska's Nirukta is ascribed to Skandasvāmin and Maheśvara's name is also associated with him in this connection. According to Dr. L. Sarup, the author of this commentary on the Nirukta is Maheśvara and not Skandasvāmin, the author of the Veda-Bhāṣya. But Pandit Bhagavaddatta controverts Dr. Sarup's view and regards the author of this Nirukta-commentary to be identical with the famous Veda-Bhāṣyakāra, Skandasvāmin.[8] (see infra).

Nārāyaṇa

According to Veṅkaṭamādhava (see note 6), Nārāyaṇa and Udgītha collaborated with Skandasvāmin in the composition of a *Ṛg-Bhāṣya*. No Veda-Bhāṣya or part of any Bhāṣya ascribed to Nārāyaṇa has so far come to light, and there is no basis for identifying our Nārāyaṇa with Gārgya Nārāyaṇa, the author of a commentary on the Asv. S. S, or with Naidhruva Nārāyaṇa, the commentator of the Asv. G.S. The only Nārāyaṇa to approximate to the Veda-Bhāṣyakāra Nārāyaṇa is the father of Mādhava who wrote a Bhāṣya on the Sāmaveda. In the Introduction to his Sāmaveda-Bhāṣya it is said that this Bhāṣya was written by Mādhava, the son of Nārāyaṇa. As it has been aptly observed by Dr. C. Kunhan Raja in the Foreword to his edition of the Sāmaveda with the Bhāṣyas of Mādhava and Bharatasvāmin, there is a close similarity in wording, style and ideas between the introductory portions of Skandasvāmin's Ṛgveda-Bhāṣya and Mādhava's Sāmaveda-Bhāṣya. Besides, Mādhava also mentions a Ṛgveda-Bhāṣya.

Therefore it is not unreasonable to assume that Mādhava, the son of Nārāyaṇa, in the composition of his Sāmaveda-Bhāṣya has been influenced by the ideas and style of his father who wrote a Ṛg-Bhāṣya in collaboration with Skandasvāmin.

Udgītha

As we have pointed out above (see note 6), Udgītha is said to be a collaborator of Skandasvāmin and Nārāyaṇa in the composition of a Ṛg-Bhāṣya. Like Skandasvāmin's Bhāṣya Udgītha's Bhāṣya is now available in fragments only. The extant Udgītha-Bhāṣya is on RV. X, 5, 4 to X, 12, 5 and X, 13, 2 to X, 83, 6. Since Udgītha's style of interpretation bears close similarity to that of Skandasvāmin, this fact lends support to the view that they were contemporaries and collaborated in the composition of a commentary on the RV. Sāyaṇa[9] in his Ṛgveda-Bhāṣya and Ātmānanda in his commentary on the Asya-Vāmīya Hymn mention Udgītha's name. Dr. C. Kunhan Raja in the Introduction to the Descriptive Catalogue of Sanskrit MSS. in the Adyar Library (Vol. I B, p. xxv) makes the following significant observation about Udgītha: "From a reference in Haradatta's commentary on the Āśvalāyana-Gṛhya-Mantras, it is found that Udgītha must have written the commentary for portions of the 8th Maṇḍala, since the reference is to the Vālakhilya Sūktas. It reads as follows: *anena karmaṇā khila-mantra-dvayam paṭhitvā vyākhyātam Udgīthāchārvair vyākhyānam kurvadbhiḥ.*"

In the colophon of his Bhāṣya at the end of the Adhyāyas Udgītha gives the following information about himself: "*Vanavāsīvinirgatāchārvasya Udgīthasya kṛtā Ṛgveda-Bhāṣye ...Adhyāyaḥ Samāptaḥ.*" It indicates that he had migrated from his native place named *Vanavāsī* to another place (probably *Valabhī*) where he carried out his literary pursuits. According to some scholars, *Vanavāsī* was the name of the chief town of a country of that name in the South.[10]

Mādhava, the son of Nārāyaṇa

As pointed out above, Mādhava, the son of Nārāyaṇa, has written a Bhāṣya on the Sāmaveda. His Bhāṣya seems to have been influenced in ideas and style by an earlier Ṛg-

Bhāṣya which might have been jointly authored by his father Nārāyaṇa and the famous commentator Skandasvāmin, because Mādhava's Bhāṣya mentions a Ṛg-Bhāṣya and shows numerous verbal agreements in the Introduction with the introductory portion of Skandasvāmin's Bhāṣya as pointed out above. This fact lends support to the view that our Bhāṣyakāra Mādhava might have been the son of Nārāyaṇa who is said to have collaborated with Skandasvāmin in the composition of a Ṛg-Bhāṣya.

Another important feature of Mādhava's Bhāṣya is that its opening (salutatory) verse is identical with the opening verse of Bāṇa's Kādambarī. Scholars have advanced conflicting conjectures about this circumstance. In the opinion of Pandit K. Sambasiva Sastri (vide p. 4 of the Introduction to the RV. with the Bhāṣyas of Skandasvāmin and Veṅkaṭamādhava), it is Bāṇa who borrowed this verse from Mādhava's Bhāṣya. In support of this view Pandit Bhagavaddatta argues that the use of the term *trayīmayāya* in the verse points to its aptness in the beginning of a Vedic Bhāṣya only[11]. In this connection Dr. C. Kunhan Raja in the Foreword to his edition of this Bhāṣya (p. xi) offers the following alternatives: "Perhaps both Mādhava and Bāṇa had a common source; or one utilised the Maṅgalaśloka of the work of the other. Or perhaps the two are identical, Mādhava being the real name and Bāṇa being the assumed name." In support of the last alternative Dr. Raja cites the instance of Bhavabhūti and Umveka. In my opinion, since the verse in question appears to be in keeping with the ideas and style of the succeeding verses of Bāṇa's Kādambarī and appears to be isolated and inappropriate in the beginning of a Vedic Bhāṣya, some scribe fond of Bāṇa's Kādambarī might have added this verse in the beginning of Mādhava's Bhāṣya. It seems to be highly unlikely that either a Vedic commentator or a celebrated writer like Bāṇa would have borrowed the opening verse of his composition from another work. Bāṇa's autobiography and his style lend no support to the view that he is identical with the Veda-Bhāṣyakāra Mādhava who might be the son of Nārāyana, a contemporary and collaborator of Skandasvāmin.

Mādhava's explanation of Mantras is very simple, and he

seldom cites any Vedic authority or a parallel passage in support of his explanations. However, he quotes a few grammatical aphorisms here and there. This Bhāṣya is more or less a running paraphrase of the Mantras of the Sāmaveda with hardly any important notes.

Mādhavabhaṭṭa/Veṅkaṭamādhava

Mādhava, son of Veṅkaṭa, is the only pre-Sāyaṇa Bhāsyakāra whose complete Bhāṣya on the RV. is now available. The existence of another version of the Ṛgveda-Bhāṣya ascribed to Mādhava on the first Aṣṭaka has given rise to the controversy that there were two Mādhavas who commented on the RV. According to Dr. C. Kunhan Raja who published in the Adyar Library Series both the versions of the Bhāṣya side by side, Mādhava, the author of the longer version entitled *Ṛgveda-Vyākhyā* in the printed edition is not the same Mādhava, son of Veṅkaṭārya, who is undoubtedly the author of the shorter version entitled *Ṛgartha-dīpikā*. Dr. Raja expresses the view that the author of the longer version of the Bhāṣya is that Mādhava who claims in the introductory verses of his work *Mādhavānukramaṇī* (published by Dr. Raja as Appendix IV in the Ṛgvedānukramaṇī) to have composed twelve Anukramaṇīs, the last of them being in the form of a commentary on the RV. In the opinion of Dr. Raja, the above-mentioned statement is corroborated by the opening passage of the said commentary wherein it is designated as the twelfth *Anukramaṇikā*.[12] The learned editor further argues that the names of these Anukramaṇīs agree with those mentioned by Mādhava in his commentary. In order to defend his view-point Dr. Raja questions the veracity of Devarāja's statements ascribing the authorship of various Anukramaṇīs to Veṅkaṭamādhava on the plea that the passages quoted by Devarāja in his Nighaṇṭu-Bhāṣya from the Anukramaṇīs of Mādhava are not traceable to the stanzas prefixed by Veṅkaṭamādhava to his Bhāṣya on the various chapters of the RV. Another argument advanced by Dr. Raja in support of his thesis is that Veṅkaṭamādhava who speaks of previous commentators says nothing in his Bhāṣya or Kārikās about a previous commentary on the RV. by himself or about any of the Anukramaṇīs which Devarāja ascribes to Mādhava. Dr.

Raja further argues that on the other hand Mādhava, the author of the longer version of the Bhāṣya, mentions in his Bhāṣya his own Anukramaṇīs and cites quotations therefrom which agree with the quotations given by Devarāja from Mādhava's Anukramaṇīs.

However, the facts which militate against Dr. Raja's thesis cannot be easily brushed aside. It has been mentioned by Dr. Raja in the Foreword to his edition of the Mādhava-Bhāṣya that according to a stanza found at the end of the fifth Adhyāya of his Bhāṣya the name of Mādhava's village was *Gomat* which was also the village of Veṅkaṭamādhava. It has been also admitted by Dr. Kunhan Raja that some passages from the Ṛgveda-Bhāṣya attributed by Devarāja to Mādhava are traceable to Veṅkaṭamādhava's Ṛgarthadīpikā. This fact also cannot be denied that there are striking verbal agreements between the longer and the shorter versions of the Ṛgveda-Bhāṣya published side by side by Dr. Raja. The points of their agreements outnumber those of differences. The main point of difference between the two versions is that the longer version is more elaborate supported with quotations and illustrations, while the shorter version is very succinct and a sort of running paraphrase of the Mantras. In his Nighaṇṭu-Bhāṣya I, 14, 18 Devarāja attributes to the *Prathama-Bhāṣya* of Mādhava an explanation of RV. IX, 97, 54 which agrees to a large extent with Veṅkaṭamādhava's Bhāṣya on this Mantra, but also shows some agreements with the Sāyaṇa-Bhāṣya. It shows that Mādhava wrote two commentaries on the RV.; and the obvious inference is that one was brief while the other was elaborate. Since the shorter version of the Bhāṣya is available on the whole of the RV. and the longer version goes only up to the end of the first Aṣṭaka, it indicates that Veṅkaṭamādhava first completed the shorter version of his Bhāṣya and then took up the preparation of the longer version but did not live long to complete it. This is why the shorter version, i.e. the first Bhāṣya, makes no mention of his second Bhāṣya and Anukramaṇīs.

As pointed out above, Veṅkaṭamādhava's first Bhāṣya on the RV. is marked by utmost brevity, and the Vedic words to be explained have not been included in the commentary. Extolling the brevity of his commentary, the Bhāṣyakāra claims to have avoided prolixity and to have explained the Mantras in the fewest possible words. Another salient feature of this Bhāṣya is that in the beginning of his commentary on each Adhyāya he introduces it with a *Pratīka* (initial words of the first Mantra) and adds a number of verses composed by himself to deal with an important topic connected with Vedic interpretation, such as accent, tenses and moods, prepositions, particles, pronouns, compounds, metres, deities, conjugation, etc. Veṅkaṭamādhava opines that those so-called modern scholars (*adhunātanāḥ*) who have devoted their energies to the study of only the Nirukta and grammar understand only a quarter of the RV., but those who discuss the meanings of the Brāhmaṇas understand the Vedic usage (*śabda-rīti*). He regards Śākalya, Yāska and Pāṇini as adept in the meaning of the RV. (*Ṛgarthaparāḥ*).

Condemning plagiarists, Veṅkaṭamādhava says that at present deceitful persons write commentaries everywhere plagiarizing the meaning suggested by Skandasvāmin, Nārāyaṇa and Udgītha. As regards his own Bhāṣya Veṅkaṭamādhava claims that he has suggested different original meanings of a large number of hymns and stanzas without any deception; and that his meanings are different from those suggested by the earlier Bhāṣyakāras in the same way as cows are different from horses and not in the manner in which the word *āmra* is different from its synonym *sahakāra*. Veṅkaṭamādhava's claim of originality is fully justifiable. Unlike the other Bhāṣyas Veṅkaṭamādhava's commentary is not dominated by the ritualistic interpretation, though it has cited some quotations from the Brāhmaṇas here and there. Both Devarāja and Sāyaṇa (see his Ṛgveda-Bhāṣya on X, 86, 1) mention the Bhāṣyakāra Mādhava; and Sāyaṇa follows Mādhava's commentary in numerous places (compare their explanations of RV.IX, 97, 54; X, 5, 6; 50, 6; 51, 1; 68, 8; 69, 4; 75, 9; 79, 1; 86, 1.). At the end of his commentary on each Adhyāya Veṅkaṭamādhava adds some verses composed by himself to give autobiographical information. According to the information gleaned from such verses, Veṅkaṭamādhava was a native of *Gomat* village situated on the southern bank of the river Kāverī in Chola country. Dr. Raja suggests the identification of this village with the present Tiruvaduthurai village of Trichanapally district. Mādhava's father was Veṅkaṭārya, mother Sundarī, grandfather Mādhava, and maternal grand-father Bhavagola. His own gotra was Kauśika and that of his mother was Vasiṣṭha. At that time Ekavīra (v.l. Ekadhīra) was the king of the Chola country. It is not possible to fix Veṅkaṭamādhava's date with any amount of certainty. The only definite fact about his date is that he is later than Skandasvāmin and Udgītha but earlier than Devarāja and Sāyaṇa. Dr. Raja who is inclined to identify the King Ekavīra ("Jagatām Ekavīraḥ") with the king Parāntaka I described in some Inscrip-tions as Vīrachola (907-952 A.D.) places Veṅkaṭamādhava between the beginning of the seventh century and the four-teenth contury A.D.[13] But elsewhere the same scholar observes that Veṅkaṭamādhava is earlier than Sāyaṇa and may have lived about the tenth or ninth century of the Christian Era.[14] Simi- larly Dr. L. Sarup assigns Veṅkaṭamādhava to about the tenth century A.D.[15]

Uvaṭa

The earliest extant commentary on the Mādhyandina-Śākhā of the Vājasaneyi-Saṃhitā is from the pen of Uvaṭa. It is a noteworthy feature of this Bhāṣya that even though it is ritualistic in its approach, as it has got to be on account of the essential nature of the Yajurveda, yet it also attempts other types of interpretations such as a mystic and an Aitihāsika interpretation. For instance, Uvaṭa attempts a mystic interpretation of a part of the V.S. XX,23 and mentions in his commentary on V,2 the Aitihāsika interpretation of the three Mantras suggested by the Sat. Br. In his Bhāsya Uvaṭa quotes passages from several ancient works including the Nighaṇṭu, the Nirukta, the Bṛhaddevatā, and the Sat. Br. At some places he cites the Mantras of the Charakas and the Bahvṛchas. On the whole, Uvaṭa's commentary is brief and to the point. Uvaṭa does not cite or refer to any Anukramaṇī belonging to the Śukla-Yajurveda and claims to mention the Ṛṣis, deities and metres of the Mantras on the authority of the Sat. Br., his teacher and his own reasoning.[16] It shows that he did not know or recognize the Sarvānukramaṇī or any other Anukramaṇī of this Veda. In the introductory part of his Bhāṣya Uvaṭa discusses some general questions concerning

Vedic interpretation and cites a verse enunciating some important principles of interpretation.

In the colophon of his commentary he furnishes the following information about himself : "Uvaṭa, son of Vajraṭa resident of Ānandapura, composed this Bhāṣya in precise words and sentences. Having paid homage to Ṛṣis etc., Uvaṭa wrote this commentary residing at Ujjain during the reign of King Bhoja." As the period of King Bhoja's reign is generally held to be between 1018 A.D. and 1060 A.D., Uvaṭa might have written his commentary in the first half of the 11th century A.D. Ānandapura is identified with a town of this name in Gujarat. So like Skandasvāmin Uvaṭa was also a native of Gujarat. There is no force in the argument that since names ending in *aṭa* such as Kaiyaṭa and Mammaṭa belong to Kashmir, Vajraṭa and Uvaṭa must also be Kashmirian names ; for the fashion of giving a particular type of names may not necessarily belong to a region but it may also belong to an age.

In addition to the above-described Bhāṣya, commentaries on the Ṛk-Prātiśākhya, Vājasaneyi-Prātiśākhya and the Sarvānukramaṇī of the RV. were also written by Uvaṭa. Devarāja in his Nighaṇṭu-Bhāṣya (e.g. III, 4,11) mentions Uvaṭa and cites from his commentary. Since the above-referred quotation from Uvaṭa's commentary is not traceable to his VS. Bhāṣya (though it agrees to a large extent with the Mahīdhara-Bhāṣya on V.S.V, 23), Dr. C. Kunhan Raja[17] conjectures that a Ṛgveda-Bhāṣya also might have been composed by Uvaṭa. It is well known that Mahīdhara considerably draws upon Uvaṭa's VS. Bhāṣya. We shall discuss below that Durgāchārya, the commentator of the Nirukta, is also indebted to Uvaṭa's VS. Bhāṣya.

Śaunaka

Uvaṭa in his Bhāṣya on the *Puruṣa-Sūkta,* which forms 31st Adhyāya of the VS., observes that the Ṛṣi Śaunaka composed a Bhāṣya of this Hymn and explained it to Janaka for Mokṣa. In that Bhāṣya, according to Uvaṭa, first word-analysis, then the relationship of verbs with the other words, then compounds, and finally the meaning of notable words were explained.

However, nothing more is known about the Bhāṣya composed by Śaunaka.

Bhavasvāmin

In a self-composed verse in the Introduction to his commentary on the T.S. Bhaṭṭa Bhāskara says that he is writing his Bhāṣya after having studied the Bhāṣyas composed by Bhavasvāmin and others. It clearly proves that prior to Bhaṭṭa Bhāskara Bhavasvāmin was a celebrated commentator who had composed a Bhāṣya on the T.S. Besides, Keśavasvāmin in the Introduction to his Baudhāyana-Prayogasāra refers to the view of Bhavasvāmin. Devaraja in the Introduction to his Nighaṇṭu-Bhāṣya says that among others Bhavasvāmin's Veda-Bhāṣya was also consulted by him (Devarāja) for explaining the etymologies of Vedic words. But unfortunately no manuscript of Bhāvasvāmin's Bhāṣya has so far come to light.

Guhadeva or Rāhadeva

Devarāja in the Introduction to his Nighaṇṭu-Bhāṣya mentions the Veda-Bhāṣya of *Rāhadeva* along with those of Skandasvāmin, Bhavasvāmin, etc., and cites in I,3,14 the Bhāṣya of *Rāhadeva* (v.l. *Gṛhadeva*) on the etymology of the word *garagiraḥ*. However, according to Pandit Bhagavaddatta[18], the reading in the above-referred Nighaṇṭu-Bhāṣya (I,3,14) is *Guhadeva* and Rāmānuja in his Vedārtha-saṃgraha (p. 148 of Kāśī-edition, Saṃvat 1952) also makes a reverential reference to *Guhadeva*. In any case no Veda-Bhāṣya ascribed to Rāhadeva or Guhadeva is now available. Pandit Bhagavaddatta is of the view that Guhadeva's Bhāṣya might have been on the T.S., because the Mantra containing the phrase—*raśmayaścha devā garagiraḥ*—cited by Devarāja occurs in the Tait. Ar. I,9,3.

Bhaṭṭa Bhāskara

Bhaṭṭa Bhāskara who wrote his Bhāṣya called Jñāna-yajña on the T.S., is definitely earlier than Sāyaṇa who in his Ṛgveda-Bhāṣya (I, 63, 4; VI, 1, 13) quotes explanations from the Bhāṣya of the former. In fact in his commentary on the Tait.

Br. III, 6, 10,5, Sāyaṇa follows Bhaṭṭabhāskara with regard to the explanation of *Vasutāte*. Devarāja also in the Introduction to his Nighaṇṭu-Bhāṣya mentions the Veda-Bhāṣya of Bhaṭṭa Bhāskara and quotes explanations from it (Cf. I, 11, 24; 12, 11 etc.). Vedāchārya alias Lakṣmaṇa in his Sudarśana-mīmāṃsā (pp. 4 and 8) mentions the Bhāṣyakāra Bhaṭṭa Bhāskara and his Bhāṣya called *Jñāna-yajña*. In his Bhāṣya Bhāṭṭa Bhāskara speaks of Āryabhaṭṭīya, Amarakośa and Kāśikā. On the basis of this evidence Pandit Bhagavaddatta is inclined to assign Bhaṭṭa Bhāskara to the 11th century of the Vikrama Era.[19] Dr. R. Shamasastry in his Sanskrit Preface to the Mysore edition of the Tait. Br. places Bhaṭṭa Bhāskara later than Sāyaṇa on the basis of an autobiographical verse.[20] In this connection Pandit P.P.S. Sastri[21] observes that Mr. Seshagiri Sastri discussed this point in detail on pages 1-4 of "Report on a Search for Sanskrit and Tamil MSS. for the year 1893-94" and arrived at the conclusion that Bhaṭṭa Bhāskara wrote his Jñāna-yajña- Bhāṣya on the T.S. in the Śaka year 1110 corresponding to 1189 A.D., by suggesting the emendation *niṣpāpake* instead of *niṣpāvake* in the verse (see note 20), and concludes: "This date roughly approaches the age which is already assigned to Bhaṭṭa Bhāskara by tradition, viz. 950 A.D." In his Bhāṣya on I, 8, 12 Bhaṭṭa Bhāskara mentions as an illustration the name of *Narasiṃhavarmā*, son of Rājendravarman, probably a ruler of the territory. Bhaṭṭa Bhāskara in his Bhāṣya refers to the views of other Bhāṣyakāras but does not mention any name. For instance in his commentary on the T.S. 1,8,15 (which occurs in the RV.IV, 40, 5 and numerous other texts) Bhaṭṭa Bhāskara refers to the views of other commentators who interpret this Mantra in three different ways, viz. *adhyātamam*, *adhidaivam* and *adhiyajñam*. He calls his commentary *Sarvapathīna* "all-embracing", which is very brief in comparison with Sāyaṇa's commentary on the T.S. It must be pointed out that Bhaṭṭa Bhāskara who makes very brief references to the ritual application of the Mantras does not evince much interest in the ritualistic aspect of his interpretation and lays all-out emphasis on explaining the grammatical formation, accent and etymology of the words. So his Bhāṣya is concerned more with the linguistic interpretation than with the ritualistic interpretation of the T.S. In support of his explanations he profusely quotes Pāṇini and the other authorities on Sanskrit Grammar. Besides, he also refers to the Nighaṇṭu and the Nirukta. Quotations from the Tait. Br. and the Ap. S.S. are also frequently cited in his Bhāṣya. Bhaṭṭa Bhāskara wrote a commentary on the Tait. Br. also. Sāyaṇa's reference to Bhaṭṭa Bhāskara on the interpretation of *Vasutāte* as a vocative singular obviously pertains to the latter's Bhāṣya on the Tait. Br. III, 6,10,5 where this formation occurs. As pointed out above, Sāyaṇa in his commentary on the Tait. Br. III, 6, 10, 5 adopts Bhaṭṭa Bhāskara's interpretation without acknowledgement.

Ānandatīrtha and his Followers

Ānandatīrtha Bhagavatpāda alias Madhvāchārya, founder of a Vaiṣṇava sect called *Mādhava* and exponent of the Dvaita doctrine of Philosophy, wrote a metrical commentary called *Ṛg-Bhāsya* on the first forty hymns of the first Aṣṭaka of the RV. His Bhāṣya is an attempt to interpret the Mantras of the RV. in terms of their application to Nārāyaṇa, the Supreme God of the Vaiṣṇavas. In other words, the names of various Vedic deities are interpreted to refer to Nārāyaṇa. Ānandatīrtha makes his objective perfectly clear in the introductory Śloka of his Bhāṣya, in which he says that Nārāyaṇa who is called Puruṣa in the Puruṣa-Sūkta is the subject-matter of all the Vedas and Śāstras. So Ānandatīrtha's Bhāṣya which proceeds in pursuance of pre-conceived notions is obviously sectarian in its approach. With regard to this Bhāṣya Dr. Burnell in his catalogue observes: "This work is by no means deserving of its name; it is a sort of Vedānta sermon with scanty explanation of a few Ṛgvedic texts."

Ānandatīrtha was born in Karnatak, and according to his own statement in his Mahābhārata-tātparya-nirṇaya he was born when 4300 years of the Kali Era had passed. This date corresponds to 1198 A.D. He is said to have lived for 80 years. Therefore his Ṛg-Bhāṣya was composed in the 13th century A.D. He also wrote a commentary on the Gītā.

The followers of Ānandatīrtha have written over a dozen commentaries on his Ṛg-Bhāṣya as well as on the commentaries of the Bhāṣya in order to further expound and elucidate the Dvaita doctrine propounded by the founder of their sect.[21]

Jayatīrtha who was a very eminent exponent of the Mādhava School of Philosophy wrote his *Ṛg-Bhāṣya-Ṭīkā* (1365-88 A.D.) on Ānandatīrtha's commentary. Nārāyaṇāchārya wrote a commentary entitled *Madhvamantā-rthamañjarī*. Rāghavendratīrtha wrote his Mantrārthamañjarī (C. 1623-71 A.D.) on the Ṛg-Bhāṣya of Ānandatīrtha. A commentary called *Ṛg-Bhāṣya-Ṭīkā-Vivṛti* (C.1648-74 A.D.) on Jayatīrtha's commentary was written by Chalāri Narasiṃhāchārya. All the above-mentioned commentaries are now available in print. The commentaries mentioned below are available in MSS. at various places. The *Padārtha pra-kāśikā* is a commentary on Jayatīrtha's *Ṛg-Bhāṣya-Ṭīkā* by Śrīnivāsatīrtha, a disciple of Yādavāchārya. Śrīnivāsatīrtha was a scholar of not only Dvaita School of Philosophy but also of Nyāya and Pāṇinian grammar. Nārāyana,a disciple of Jayatīrtha, wrote a commentary called *Bhāva-Ratna-Prakāśikā* on the latter's commentary. Similarly Keśavāchārya wrote a commentary entitled *Ṛg-Bhāṣya-Ṭippaṇī* on Jayatīrtha's commentary. A commentary known as *Ṛg-Bhāṣya-Ṭīkā-Prakāśa* on Jayatīrtha's commentary was written by Satyanāthayati, a disciple of Satyanidhitīrtha. The *Ṛgarthoddhāra* is still another commentary on Jayatīrtha's commentary by a follower of the Mādhava sect (Narasiṃha Bhikṣu?). A commentary called *Ṛg-Bhāṣya-Ṭīkā* (*Bhāvārthakośa*) on Ānandatīrtha's commentary was written by Muddu Veṅkaṭa Kṛṣṇa; and Rāmachandratīrtha also wrote a commentary called *Ṛg-Bhāṣya-Ṭīkā* on Ānandatīrtha's Bhāṣya. Lakṣmīnārayaṇa's *Ṛg-Bhāṣya-Tīppaṇī* is also a commentary on Mādhava's Bhāṣya. The *Ṛgartha-Chūḍāmaṇi* by an unknown author claims to explain the meaning of the Ṛks in accordance with the ideas of the Ṛg-Bhāṣya (of Ānandatīrtha). A commentary called *Ṛgartharatnamālā* was also written by a follower of Ānandatīrtha on his Ṛg-Bhāṣya. As the author of the Ṛgartharatnamālā mentions *Ṛg-Bhāṣyārtha-tattva-Prakāśikā* (probably the same as Padārtha-Prakāśikā), he appears to belong to a late date.

Since the commentaries written by Ānandatīrtha's followers follow the beaten track and attempt to project their own pre-conceived notions in the Veda, their exegetical value is very limited.

Ātmānanda

Ātmānanda wrote a Bhāṣya on the RV. hymn I, 164 which is called *Asya-Vāmīya-Sūkta* after its initial words *asya vāmasya*. He claims to be a descendant of the Ṛṣi of this Sūkta. In the beginning of his Bhāṣya Ātmānanda says that ancient commentators such as Skanda, Bhāskara etc., attempt the ritualistic or naturalistic interpretation and ignore the mystic interpretation of the Hymn. But this Hymn is, in his opinion, mystic in import. Therefore, Ātmānanda interprets the Hymn from the point of view of the Advaita School of Vedānta, and says that his interpretation is based on the Viṣṇudharmottara. Moreover, in support of his interpretation (Cf. his Bhāṣya on RV. I,164,46) he sometimes cites *Kalpa* which in the opinion of Pandit Bhagavaddatta stands for *Puṣkaroktakalpa.* In his Bhāṣya Ātmānanda mentions a large number of Vedic authorities and important works such as Skanda, Udgītha, Bhāskara, Śaunaka, Vedamitra, Viṣṇudharmottara, Nirukta, Purāṇas, Vijñāneśvara, Upaniṣads, etc. But he does not mention Sāyaṇa. On the basis of this negative evidence some scholars are inclined to hold that Ātmānanda is earlier than Sāyaṇa but later than Vijñāneśara who wrote a commentary on the Yājñavalkya Smṛti in the 11th century A.D. So far there is no positive evidence to fix his date with any amount of certainty.

Bharatasvāmin

Bharatasvāmin Kāśyapa wrote a commentary on the Sāmaveda, which Dr. C. Kunhan Raja published in the Adyar Library Sanskrit Series in the year 1941 along with Mādhava's commentary of the Sāmaveda (see above). In comparison with the Mādhava-Bhāṣya the Bhāṣya of Bharatasvāmin is very brief. In his commentary Bharatasvāmin quotes from Pānini, Ait. Br., Tait. Ar., Ait. Ar., Nirukta, T.S., P. Br., RV. etc., and this gives ample proof of his Vedic erudition. His Bhāṣya is undoubtedly a learned composition. This is why Bharatasvāmin as a Bhāṣyakāra is cited by Devarāja and Sāyaṇa (Ṛgveda-Bhāṣya VI,1,13).

According to autobiographical information furnished

by Bharatasvāmin in his Bhāṣya, his father was Nārāyaṇa, mother Yajñadā, and teacher Nāganātha. It is further said that Bharatasvāmin composed this Bhāṣya living happily at *Śrīraṅga* during the reign of the Hoysla King Ramanātha who, according to Burnell, reigned between 1272 A.D. and 1310 A.D. Therefore Dr. Raja opines that Bharatasvāmin wrote his commentary about 1300 A.D. Even though no definite date can be assigned to the composition of Bharatasvāmin's Bhāṣya, it is definite that he was earlier than Devarāja and Sāyaṇa. Bharatasvāmin wrote commentaries on some Brāhmaṇas of the S.V., such as the Sāmavidhāna Brāhmaṇa. Did he also write a commentary on the RV., M.S., K.S., or T. Br., wherein the Ṛgvedic verse VI,1, 13 occurs? For, Sāyaṇa in his commentary on RV. VI,1,13 refers to the opinion of Bharatasvāmin who regards *Vasutāte* (analysed into two words by Śākalya) as a locative singular of a single word, but this verse does not occur in the S.V.

Sāyaṇa

Sāyaṇa occupies a unique position in the history of Vedic exegesis. At present as many as *twenty-five* scholarly works are found ascribed to Sāyaṇa. Out of them five are Veda-Bhāṣyas, eleven Brāhmaṇa-Bhāṣyas, two Āraṇyaka-Bhāṣyas, and seven works are on other subjects as listed below.

Sāyaṇa's Veda-Bhāṣyas :

1. The Taittirīya-Saṃhitā-Bhāṣya.
2. The Ṛgveda-Saṃhitā-Bhāṣya.
3. The Śukla-Yajurveda-Kāṇva-Saṃhitā-Bhāṣya.
4. The Sāmaveda-Saṃhitā-Bhāṣya.
5. The Atharvaveda-Saṃhitā-Bhāṣya.

Sāyaṇa's Brāhmaṇa-Bhāṣyas :

1. The Taittirīya-Brāhmaṇa-Bhāṣya.
2. The Aitareya-Brāhmaṇa-Bhāṣya.
3. The Śatapatha-Brāhmaṇa-Bhāṣya (incomplete).
4. The Tāṇḍya-Mahā-Brāhmaṇa-Bhāṣya.
5. The Ṣaḍviṃśa-Brāhmaṇa-Bhāṣya.
6. The Sāmavidhāna-Brāhmaṇa-Bhāṣya.
7. The Ārṣeya-Brāhmaṇa-Bhāṣya.

8. The Devatādhyāya-Brāhmaṇa-Bhāsya.
9. The Vaṃśa-Brāhmaṇa-Bhāṣya.
10. The Upaniṣad-Brāhmaṇa-Bhāṣya.
11. The Saṃhitopaniṣad-Brāhmaṇa-Bhāṣya.

Sāyaṇa's Bhāṣyas on the Āraṇyakas:

1. The Taittirīyāraṇyaka-Bhāṣya.
2. The Aitareyā raṇyaka-Bhāṣya.

The other Works ascribed to Sāyaṇa :

1. The Mādhavīyā Dhātuvṛtti.
2. The Subhasita-Sudhā-Nidhi.
3. The Alaṅkāra-Sudhā-Nidhi.
4. The Puruṣārtha-Sudhā-Nidhi.
5. The Yajñatantra-Sudhā-Nidhi.
6. The Prāyaśchitta-Sudhā-Nidhi.
7. The Āyurveda-Sudhā-Nidhi.

We shall here discuss the salient features of his Veda-Bhāṣyas only.

The Taittirīya-Saṃhita-Bhāṣya : In the Introduction to his Ṛgveda-Bhāṣya Sāyaṇa himself has made it clear that first of all he wrote his Bhāṣya on the T.S., because it is of prime importance for the performance of sacrifices. Another reason for composing his first Veda-Bhāṣya on the T.S. might have been that Sāyaṇa was a follower of the Baudhāyana School of this Veda. As the main aim of Sāyaṇa's commentary on the T.S. is to explain the sacrificial procedure, he takes great pains to present all possible details of the ritualistic aspect of the Mantras and cites copious quotations from the Brāhmaṇas and the Śrauta-Sūtras, especially from the Tait. Br., Baudh. S.S., and Ap. S.S. Besides, he derives help from the Pūrva-Mīmāṃsa and Pāṇini also in support of his explanations as claimed by him in the Introduction to his Bhāṣya.[23] As we have pointed out above, Sāyaṇa in his Ṛgveda-Bhāṣya refers to the interpretations of Bhaṭṭa Bhāskara and accepts them without acknowledgement in his Bhāṣya on the T. Br. III, 6, 10, 5. Similarly in his Bhāṣya on the T.S. also Sāyaṇa follows in many places the explanations offered by Bhaṭṭa Bhāskara. For instance, in his Bhāṣya on the T.S.I,8,12 Sāyaṇa cites by way of illustration the same name *Narasiṃhavarmā*, son of *Rājendravarman*, as is cited by Bhaṭṭa Bhāskara in this connection. Sāyaṇa might have derived help for his commentary from some other previous commentators also, but he does not mention any commentator by name.

The Ṛgveda-Saṃhitā-Bhāṣya : Among the extant Bhāṣyas on the RV. Sāyaṇa's Bhāṣya is most comprehensive and lucid. Sāyaṇa's attempt in his Bhāṣya, especially on the first Aṣṭaka, to explain in detail the grammatical formation, etymologies and accent of the Vedic words is worthy of praise and can be matched to a certain extent by only Bhaṭṭa Bhāskara's Bhāṣya on the T.S. In this admirable task Sāyaṇa has made full use of the Pāṇinian grammar, Nighaṇṭu, Nirukta, Uṇādisūtras, etc. and has suggested original and novel etymologies of a good number of Vedic words.

In the beginning of his commentary on each hymn Sāyaṇa first of all cites Kātyāyana's Sarvānukramaṇī to indicate the number of Ṛks, deity, Ṛṣi and metre of the hymn or of the verses comprised in it. Then he refers to the Asv. S.S and the Ait. Br. to point out the ritual application of the hymn or its Ṛks. If Sāyaṇa is aware of any *Itihāsa* connected with the hymn, in the beginning of its Bhāṣya he quotes the concerned Itihāsa together with its source such as the Bṛhaddevatā and the Śāṭyāyana Brāhmaṇa. There is no doubt that the ritualistic explanations of the Mantras dominate the Sāyaṇa-Bhāṣya. But Sāyaṇa does not hesitate to include in his Bhāṣya the other known interpretations of a Mantra. Therefore iu some cases Sāyaṇa offers as many as four or five different interpretations including ritualistic, naturalistic, mythological, Vedantic and grammatical. It must be said to Sāyaṇa's credit that all the different interpretations of a Mantra are not the results of his own speculations but they represent the view-points of various interpreters known to him. At some places Sāyaṇa explicitly mentions the names of previous Bhāṣyakāras such as Skandasvāmin, Udgītha, Mādhava-Bhaṭṭa, Bhaṭṭa Bhāskara Miśra, Bharatasvāmin, etc., but elsewhere refers to the views of other Bhāṣyakāras in such general terms as *Apare*, *Anye*, etc. In support of his explanations Sāyaṇa cites quotations from several important works which include the T.S., T. Br., P. Br.,

Ait. Br., Sat. Br., Kaus. Br., Charaka-Brāhmaṇa, Śāṭyāyana-Brāhmaṇa, Tait. Ar., Ait. Ar., numerous Upaniṣads, Manusmṛti, Asv. S.S., Ṛg-vidhāna, and the Mahābhārata. Besides, Sāyaṇa quotes parallel passages from the RV. to corroborate his interpretation.

Sāyaṇa's Ṛgveda-Bhāṣya is a monumental work which no student of the Veda can afford to ignore. Although some modern scholars are highly critical of the Sāyaṇa-Bhāṣya and find fault with it, yet they cannot shut their eyes to the irrefutable fact that at a crucial time in the history of Vedic studies Sāyaṇa provided much-needed prop to the tottering Vedic scholarship and saved it from total collapse. It is Sāyaṇa's Bhāṣya that imparted initial strength and confidence to modern scholarship to criticise this pre-eminent commentator, as aptly observed by Max Müller [24]: "It is well known to those who have followed my literary publications that I never entertained any exaggerated opinion as to the value of the traditional interpretation of the Veda, handed down in the theological schools of India, and preserved to us in the great commentary of Sāyaṇa. More than twenty years ago, when it required more courage to speak out than now, I expressed my opinion on that subject in no ambiguous language, and was blamed for it by some of those who now speak of Sāyaṇa as a mere drag in the progress of Vedic scholarship. Even a drag, however, is sometimes more conducive to the safe advancement of learning than a whip; and those who recollect the history of Vedic scholarship during the last five and twenty years, know best that, with all its faults and weaknesses, Sāyaṇa's commentary was a sine qua non for a scholarly study of the Ṛgveda. I do not wonder that others who have more recently entered on that study are inclined to speak disparagingly of the scholastic interpretations of Sāyaṇa. They hardly know how much we all owe to his guidance in effecting our first entrance into this fortress of Vedic language and Vedic religion, and how much even they, without being aware of it, are indebted to that Indian Eustathius......If now we can walk without Sāyaṇa, we ought to bear in mind that five and twenty years ago we could not have made even our first steps, we could never, at least, have gained a firm footing without his leading strings. If therefore we can now see further then he could, let us not forget that we are standing on his shoulders."

Despite our gratitude to Sāyaṇa we should not turn a blind eye to the shortcomings of his Bhāṣya to avoid his mistakes and make further advancement in the realm of Vedic exegesis. Sāyaṇa's interpretation of several Mantras is arbitrary and fanciful in accordance with his pre-conceived notions, and suffers from lack of consistency. He suggests one meaning of a word in one Mantra and an altogether different meaning of the same word in a similar context in the interpretation of another Mantra. It seems to suggest, as we shall discuss below, that the entire Ṛgveda-Bhāṣya is not the work of one scholar but the joint endeavour of several scholars. It must be admitted that some of the interpretations suggested by Sāyaṇa are more appropriate than those of the other commentators and even modern scholars.[25]

The Sāmaveda-Saṃhitā-Bhāṣya: Sāyaṇa in his Introduction to this Bhāṣya says that he wrote his Bhāṣya on the S.V. after composing his Bhāṣya on the T.S. and the RV., because the Mantras of the S.V. are dependent on those of the RV. In the Introduction of his Sāmaveda-Bhāṣya Sāyaṇa has discussed various topics concerning the S.V. In order to give information about the Ṛṣi, deity, metre etc. of a Mantra Sāyaṇa at places cites a versified Anukramaṇī. In his Bhāṣya he quotes many important works including the Nidāna-Sūtra.

The Śukla-Yajurveda-Kāṇva-Saṃhitā-Bhāṣya: After completing his Bhāṣyas on the T.S., RV., and S.V., Sāyaṇa wrote a commentary on the Kāṇva-Saṃhitā of the Śukla-Yajurveda as stated by him in his Introduction to this Bhāṣya. In addition to the thirteen introductory verses Sāyaṇa has written a detailed prose Introduction to this Bhāṣya discussing various issues connected with the Kāṇva-Saṃhitā. After narrating the Purāṇic legend relating to the schism between the Kṛṣṇa and Śukla Śākhās of the Yajurveda Sāyaṇa explains the term *Vājasaneya* and enumerates the fifteen Śākhās of the Vājasaneyins, and then he elucidates the meaning of Kāṇva Śākhā. Afterwards he discusses the terms Svādhyāya, Dharma etc., following the line of argumentation adopted by the Mīmāṃsakas. In the Introduction Sāyaṇa considers the Sat. Br.

to be an interpretation of the Mantras, and gives an outline of the subject-matter of different chapters of the Śaṃhitā. In this Bhāṣya Sāyaṇa has derived considerable help from the Kātyāyana-Śrauta-Sūtra to explain the sacrificial procedure. Unlike the Ṛgveda-Bhāṣya this Bhāṣya seldom quotes from the Pāṇinian gramar, Nirukta and other important works, although several important authorities such as the Śvetāśvataropaniṣad, Manu, Bādarāyaṇa, Sat. Br., Jaimini, Āpastamba, Charaṇa-vyūha, Vivaraṇa granth of Prakāśātmāchārya, etc., have been cited in the Introduction.

Sāyaṇa's commentary on the first twenty Adhyāyas of this Saṃhitā was published as early as 1915 and the MSS. of his Bhāṣya on the remaining Adhyāyas were not then easily available. So an erroneous impression gained currency that Sāyaṇa wrote his Bhāṣya on the first twenty Adhyāyas only or that his Bhāṣya on the remaining Adhyāyas was lost. And this impression was confirmed by the statement of a later commentator Anantāchārya who says in his commentary on the Kāṇva-Saṃhitā that Sāyaṇa wrote a Bhāṣya on the first twenty Adhyāyas only. But the discovery of the Sāyaṇa-Bhāṣya on the remaining Adhyāyas of this Saṃhitā has disproved this contention of Anantāchārya; and very recently Sāyaṇa's commentary on the second half of the Kāṇva-Saṃhitā has been published by Pandit Chintamani Misra Sarma from Varanasi in the Sarasvatibhavana-Grantha-Mala.

The Atharvaveda-Samhita-Bhāṣya: Sāyaṇa's commentary on the AV. is the last among his Veda-Bhāṣyas. In the Introduction to this Bhāṣya it is said that Sāyaṇa wrote the commentary on the AV. at the instance of king Harihara who is identified as Harihara II. In the introduction to this Bhāṣya Sāyaṇa discusses various important topics such as *Travī Vidyā* and the AV., the *Brahmaveda* epithet of the AV., the importance of the AV., Svādhyāya-Dharma, the Veda as supreme authority, the Veda as divine revelation, nine Śākhās of the AV., and Ātharvaṇa rituals, etc. In connection with the rituals of the AV. Sāyaṇa in the Introduction cites a Śloka of Upavarṣa which mentions five important ritualistic treatises of the AV., viz. Nakṣatra-kalpa, Vaitāna-Sūtra, Kauśika-Sūtra, Āṅgirasa-Kālpa and Śānti-Kalpa. Although Sāyaṇa says in the Introduction that he is commenting on the AV. consisting of twenty Kāṇḍas, at present his commentary is available on Kāṇḍas 1,2,3,4,6-8,11,17-19 and 20 (1-37) only. In order to explain the ritual application of the Mantras Sāyaṇa cites the Kauśika-Sūtra and the Vaitāna-Sūtra. Moreover, he also quotes from several other works such as the RV., T.S., T.Br., T.Ar., Ait. Br., Ait. Ar., Nirukta, Pāṇini etc.

A noteworthy feature of this Sāyaṇa-Bhāṣya is that it contains hundreds of readings which are not found in the Vulgate edition or in any of the extant MSS. of the AV. If a new edition of the AV. is prepared on the basis of the readings of this Bhāṣya, it would be substantially different from the Vulgate. The recension of the AV. relied upon by Sāyaṇa seems to have been irretrievably lost.

The Authorship of the Veda-Bhāṣyas ascribed to Sāyaṇa: Now we are confronted with the question whether all the above-described Veda-Bhāṣyas ascribed to Sāyaṇa were composed by him alone or they were written by several scholars under his direction and guidance. On the basis of a thorough examination of these Bhāṣyas many modern scholars are of the opinion that Sāyaṇa is not the sole author of all these Bhāṣyas. Dr. P.D. Gune has put forward the view that several scholars collaborated in the composition of the Ṛgveda-Bhāṣya, for there is a marked difference in the style of composition of the commentary on different Aṣṭakas.[26] A comparative study of the different portions of the Ṛgveda-Bhāṣya has convinced me also that the entire commentary is not from the pen of a single author although Sāyaṇa might have made a significant contribution to its composition, because the Bhāṣya at many places contains quite contradictory and inconsistent interpretations of one and the same word. If we examine Sāyaṇa's interpretation of one and the same word and Mantra in his various Veda-Bhāṣyas, we find startling differences in his interpretations which point to the irresistible conclusion that all these Bhāṣyas with such contradictory and irreconcilable views could not have been written by a single author. Readers may consult my previous work entitled *Vaidika Vyākhyā-Vivechana* for a comparison of Sāyaṇa's Veda-Bhāṣyas on some important words and verses.

In his Introduction to the second edition of the Ṛgveda-Bhāṣya Max-Müller has drawn attention to the fact that Sāyaṇa in his commentary on RV. I, 164,31 cites a passage[27] from the Ait. Br. styling it as "our Brāhmaṇa". If this statement turns out to be factual, it would prove that the author of this portion of the Bhāṣya was a Ṛgvedin Brāhmaṇa, follower of the Ait. Br., different from Sāyaṇa who himself was a Yajurvedin, follower of the T. Br. The above-mentioned quotation is traceable neither to the Ait. Br. nor to the T. Br., but is found verbatim in the Ait. Ar. II, 1,6,6. As the Ait. Ar. is traditionally regarded as part of the Ait. Br., the author of this portion of the Bhāṣya must have been a follower of the Ait. Br., who first cites this passage from his own Brāhmaṇa and then another similar passage from the T. Ar. V,6,4 without describing it as his own Brāhmaṇa.

A piece of external evidence also seems to support the view that several scholars collaborated with Sāyaṇa in the composition of his Veda-Bhāṣyas. According to an inscription[28] of 1386 A.D., the founder of the Vedic path (*Vaidika-Mārga-Pratiṣṭhāpaka*) King Harihara II honoured, by donating *agrahāra* in the presence of Vidyārṇyaśrīpāda, the three Brāhmaṇas, viz. Nārāyaṇa Vājapeyayājin, Narahari Somayājin and Paṇḍarī Dīkṣita, who were esteemed as pioneers of the Bhāṣyas on the four Vedas (*Chaturveda-Bhāṣya-Pravartakāḥ*) and followers of the path of virtue and Veda (*Dharma-Brahmādhvanya*). It is quite likely that these scholars might have assisted Sāyaṇa in the composition of his Veda-Bhāṣyas. In the Introduction to his Bhāṣya on the AV. Sāyaṇa expresses his sense of appreciation and gratitude to both Vidyārṇya and Harihara.

It would not be unreasonable to infer from the internal and external evidence that, although Sāyaṇa did not personally author all the Veda-Bhāṣyas and the other Bhāṣyas ascribed to him, he himself drew a plan of their composition, contributed his share, and finally got the plan executed with the assistance and collaboration of a number of dedicated and competent scholars working under his guidance and supervision. There is no doubt that Sāyaṇa himself was a profound scholar who inspired other scholars with his erudition and sense of dedication to the cause of Vedic learning.

Biographical Information about Sāyaṇa: The works ascribed to Sāyaṇa and some other works furnish a good deal of biographical information about him, which is summed up below. Sāyaṇa's father was Māyaṇa, mother Śrimatī, and Gotra Bhāradvāja. He belonged to the Baudhāyana school of the T.S. In the Introduction to his several Bhāṣyas he mentions the name of his teacher Vidyātīrtha. According to an inscription,[29] Sāyaṇa's teacher was *Śrikaṇṭhanātha* who might have been the same as *Śrīkaṇṭha* whom Sāyaṇa's younger brother Bhoganātha in his *Mahāgaṇapatistava* mentions as another teacher of Sāyaṇa. Bhoganātha was a famous poet who composed several poetic works such as *Tripura-vijaya, Udāharaṇamālā, Śṛṅgāramañjarī, Mahāgaṇapatistava* and *Gaurī nāthāṣṭaka.* Sāyaṇa's elder brother Mādhava was both an able administrator and profound scholar who worked as a Minister of Kings Harihara and Bukka of Vijayanagara Empire, and authored several learned works. In the Introduction to his Bhāṣya on the T.S Sāyaṇa says that when king Bukka directed Mādhavāchārya to write Veda-Bhāṣyas Mādhavāchārya told the King that his (Mādhava's) younger brother Sāyaṇārya who was well versed in all the Vedas should be appointed as a Vedic commentator; and that accordingly King Bukka instructed Sāyaṇa to write Veda-Bhāṣyas. This is why Sāyaṇa associates Mādhava's name with his Bhāṣyas and calls them *Mādhavīya Vedārthaprakāśa.* However, Mādhava's name does not figure in the Introduction to Sāyaṇa's commentaries on the AV., SV. and Kāṇva-Saṃhitā, and the names of only Sāyaṇa and his patron King are mentioned there, while Sāyaṇa's commentaries on the T.S. and the RV. contain the following introductory verses:

Ye pūrvottaramīmāṃse te vyākhyayātisaṃgrahāt,
Kṛpālur Mādhavāchāryo vedārthaṃ vaktum udyataḥ.

According to evidence available from his writings Sāyaṇa worked as a minister of Kings Bukka and Harihara Second. Sāyaṇa is said to have died in 1387 A.D. after attaining the age of 72 years,[30] which means he was born in 1315 A.D. Therefore, his Veda-Bhāṣyas might have been written in the second half of the 14th century A.D.

Mudgala

Mudgala is a post-Sāyaṇa Bhāṣyakāra who has prepared a summary of Sāyaṇa's Ṛgveda-Bhāṣya by omitting all discussion on the grammatical formation, accent and divergent interpretations of Vedic words. In the Introduction to his Bhāṣya Mudgala claims that having fully considered the previous Bhāṣya regarded as abstruse he has derived its essence in the same way as butter is churned out from milk and gold is extracted from sands. He might have prepared such a summary of the whole of the Sāyaṇa-Bhāṣya, but at present Mudgala's commentary on the 1st Aṣṭaka (I, 1-21) and part of the 4th Aṣṭaka (V, 9,1 to VI, 9,6) of the RV. is available which has been published by Dr. Vishva Bandhu along with the Bhāṣyas of Skanda, Veṅkaṭamādhava and Udgītha. There is no definite information about the exact date of composition of Mudgala-Bhāṣya. However, Pandit Bhagavaddatta conjecturally assigns Mudgala-Bhāṣya to Saṃvat 1470-1479 on the basis of an incomplete reading *Samvat-147*—found at the end of its manuscript preserved in the India Office Library.

Mahīdhara

Mahīdhara wrote a commentary called *Veda-dīpa* on the Mādhyandina-Saṃhitā of the Śukla-Yajurveda. A comparison of his commentary with that of Uvaṭa clearly shows that Mahīdhara has largely drawn upon the Uvaṭa-Bhāṣya. In the Introduction to his Bhāṣya Mahīdhara himself admits that he is writing his commentary after consulting the Bhāṣyas composed by Uvaṭa and Mādhava. In this connection Dr. L. Sarup advances the conjecture that Mādhava mentioned by Mahīdhara is probably to be identified with Mādhava, son of Veṅkaṭa[31]; and on this basis Dr. Sarup places Mahīdhara in the beginning of the 12th century A.D. But Pandit Bhagavaddata[32] refutes Dr. Sarup's view and holds that Mādhava mentioned by Mahīdhara in the introductory verse is identical with Sāyaṇa Mādhava and not Veṅkaṭamādhava, because the passage from Mādhava's Bhāṣya quoted by Mahīdhara in his commentary on the V.S. XIII, 45 is traceable to Sāyaṇa's commentary on the Kāṇva-Saṃhitā, XIV, 47. The assertion of Pandit Bhagavaddatta is correct as the passage in question is actually found in the Sāyaṇa-Bhāṣya on the Kāṇva-Saṃhita. Moreover, there is no possibility of the occurrence of the said passage of Mādhava-Bhāṣya in the commentary of Veṅkaṭamādhava, because the concerned Mantra does not belong to the RV.

Although Mahīdhara has derived considerable help from the commentaries of Uvaṭa and Sāyaṇa, yet Mahīdhara's commentary is not devoid of originality. In his commentary he frequently quotes passages from the Sat. Br., Kat. S.S., Nirukta, Pāṇini, etc., and suggests original interpretations of several words and Mantras.

Another work entitled *Mantramahodadhi* is found ascribed to Mahīdhara. The introductory verse of this work is very similar to the one found in the Introduction to his Veda-Bhaṣya. Therefore most of the scholars are inclined to place Mahīdhara in the 16th century A.D., as the date of composition of the Mantra-mahodadhi given in its colophon is 1588 A.D.

Anantāchārya

Anantāchārya alias Anantabhaṭṭa wrote a commentary called Bhāvārthadīpikā (sometimes designated as *Veda-dīpa* also) on the second half (Adhyayas 21-40) of the Kāṇva-Saṃhitā. In the Introduction to his Bhāṣya Anantāchārya says that since the first twenty Adhyāyas only of the Kāṇva-Saṃhitā were explained by Mādhavāchārya, he (Anantāchārya) would explain the remaining twenty Adhyāyas. This misconception of Anantāchārya, which has been now proved to be baseless by the discovery of Sāyana's Bhāṣya on the remaining Adhyāyas, might have arisen as a result of the non-availability of Sāyaṇa's commentary on the entire Saṃhitā at that time. In his commentary he has derived full help from the Sat., Br., Kat. S.S., Nirukta and earlier Veda-Bhāṣyas. The influence of Mahīdhara-Bhāṣya is also discernible on the Bhāṣya of Anantāchārya who in a few places styles his Bhāṣya as *Veda-dīpa* like the name of the Mahīdhara-Bhāṣya. Moreover, Anantāchārya wrote commentaries on the Sat. Br. (Kāṇva-recension), Vājasaneyi-Prātiśākhya, and Bhāṣika-Sūtra. Vidhāna Pārijāta, Kāṇva-Kaṇṭhābharaṇa and Kātyāyana-Smārta-Mantrārtha-Dīpikā are also ascribed to Anantāchārya. In the Introductions and Colophons of his works he has given ample biographical information. His father was Nāgadeva and mother Bhāgīrathī. Anantāchārya was a follower of Kāṇva-Śākhā and lived at Kāśī. As the date of composition of his work Vidhāna-Pārijāta given in its colophon is 1625 A.D., it indicates that he might have written most of his works in the first half of the 17th century A.D.

Ānandabodha

Ānandabodha wrote a commentary called *Kāṇva-Veda-Mantra-Bhāṣya* (or *Kāṇva-Veda-Mantra-Bhāṣya-Saṃgraha*) on the Kāṇva-Saṃhitā, which has been recently published by Dr. Subhadra Jha. In the Colophon of his Bhāṣya Ānandabodha mentions his full name as *Ānandabodhabhaṭṭopādhyāya Chaturvedin* and that of his father as *Jātavedabhaṭṭopādhyāya.* Nothing definite can be said with regard to the date of this Bhāṣya excepting that it is later than Sāyaṇa.

Veṅkaṭeśa Naidhruva

One Veṅkaṭeṣa Naidhruva, whose date cannot be determined on the basis of available evidence, wrote on th- Kṛṣṇa-Yajurveda a brief commentary which is variously named as *Yajurveda-Bhāṣya-Saṃgrah*, or *Yajurveda-Bhāṣya-Saṃgraha-Sāra* or *Vedārtha-Saṃgraha-Sāra.* The commentary is very brief and nothing more than a running paraphrase of the Mantras without any quotations from or references to other works. The commentary is incomplete and fragmentary.

The Bhāṣyakāras of Collections of Ritual Mantras and Select Mantras

In addition to the above-mentioned Bhāṣyakāras who wrote Bhāṣyas on the Vedic Saṃhitās, some Bhāṣyakāras mostly belonging to the mediaeval period attempted to explain from a ritualistic or sectarian point of view or with some other object in view the collections of ritual Mantras or selcet Mantras. We give below brief information about some important Bhāṣyakāras of this category.

Haradatta

Haradatta or Haradattamiśra is a name to conjure with in the domain of Vedāṅga-studies. He is famous as a commentator of the Asv. G.S., Ap. G.S., Ap. D.S. and Gautama D.S. The collection of ritual Mantras (Gṛhya Mantras) to be recited at the performance of the Gṛhya rites described in the Asv. G.S. has been interpreted by Haradatta Miśra and published under the title *Āśvalāyana-Gṛhya-Mantra-Vyākhyā* in the Trivandrum Sanskrit Series. In the colophon of the lst Adhyāya of his commentary it is said in a verse that the Mantras to be recited at the rites of the Asv. G.S. have been explained by *Chakrapāṇi.* Is *Chakrapāṇi* his another name or a title or a later interpolation? This requires further investigation. Haradatta is the author of a commentary on another collection of ritual Mantras which is called *Āpastambīya Mantrapāṭha* or *Ekāgnikāṇḍa* forming 25th and 26th Praśnas of the Āpastamba-Kalpa. In keeping with the object of the recitation of ritual Mantras at Gṛhya rites Haradatta's interpretation is essentially ritualistic in approach. Like his all other commentaries Haradatta's commentaries on the above-mentioned collections of ritual Mantras display his mastery over the Pāṇinian grammar.

The question of Haradatta's date and his identification with the author of the Padamañjarī has been hotly debated by eminent scholars. Without going into this controversy I would refer to Dr. P.V. Kane's History of Dharmaśāstra (Vol. I, Part II, pp. 742 ff.) according to which Haradatta who belonged to the South (most probably to Tamil Nadu) and wrote the above-mentioned commentaries was identical with Haradatta, the author of the Pada-mañjarī, and flourished between 1100 A.D. and 1300 A.D. Prof. Belvalkar in his *Systems of Sanskrit Grammar* (pp. 39-40) assigns Haradatta, the author of the Padamañjarī, to c. 1100 A.D.

Guṇaviṣṇu

Guṇaviṣṇu explained the collection of ritual Mantras to be recited at the rites described in the Gobhila-Gṛhya-Sūtra. This collection of ritual Mantras is known as *Mantra-Brāhmaṇa,* because it forms part of the Chhāndogya-Brāhmaṇa. Prof. Durgamohan Bhattacharya who published this collection of ritual Mantras under the title of *Chhāndogya-Brāhmaṇa* with the commentary of Guṇaviṣṇu has discussed in the Introduction the various questions concerning Guṇaviṣṇu. Dr. Bhattacharya opines that Guṇaviṣṇu who belonged to Bengal flourished sometime before the 12th century A.D., as he (Guṇaviṣṇu) is quoted and explicitly mentioned in Halāyudha's Brāhmaṇa-Sarvasva, a work composed during the reign of King Lakṣmaṇasena of Bengal. Dr. Bhattacharya believes that Sāyaṇa is indebted to Guṇaviṣṇu for several explanations embodied in the Sāyaṇa-Bhāṣyas. This assertion of Dr. Bhattacharya needs to be examined in view of the fact that Devarāja who in his Nighaṇṭu-Bhāṣya mentions a number of important Bhāṣyakāras is not aware of Guṇaviṣṇu's work which must have been mentioned by him if it had been so outstanding as to be relied upon by Sāyaṇa.

Halāyudha

Halāyudha wrote a commentary to explain the meaning of the select Vedic Mantras to be recited by Brāhmaṇas at the time of performing all sorts of religious observances and rites beginning from conception to death and from morning prayer to the muttering of Mantras at the time of sleeping at night. He has given the title "*Brāhmaṇa-Sarvasva*" to this work. In the Introduction Halāyudha says that he has to explain the Mantras to be used by the followers of the *Kāṇva-Śākhā* of the Śukla-Yajurveda in the performance of their religious rites beginning from the brushing of teeth to going to sleep and for the performance of Saṃskāras from conception to marriage. Besides, Halāyudha acknowledges the help derived by him in this connection from Uvaṭa's Bhāṣya on the VS. Moreover, in his work Halāyudha refers to several ancient works and Bhāṣyas including Karka's commentary on the Par. G.S. and the Veda-Bhāṣya of Mugudāchārya. In the Introduction to the Brāhmaṇa-Sarvasva Halāyudha claims to have written the following four works also: *Mīmāṃsā-Sarvasva*, *Vaiṣṇava-Sarvasva*, *Śaiva-Sarvasva* and *Paṇḍita-Sarvasva.*

Giving autobiographical information in the Introduction to the Brāhmaṇa-Sarvasva Halāyudha says that the King Laksmaṇasena conferred on him (Halāyudha) the title of *Rājapaṇḍita* in childhood, appointed him to the office of *Mahāmaha* in early youth, and made him *Dharmādhikārin* in the later part of youth. It shows that Halāyudha was a court-poet of the King Lakṣmaṇasena of Bengal. Therefore most of the scholars are inclined to place Halāyudha in the second half of the 12th century A.D.

Murārimiśra

Murārimiśra wrote a commentary to explain the meaning of the Mantras to be recited at the performance of Gṛhya rites described in the Par. G.S., and therefore it is called *Pāraskara-Mantra-Bhāṣya.* In the Introduction to his Bhāṣya Murārimiśra says that he is writing the *Pāraskara-Mantra-Bhāṣya* after deriving help from the *Gṛhya-Prakāśa-Bhāṣya* of his father Vedamiśra. In the colophon of his Bhāṣya on the Mantras of the first Kāṇḍa of the Par. G.S, Murārimiśra informs us that his father Vedamiśra who wrote Gṛhya-Bhāṣya was the son of Dīkṣita. Although Murārimiśra's commentary is quite elaborate, yet it does not show his profound scholarship of the Vedic language; otherwise he would not have explained the subjunctive form *Vahāśi* as "*vahasi, varṇāgamah; ḍāch vā*" (see his Bhāṣya of the Mantra beginning with "*ayāśchāgne*"). There is no definite evidence for determining the exact date of Murārimiśra. However, on the basis of the dates written on the MSS. of this work Pandit Bhagavaddatta[33] is inclined to hold that it seems to have been written not later than Saṃvat 1430.

Devapāla

Devapāla, the commentator of the Laugākṣi-Gṛhya-Sūtra alias Kāṭhaka-Gṛhya-Sūtra, explains fully in his commentary on this Gṛhya-Sūtra the meaning of the Mantras to be recited at the performance of the Gṛhya rites. The explanation of the Mantras does little credit to Devapāla's Vedic scholarship and betrays his ignorance of the rules of Vedic grammar and Vedic usage. He does not seem to be acquainted with the meaning of subjunctive forms. As he refers to the local customs of Kashmir, he might have written this commentary in Kashmir where this Gṛhya-Sūtra was prevalent. In the colophon of his commentary it is written: "*iti Chārāyaṇīya-Mantra-Bhāṣyam*". In the colophon of the commentary of 29th Kaṇḍikā dealing with marriage it is said that this Bhāśya has been written by Devapāla, son of

Haripāla and grandson of Bhaṭṭopendra belonging to Jālandhara (p. 302 of Kashmir Sanskrit Series edition). However, in the colophon of his Bhāṣya on the 25th Kaṇḍikā (p. 277 of the Kashmir edition) the word *Jayapuravāstavya* is added after *Jālandharīya*. It shows that Devapāla was a resident of Jayapura. The editor of this commentary, Pandit Madhusudan Kaul (vide p. 5 of the Introduction) raises the question whether this Jayapura can be identified with the present village *Zovur* about seven miles from the Rajgarh Palace towards the south-east of Srinagar. Devapāla appears to be a later writer but there is no definite information or indication about his exact date.

Śatrughna

Śatrughna explains in his work entitled *Mantrārtha-Dīpikā* the meaning of the Mantras to be recited at the performance of daily religious observances such as ablution, morning and evening worship, and at other Gṛhya rites. In the Introduction Śatrughna acknowledges his indebtedness to Uvaṭa, Guṇaviṣṇu and Halāyudha for the help taken from their works in the composition of the Mantrārtha-Dīpikā. He clearly admits in the Introduction that he has generally adopted the interpretation of the Mantras suggested by the earlier commentators and presented in a simple form the difficult interpretations of his predecessors. He flourished in the second half of the 16th century A.D.

Dinakara-Bhaṭṭa

Dinkara-Bhaṭṭa has written a commentary entitled *Ṛgarthasāra* (or *Ṛgartha-Vyākhyā-sārā*) on the selected Ṛks from the eight Aṣṭakas of the RV. and on the prose portions culled from the Ait. Br. In the Introduction to his work Dinakara claims that he is explaining the meaning of the Ṛks representing the essence of the RV. in accordance with the Bhāṣya (which Bhāṣya?) but at places also at variance with the Bhāṣya. Dinakara's commentary is brief and simple. According to the autobiographical information given in the Introduction and the colophon of the work its author was the son of Rāmakṛṣṇa and Umā and grandson of Nārāyaṇa-Bhaṭṭa. These autobiographical data prove our author to be identical with Dinakara alias Divākara who was the eldest brother of Kamalākara-Bhaṭṭa, the famous author of the Niraṇaya-Sindhu and several other works. As Dr. P.V. Kane assigns the literary activity of Kamalākara-Bhaṭṭa to the period between 1610 A.D. and 1640 A.D., Dinakara-Bhaṭṭa might have flourished at almost the same time.

A manuscript of the *Ṛgartha-sāra* dated Saṃvat 1867 is available in the library of the Oriental Institute, Baroda. The *Ṛgartha-sāra* was published by Dr. Aryendra Sharma from Hyderabad in 1959.

Nīlakaṇṭha

Nīlakaṇṭha has ingeniously interpreted a selection of 250 Ṛks under the title *Mantra-Bhāgavata-Vyākhyā* (*Mantra-Rahasya-Prakāśikā*) to prove in the RV. the existence of the Kṛṣṇa-story as narrated in the Bhāgavata-Purāṇa. The work has been divided into four Kāṇḍas. According to the autobiographical information contained in the colophon, Nīlakaṇṭha was the son of Govindasūri of Chaturdhara family. As Nīlakaṇṭha, the commentator of the Mahābhārata, is also the son of Govinda and belongs to Chaturdhara family, there is no doubt that the author of the *Mantra-Bhāgavata-Vyākhyā* is the same person as the commentator of the Mahābhārata. In his commentary on the Mahābhārata Nīlakaṇṭha mentions Śrīdhara, the commentator of the Bhāgavata-Purāṇa as his teacher and refers to his (Śrīdhara's) commentary. Nīlakaṇṭha in his Mahābhārata-commentary betrays his knowledge of Marāṭhī which indicates that he belonged to Mahārāṣṭra.

Dyā Dviveda

Dyā Dviveda has explained the meaning of 188 selected Ṛks to illustrate 166 verses of didactic maxims in his interesting and instructive work entitled *Nītimañjarī* which has been divided into 8 Aṣṭakas. Although Dyā Dviveda generally draws upon the Sāyaṇa-Bhāṣya of the RV. for the explanations of the Mantras, yet he adopts only the Aitihāsika interpretation of the Mantras and leaves out their other alternative explanations. In keeping with the Aitihāsika system of interpretation Dyā

Dviveda prefaces his explanation of a Ṛk with the narration of a legend supposed to be connected with it. In addition to the Sāyaṇa-Bhāṣya, ihe Bṛhaddevatā, the Brāhmaṇas and Ṣaḍguru-śiṣya's Vedārthadīpikā have also been utilized by Dyā Dviveda to cite legends in his work. In his commentary on the Ṛks Dyā Dviveda cites the Brāhmaṇas, the Nighaṇṭu, the Nirukta and the Pāṇinian grammar. His Nītimañjari is of great help to the students of Vedic mythology.

According to an introductory verse, Dyā Dviveda's parents were Lakṣmī and Lakṣmīdhara, his grandfather was Atri, and great-grand-father was Mukunda. The editor of the Nītimañjari, Pandit S.R. Joshi, cites in the Introduction (p. xix) the descriptive colophon of a manuscript of this work to the effect that Dyā Dviveda completed his Nītimañjarī on the first day of the bright fortnight of the month of Māgha in Saṃvat 1550 corresponding to the year 1494 A.D. which has been accepted by A.B. Keith also in his *History of Sanskrit Literature*, p. 239.

Kāśīnātha Upādhyāya

Kāśīnātha Upādhyāya has interpreted a number of Ṛks in his commentary called *Viṭṭhala-Ṛṅ-Mantra-Sāra-Bhāṣya* with a view to proving that the cult of the god Viṭṭhala is based on the Veda. In the Introduction to his commentary our commentator clearly states that the Mantras propounding the god Viṭṭhala are being explained here. In this connection he first of all cites the hymn (RV. I, 95) beginning with the words "*Dve virūpe charataḥ svarthe*", and interprets in his ingenious manner all its 11 verses. Then he takes up the interpretation of RV. I, 164,31 to prove his thesis. In order to justify the subjective and sectarian interpretation placed by him on the selected Ṛks Kāśīnātha Upādhyāya refers to the diverse interpretations of several Mantras suggested in the Nirukta, Patañjali's Mahābhāṣya etc.

Kāśīnātha Upādhyāya wrote also a number of other scholarly works such as *Dharmasindhu* (also known as *Dharmasindhusāra*), *Prāyaśchittenduśekhara*, and a commentary on the *Vedastuti* portion of the Bhāgavatapurāṇa (X, 87). According to the information gleaned from his works and other sources,

Kāśīnātha Upādhyāya's family which originally belonged to a village named Golavali in the Ratnagiri District of Mahārāśtra migrated to Pandharpur; and Kāśīnātha Upādhyāya became a Saṃnyāsin and died in the year 1805 A.D.[34]

Kālanātha

Kālanātha has written a commentary on about 250 selected Mantras of the Yajurveda under the title of *Yajurmañjarī*. In the Introductory verse of his work the commentator states that he has written this work after consulting the Bhāṣya and various Kalpas. According to the autobiographical information contained in the Introductory verses of the work, Svayambhū-bhaṭṭa was the father of Kālanātha; and our author was a protege of King Vāghara whose capital was at a town named *Uchcha* in the west. In the opinion of Pandit Bhagavaddatta the town named Uchcha was situated in the former Bahavalpur State (now in Pakistan) which at one time formed part of Rajasthan; and Kālanātha might have flourished earlier than Saṃvat 1232, because the Muslim occupation of the former Bahavalpur state started from Saṃvat 1232, and a manuscript of the work dated Saṃvat 1581 is available in the library of the Asiatic Society of Bengal, Calcutta.[35]

Kālanātha's commentary is little more than an abridged version of Uvaṭa's Bhāṣya. It is therefore clear that the Bhāṣya which Kālanātha claims to have consulted is none other than the Uvaṭa-Bhāṣya and that Kālanātha does not show any significant originality in spite of his high pretensions to profound learning.

Vararuchi

The manuscript of a work entitled *Nirukta-Samuchchaya* ascribed to Vararuchi and written in Malayalam script is available in the Adyar Library, Madras (vide Descriptive Catalogue of Sanskrit MSS. in the Adyar Library, Vol. I B, p.6 under No. 28). One edition of this work was brought out by Dr. C. Kunhan Raja and another by Pandit Yudhishṭhira Mīmāṃsaka. Apparently the title of the work seems to suggest that it is connected with the Nirukta. But in fact it is a commentary on about 100 Mantras. In the beginning of the work its author claims that he is explaining the Mantras for the benefit of people of low intelligence in accordance with the principles of the Nirukta.

The whole work has been divided into four Chapters called *Kalpas*. In the beginning of the first *Kalpa*, the author emphasizes the importance of etymology for the interpretation of Vedic Mantras, and cites in this connection some passages from the Nirukta to highlight the significance of Vedic interpretation. Twenty-eight Vedic Mantras, together with one Sūtra-Mantra (*Yadasya Karmaṇaḥ* etc.) have been explained in the first *Kalpa*. The author explains in the second *Kalpa* twenty-two Vedic Mantras prescribed for the performance of daily religious rites. In the third *Kalpa* twenty Vedic-Mantras together with two Sūtra-Mantras relating to the performance of Śrauta sacrifices such as Darśa-Pūrṇamāsa are explained. In the beginning of the fourth *Kalpa* the author says that, in keeping with the maxim that a person who understands the thirty-one categories of Ṛks understands the Mantras, thirty-one types of Mantras are explained.

It is evident from a perusal of this work that its author is a learned person who seems to have studied the Pāṇinian grammar as well as the Nirukta, and consulted some old commentaries on the Vedas. However, he is not deeply versed in Vedic lore and betrays his ignorance of Vedic accent and Vedic idiom in some places wherever he tries to adopt an independent path. For instance, in the interpretation of RV. I, 24,3 (I, 18) he wrongly interprets the vocative *avan* as a present participle (*rakṣan*), ignoring the accent. Similarly in the interpretation of RV. I, 115,1 (II, 36) he explains the word *anīkam* as "*an army*", ignoring Vedic usage and following later lexicographers (Cf. Amarakośa II, 78). A minute comparison of the *Nirukta-Samuchchaya* with Sāyaṇa's commentary on the RV. clearly shows that the former is indebted to the latter not only in respect of the general ideas but also in respect of the phraseology adopted in the interpretation of numerous Mantras. Compare, for instance, the interpretations of RV. V, 31,2 (1,7); X, 128,1 (I,10); X, 121.10 (III,60): I, 8,1 (III,66); X,180 1(III,67); X,117,6 (IV,77); X,129,2 (IV,95), etc. Since Sāyaṇa is indebted to Durga's commentary, as discussed by us elsewhere, the author of the *Nirukta-Samuchcharya* must have also consulted Durga's commentary and the pre-Sāyaṇa Ṛg-Bhāṣyas of Skanda and Veṅkaṭamādhava. The internal evidence supports this view. For instance, in the interpretation of RV. 1, 24,11 (II,39), the *Nirukta-Samuchchaya* copies verbatim from Durga's commentary (N. II, 1) including the saying "*sarvo hi yāchyamānaḥ krudhyati.*" Similarly the author of our work might have borrowed some interpretations from the Nirukta-Ṭīkā ascribed to Skanda and Maheśvara. Compare, for instance, the alternative interpretation of *tattvā* of RV. I, 24,11 as *tanitvā* in both these works. All these facts point to the conclusion that the Nirukta-Samuchchaya is a very late and post-Sāyaṇa work.

THE COMMENTATORS OF THE NIGHAṆṬU AND THE NIRUKTA

Yāska's Nirukta which is sometimes termed as a Bhāṣya by the later commentators is no doubt the earliest commentary on the Nighaṇṭu. But the Nirukta has not explained all the words included in the Nighaṇṭu, and is very terse and difficult to understand at numerous places. Therefore the later commentators felt the necessity of writing commentaries on the Nighaṇṭu as well as on the Nirukta.

Devarāja Yajvan

Devarāja Yajvan has written a commentary on all the words compiled in the Nighaṇṭu. In other words, he has given the etymology of all the words of the Nighaṇṭu and illustrated their Vedic usage. So he has given the title *Nighaṇṭu-Nirvachana* to his commentary.

In the Introduction to his commentary Devarāja says that although Yāska in his Nirukta has given the derivation of each and every word contained in the Naigama-Kāṇḍa and Devatā-Kāṇḍa of the Nighaṇṭu and illustrated their Vedic usage, he (Yāska) has explained the etymology of only a small proportion of 1341 Vedic words contained in the Naighaṇṭuka-Kāṇḍa of the Nighaṇṭu. Therefore, Devarāja opines, there is an urgent need of not only deciding the correct reading of all such words but also of giving their derivation and Vedic usage. Devarāja further says that in order to fulfil this desideratum he has composed this work after consulting several Anukramaṇīs and the Bhāṣya written by Veṅkaṭāchārya, son of Mādhava; the Nirukta and its commentary by Skandasvāmin; the Veda-Bhāṣya written by Skandasvāmin, Bhavasvāmin, Rāhadeva (v.l. Guhadeva) Śrīnivāsa, Mādhavadeva, Uvaṭabhaṭṭa, Bhāskaramiśra, Bharatasvāmin etc.; the Pāṇinian grammar, Uṇādi and its commentary; the Nighaṇṭu-Vyākhyā written by Kṣīrasvāmin, Anantāchārya etc.; the grammar written by Bhojarāja; the grammatical formation of all the words explained by Kamalanayana; and the manuscripts brought from different parts of the country. In his commentary Devarāja often cites explanations from the works of several authors mentioned above. There is no doubt that Devarāja's commentary on the Nighaṇṭu is a scholarly work which is indispensable for all students of the Veda and the Nirukta.

In the introductory verses of his work Devarāja mentions the names of his father and grandfather as Yajñeśvara and Devarāja-Yajvan respectively, and says that he was the resident of a village near the city of Seringapatam (*Raṅgeśapurī-Paryanta grāma-Vāstavyaḥ*).

As regards the date of Devarāja, Dr. C. Kunhan Raja regards him posterior to Sāyaṇa on the plea that Devarāja gives passages from Mādhava, which are not in Veṅkaṭa-mādhava, which are opposed to the explanations in Veṅkaṭa-mādhava, and which are seen verbatim in Sāyaṇa.[36] But both Dr. L. Sarup and Pandit Bhagavaddatta do not agree with Dr. Raja and consider Devarāja to be earlier than Sāyaṇa. Pandit Bhagavaddatta has successfully refuted Dr. Raja's arguments and shown that the passages referred to by Dr. Raja have been taken by Devarāja actually from the Ṛgveda-Bhāṣya of Veṅkaṭamādhava and not from the Ṛg-Bhāṣya of Sāyaṇa.[37] Moreover, Dr. Sarup[38] refers to a passage of the Sāyaṇa-Bhāṣya on the RV. I, 62,3 where Sāyaṇa seems to quote Devarāja's commentary on the word *Usriyā* (II, 11,3) under the title of Nighaṇṭu-Bhāṣya, because there is a close similarity between the quotation and Devarāja's commentary and no other work known as Nighaṇṭu-Bhāṣya has so far come to light. As Devarāja (I, 14,9) mentions Haradatta's Padamañjarī and the Veda-Bhāṣya of Bharatasvāmin (see above), the date of Devarāja cannot be earlier than the 13th century A.D. But he is not later than the middle of the 14th century A.D., because he is quoted by Sāyaṇa. Therefore both Dr. Sarup and Pandit Bhagavaddatta assign Devarāja to the beginning of the 14th century A.D.; and this view appears to be correct.

It may be pointed out here that a manuscript of Devarāja's commentary on the Nighaṇṭu in Malayalam script has been inadvertently listed as *Nirukta-Bhāṣyam* at serial No. 8657 (M.S. No. 10594) in the Alphabetical Index of the Sanskrit MSS. in the University MSS. Library, Trivandrum, Vol. I (A-NA), 1957. I have myself consulted this manuscript and verified that it is his *Nighaṇṭu-Bhāṣya*.

Bhāskararāya and Nārāyaṇa Yajvan

In the Tanjore Maharaja Serfoji's Sarasvati Mahal Library there are two MSS. of Bhāskararāya's *Vaidika-Kośa* with the commentary of Nārāyaṇa Yajvan. Bhāskararāya who enumerates in verses the words of the Nighaṇṭu divides all the words listed in the Nighaṇṭu into two main Kāṇḍas, namely *Nānāpada-Kāṇḍa* and *Ekapada-Kāṇḍa*, and further sub-divides the Nānāpada-Kāṇḍa into three Vargas, viz. *Bhvādi-Varga*, *Karmādi-Varga*, and *Bahvādi-Varga*; and sub-divides the *Ekapada-Kāṇḍa* into two Vargas, namely, *Jahādi-Varga* and *Āśuśukṣṇyādi Varga*. I give below a sample of Bhāskararāya's *Vaidika-Kośa* enumerating 21 names of earth in verses:

Bhūr bhūmir avanir gotrā gaur iḷā nirṛtir mahī|
Gmā jmā kṣmā kṣā kṣiti kṣāmā kṣoṇī Pṛthvyaditī ripaḥ||
Urvī Pūṣā gāturiti bhūnāmānyekaviṃśatiḥ||

In the introductory verse it is said that the words listed in the *Vaidika-Nighaṇṭu* have been composed in Ślokas by Somapāgnichit Bhāskararāya. In the colophon the full name of the author is given as Bhāskararāya Dīkṣita Agnichit son of Gambhīrarāja Dīkṣita Bhāratī. Nothing is known about the date and place of our author. However, a work entitled *Sahasra-bhojana-Sūtra-Vyākhyā* by Bhāskararāya son of Gambhīrarāya Dīkṣita has been mentioned by Dr. P.V. Kane in his History of Dharmaśāstra (Vol. I, Part II, p. 1144). This commentary seems to be another work of our author.

Nārāyaṇa Yajvan has written a commentary on the *Vaidika-Kośa*, i.e. on the words of the Nighaṇṭu enumerated in Ślokas, by Bhāskararāya. In other words, Nārāyaṇa Yajvan has explained the etymology of these words. He admits in the introductory verses that although the etymology of these words has been already explained by earlier scholars, yet he is doing so here briefly according to his knowledge. In his commentary Nārāyaṇa Yajvan often cites explanations from the works of Skandasvāmin, Bhaṭṭa Bhāskara, Bhaṭṭoji Dīkṣita, etc. It shows that Nārāyaṇa Yajvan was posterior to Bhaṭṭoji Dīkṣita and thus not earlier than the middle of the 17th century A.D.

Durgāchārya

Durgāchārya wrote a commentary on the Nirukta repeating and explaining every word of Yāska. Therefore Durga's commentary is important not only for the understanding of the Nirukta but also for constructing and correcting the text of the Nirukta. In addition to the Nirukta, the Mantras cited in it to illustrate Vedic usage have also been fully explained by Durga. And the interpretation of the Mantras attempted by Durga was regarded by the later commentators like Sāyaṇa so important that they follow it in several cases. For instance, Sāyaṇa in his Bhāṣya on RV. X, 29,1 copies verbatim Durga's explanation of *vāyo nyadhāyi* etc. as *vāyām ātmīyam putram nidadhāti* etc. (N.VI, 28) against the interpretation of *Vāyo* as a nominative singular form by the other commentators (see note 6 of Chapter V). Moreover, Sāyaṇa in his Bhāṣya on on RV. X, 30,11 acknowledges the fact that the commentary on this Ṛk has been quoted from the *Nirukta-Ṭīkā* which is obviously Durga's commentary as is proved by its verbatim agreement with Sāyaṇa's quotation.

It is a special feature of Durga's commentary that the commentator does not mention by name any of his predecessors, Veda-Bhāṣyakāra, or any other authority, but employs such general terms as *anye, apare, eke, kechit* etc. to refer to the views expressed by the other commentators. In some places Durga expresses his opinion on the readings of the Nirukta, e.g. on N.V, 17. There is no doubt that Durga's commentary is marked by erudition and exactitude.

Most of the present information about the life and date of Durga is based on mere conjecture, because unlike the other commentators Durga has not furnished any clue about himself in the Introduction as well as in the colophon of his commentary. The colophon of his commentary on the 11th Chapter of the Nirukta, which declares the commentator, *Āchārya Bhagavad Durgasimha*, to be a resident of *Jambū-mārgāśrama*, does not seem to be his own statement but seems to have been added by an admirer or disciple of his, because no author would employ for himself the honorofic title of *Bhagavad* nor is such a statement found in the colophon of any other Chapter of his commentary. Even if the above statement made by any of his admirers or disciples is accepted as based on facts, the identification of *Jambū-mārga* is also not free from doubt. Dr. L. Sarup identifies *Jambū-mārga* with Jammu.[39] But Pandit Bhagavaddatta identifies *Jambū-mārga* with a place named *Jambū-sara* near Baroda in Gujarat, because Durga in his commentary often quotes from the MS. which was prevalent in Gujarat at that time.[40] According to the Viṣṇu Purāṇa III, 13,33 *Jambū-mārga* was a vast forest teeming with deer; and the Mbh. thrice mentions *Jambū-mārga* as a sacred *Tīrtha.* In the Mbh. XIII, 25,51 *Jambū mārga* is mentioned after the river Narmadā and *Śūrpārka* Tīrtha and before *Kokāmukha, Kanyā-hrada* and *Prabhāsa*; and in the Mbh. III, 82,40 the same Tīrtha is mentioned after *Puṣkara* and before *Narmadā* and the other Tīrthas situated in Western India. The Mbh. III, 89,13 mentions *Jambū-mārga Āśrama* among the Tīrthas of the West such as the rivers Narmadā and Viśvāmitra, the *Maināka* mountain, and *Puṣkara.* It is abundantly clear from the above-mentioned facts that *Jambū-mārga Āśrama* was a Tīrtha in Western India (either in Gujarat or in Rajasthan), and there is no basis for identifying it with Jammu in the north.[40a] Similarly there is not much force in Dr. Sarup's argument that "the fact that he (Durga) lived in a hermitage and was addressed as *bhagavat* indicates that he was an ascetic and belonged to some particular order of Saṃnyāsa," because *Jambū-mārga Āśrama* as pointed out above was the name of a sacred place (*Tirtha*) mentioned in the Mbh. III, 89,13 and not a hermitage of ascetics. Moreover, the addition of the honorofic title *bhagavat* to Durga's name by any of his disciples or admirers does not necessarily prove that Durga was a Saṃnyāsin, because this title is found added to the names of many ancient Āchāryas, e.g. *Bhagavān Bodhāyanaḥ*. There is also another circumstance which indicates that Durga was not a Saṃnyāsin. In his commentary on N.IV, 14 Durga does not explain the Ṛgvedic stanza III, 53,22 saying: "The stanza where this word (*lodham*) occurs expresses hostility towards Vasiṣṭha, and I am a descendant of Vasiṣṭha, belonging to the *Kapiṣṭhala* Śākhā. Therefore I do not explain this stanza." Durga's mention of his Gotra and Śākhā shows that he was not a Saṃnyāsin, because those who have entered the order of of Saṃnyāsa renounce all distinctions of Gotra, Śākhā, etc. Dr. Sarup's conjecture appears to be probable that Durga himself wrote his commentary up to the end of the 11th chapter, whose colophon was added by a disciple who also wrote the commentary on the 12th chapter, and faithfully refrained himself from adding the name of Durga in the colophon of the 12th Chapter.[41]

The most dependable piece of evidence about the lower limit of the date of Durga is a manuscript of his commentary dated 1387 A.D. in the Bodleian Library Oxford. The manuscript was copied at Bhṛgu-kṣetra (Broach) during the reign of Mahārāṇā Durgasiṃhavijaya. The copying of Durga's commentary in 1387 A.D. conclusively proves that he had flourished much earlier than this date. This lower limit of Durga's date is corroborated by Sāyaṇa who quotes in his Ṛg-Bhāṣya Durga's interpretation of Ṛk referred to above. There is, however, a sharp difference of opinion among scholars with regard to the upper limit of Durga's date. Dr. Sarup regards Durga as posterior to or as a contemporary of Devarāja, the author of the Nighaṇṭu-Bhāṣya, on the plea that Devarāja who is familiar with the extant commentaries on the Vedas, the Nighaṇṭu, and the Nirukta, does not mention Durga in the long list of the authorities used by him (Devarāja) for the purpose of his own work.[42] On the basis of this *argumentum ex silencio* Dr. Sarup puts the upper limit of Durga's date later than the beginning of the 14th century A.D. On the other hand, Pandit Bhagavad-datta assigns Durga to the 6th century A.D. and regards him as anterior to Udgītha and Skanda on the ground that the close similarity between Durga's commentary and the Udgītha-Bhāṣya as well as between Durga's commentary and the commentary of Skanda-Maheśvara indicates that both Udgītha and Skanda-Maheśvara had before them Durga's commentary at the time of writing their respective commentaries.[43]

However, a minute analysis of the verbal agreements between the Udgītha-Bhāṣya and Durga-Ṭīkā on the one hand and between Durga-Ṭīkā and the Skandasvāmi-Bhāṣya on the other does not lend support to Pandit Bhagavaddatta's thesis and leads us to the opposite conclusion that it is, in fact, Durga who borrows interpretations and phraseology from the commentaries of Udgītha and Skandasvāmin and endeavours to improve upon them in various ways.

In respect of the interpretation of over two dozen Ṛks there is a very close, striking and almost verbal agreement between the Udgītha-Bhāṣya and Durga's commentary.[44] A minute examination of such close verbal agreements between these two works makes it abundantly clear that it is Durga who succinctly and discreetly copies from the Udgītha-Bhāṣya and tries to improve upon it in some places either through elaboration or condensation. In some places Durga either explains a difficult word of the Udgītha-Bhāṣya or paraphrases it by an easy word. For instance, while interpreting the RV. X, 5, 5 Durga (N.V. 1) first copies verbatim Udgītha's interpretation of the Vedic word *aruṣīḥ* as "*ārochanāḥ*" and then explains Udgītha's interpretative word *ārochanāḥ* by adding the gloss "*dīptā ityarthaḥ*"; and similarly Durga seeks to improve upon Udgītha's interpretation of the Vedic word *vāvaśānaḥ* of the same stanza as "*vāvaśyamānaḥ atyartham sabdyamānaḥ*" by prefixing the explanation "*kāmayamānaḥ*" and by paraphrasing Udgītha's *śabdyamānaḥ* as follows: "*kāmayamānaḥ vāvaśyamānaḥ vā śabdam kurvāṇaḥ*". With regard to the interpretation of the RV. X, 71, 2 Durga (N. IV, 10) not only copies verbatim some portion of the Udgītha-Bhāṣya with slight modifications but also seems to refer to Udgītha's explanation of the Vedic words *vācham akrata* as "they acquire the knowledge of speech." It may by noted that in his attempt to show his originality Durga first explains the Vedic word *sakhyāni* of this stanza as *sakhibhāvān* but later adds Udgītha's interpretation "*Jñānāni*" by altering it into *vijñānāni*; and similarly he substitutes the words *vijñānākhyā* for Udgītha's lengthy explanation of lakṣmī as "*kāryakāraṇa-svarūpa-parijñāna-lakṣaṇa*". In the interpretation of the RV. X, 10, 13 Durga (N. VI, 28) copies Udgītha verbatim to a very large extent but introduces a few changes, and glosses Udgītha's explanation "*anukampyaḥ*" by "*śochya ityārthaḥ*". There are numerous instances of such minor changes of phraseology introduced by Durga in the Vedic interpretation copied from the Udgītha-Bhāṣya.

Similarly there is a very close and verbal agreement between Durga's commentary and the Skandasvāmi-Bhāṣya in respect of the interpretation of a large number of Ṛks.[45] In this case, too, Durga follows the same method of copying as he does in the case of the Udgītha-Bhāṣya discussed above, i.e., he introduces some alterations here and there and makes his explanation generally more compact and concise in comparison with the loose, diffuse and verbose style of Skandasvāmin. Compare, for instance, Durga's explanation (N. III, 20) with the Skanda-Bhāṣya of the RV. I, 24, 10. A minute comparison of the two works leaves no doubt that it is Durga who is copying from Skanda's Bhāṣya.

In additon to the above-mentioned points, commonsense also does not support the hypothesis that both the celebrated Veda-Bhāṣyakāras, Udgītha and Skandasvāmin, whose names are mentioned respectfully by the later commentators such as Veṅkaṭamādhava, Uvaṭa and Devarāja Yajvan, should have copied verbatim from the work of Durga who is not spoken of by any of these commentators. Moreover, I have discovered some very close and striking agreements between Durga's commentary and Uvaṭa's Vājasaneyi-Saṃhitā-Bhāṣya in respect of the interpretation of some Vedic stanzas.[46] A minute comparison of the two works shows that Durga not only copies varbatim from Uvaṭa but also paraphrases by easy words the difficult words employed by his predecessor in his Bhāṣya. For instance, in the interpretation of the VS. 12, 68 Uvaṭa employs in his Bhāṣya the original words of the text *Yunakta* and *vitanudhvam* without explanation, whereas Durga (N.V, 28) not only copies the Uvaṭa-Bhāṣya but also paraphrases the above-cited words by such easy words as *Yojayata* and *vitanuta*. In the interpretation of the VS. 29, 1 Durga (N. III, 20) copies verbatim Uvaṭa's explanation of the Vedic word *pinvamānaḥ* as "*pibannityarthaḥ*" leaving out the other explanatory preceding words of the Uvaṭa-Bhāṣya.

The only inference that can be drawn from the close verbal agreements which Durga's commentary betrays with the Veda-Bhāṣyas written by Udgītha, Skandasvāmin and Uvaṭa is that either all the three eminent Vedic interpreters copied verbatim from Durga's work without acknowledgement or Durga had before him the above-mentioned three Veda-Bhāṣyas and freely copied from them. It appears to be highly unlikely that if Udgītha, Skanda and Uvaṭa copied from Durga's commentary on selected Vedic hymns, cited in the Nirukta, Durga's name would not have come to the notice of Veṅkaṭamādhava and Devarāja Yajvan who have mentioned the names of so many Vedic interpreters. So the only conclusion that can be drawn from the foregoing facts is that it is Durga who is indebted to Udgītha, Skandasvāmin and Uvaṭa for the interpretation of the Vedic Mantras cited in the Nirukta.

Skanda Maheśvara

Another commentary on the Nirukta ascribed to Skanda-Maheśvara was published by Dr. L. Sarup from Lahore. With regard to the authorship of this commentary Dr. Sarup observes that although it is partly described in MSS. as a work of Skandasvāmin it is really a commentary of Maheśvara on the work of Skandasvāmin.[47] But Pandit Bhagavaddatta[48] contests Dr. Sarup's opinion and puts forward the views that this commentary is the joint composition of both Skandasvāmin and Maheśvara; that the chapters which are found ascribed in the colophon to Skandasvāmin are his composition and the others ascribed to Maheśvara in the colophon were written by him; and that Maheśvara was perhaps a disciple of either Skandasvāmin or Udgītha. In order to prove his point that Skanta, the author of the present commentary on the Nirukta is identical with the Veda-Bhāṣyakāra Skandasvāmin, Pandit Bhagavaddatta has referred to some similarities between the wording of the two works.

There is no doubt that Devarāja often mentions and quotes from Skandasvāmin's commentary on the Nirukta and stresses the fact that one and the same Skandasvāmin had written both a Veda-Bhāṣya and a Nirukta-Ṭīkā. But Devarāja does not mention the name of both Durga and Maheśvara, whereas Maheśvara in the Introduction to this commentary on the Nirukta explicitly mentions *Barbarasvāmin*, *Bhagavad Durga* etc., as previous commentators. This fact clearly proves that Maheśvara's work is definitely later than Durga's commentary. It may be noted that the reading *Barbarasvāmi* is doubtful and some MSS. read *Vyākhyāsyāmi* instead which could mean the Nirukta-Ṭīkā by Skandasvāmin. Since no work ascribed to Barbarsvāmin has come to light or has been mentioned by any other author, the probability is that Maheśvara is here referring to Skandasvāmin's Nirukta-Ṭīkā which was anterior to Durga's commentary.

It seems that Maheśvara wrote his commentary on the Nirukta basing his explanations on Skandasvāmin's commentary, as opined by Dr. Sarup; and due to its motley character the commentary has been ascribed in some parts to Skandasvāmin and in other parts to Maheśvara. In the colophon of two chapters the Commentary is ascribed to *Śabara-svāmin* (Cf. T.R. Chintamani, Madras Journal of Oriental Research, Vol. I, No. I, p. 85).

Notes and References

1. V. Pr. I, 19.
2. Asv. G.S. III, 4,4; Kaus. G S. II, 5,3; Sankh. G.S. IV, 10, 3.
3. Mbh. II, 11, 35-*Bhāṣyāṇi tarka-yuktāni dehavanti viśāmpate*; *II, 36,7—Sarva-bhāṣya-vidāṃ varaḥ*; *XII, 320, 15—Sarva-bhāṣya-vidāṃ madhye chodayāmāsa bhikṣukī* (Sulabhā); XIII, 90,34 – *Ye cha bhāṣya-vidaḥ kechid ye cha Vyākaraṇe ratāḥ*.
4. Nānārthārṇava-saṃkṣepa (Triv. Skt. Series) Vol. I, p.8.
5. Cf. Sāyaṇa-bhāṣya on RV. I, 88,5 and V, 12,3.

6. *Skandasvāmī Nārāyaṇa Udgītha iti te kramāt/Chakrussahaikam Ṛg-bhāṣyam pada-vākyārtha-gocharam//*
(p. 3659 of Vishva Bandhu edition).
7. Indices and Appendices of the Nirukta, Introduction p. 29.
8. Vaidika Vāṅmaya kā Itihāsa, Vol. I. Part II, (The Commentators of the Vedas), Lahore, 1931, pp. 5. ff.
9. See Sāyaṇa-Bhāṣya on RV. X, 46.5. Besides, Sāyaṇa has copied verbatim from Udgītha's commentary in the interpretation of many stanzas; for instance, compare the two Bhāṣyas on RV. X, 10,13;12,2; 14,1; 18,1; 22,2; 27,13; 30,4; 34,1; 64,5; 70,10; 81,1.6
10. Cf. Monier-Williams, Sanskrit-English Dictionary, *s.v.*
11. Op. cit., p. 133.
12. The opening passage of the Ṛgveda-vyākhyā : *om namo Bhagavate Vāsudevāya sārabhūtā susaṃgrahā dvādaśyanukramaṇikā kriyate*
13. Preface to the Ṛgvedānukramaṇī, p. xvii.
14. Proceeding of the Fifth Indian Oriental Conference, p. 246.
15. Op. cit., p. 34.
16. Third Śloka in the introductory part of his Bhāṣya :
Gurutastarkataśchaiva tathā śātapathaśruteḥ,
Ṛṣīn vakṣyāmi mantrāṇām devatāśchhandasaṃ cha yet.
17. Op. cit. (A I.O,C., V), p. 261.
18. Op. cit., p. 112.
19. Op. cit., p. 115.
20. *Eṣa niṣpāvake śake kuśikānvayajanmanā,*
Bhaṭṭabhāskaramiśreṇa Jñanayajñaḥ prakīrtitaḥ.
21. A Descriptive Catalogue of Sanskrit Manuscripts in the Tanjore Maharaja Serfoji's Sarasvati Mahal Library, Vol. III, Preface to the contents of vols. I-III, pp. xxvi-xxviii.
22. See B.N.K. Sharma's "History of Dvaita School of Vedanta and its Literature" in 2 volumes, Bombay, 1960-61, for detailed information on the subject.
23. Introduction to the Sāyaṇa-Bhāṣya on the T.S. :—
Brāhmaṇam Kalpasūtre dve mīmāmsām Vyakṛtim tathā,
Udāhṛtyāth taiḥ sarvaiḥ mantrārthaḥ spaṣṭam īryate.
24. SBE, Vol. 32, Introduction, p. xxx.
25. See our work "*Vaidika-Vyākhyā-Vivechana*"—especially the Introduction—for a discussion on the comparative assessment of various interpretations.
26. Sir Asutosh Mookerjee Silver Jubilee Volumes, Orientalia, Part III, pp, 467-476.
27. "*Eṣa vai gopā eṣa hīdam sarvam gopāyati*" *ityadi asmadbrāhmaṇam.*
28. See Mysore Archaeological Report for 1908, p. 54 and the Indian Antiquary for 1916, p. 19.
29. Bhagavaddatta: Op. cit., p. 56.
30. Bhagavaddatta: Op. cit., p. 56; Aufrecht: Catalogus Catalogurum, P. 711.

31. Op. cit., p. 74.
32. Op. cit., p. 13.
33. Op. cit., p. 105.
34. P.V. Kane, History of Dharmaśātra, Vol. I, Part II, p. 978.
35. Op. cit., p. 103.
36. Proceedings of the Indian Oriental Conference, p. 229.
37. Op. cit., pp. 26-30; 210-11.
38. Preface to the Nighaṇṭu and the Nirukta, pp. 25 ff.
39. Ibid., p. 29.
40. Op. cit., p. 224.

40A. According to Braj Mohan javalia. *jambū-mārga* is a place in Rajasthan near Bundi, vide his paper in the *Śodhapatrikā* 23(2) April June, 72, pp. 23-27.

41. Op. cit., p. 31.
42. Op. cit., p. 28.
43. Op. cit., pp. 9-14, 223.
44. RV. X, 5.5 (N.V, 1); 5,6 (N.VI,27); 10,10(N.IV, 20); 12,2(N.VI, 4); 10,13(N.VI, 28); 14,1(N.X, 20); 17,3(N.VII,9); 22,2 (N.VI,23); 26,4(N.VI, 29); 27,22(N.II, 6) 27,23(N.II, 22); 27,24(N.V, 19); 29,1 (N.VI,28); 30,11(N.VI, 22); 34,1(N.IX, 8); 39,4(N.IV, 19); 43,5 (N.V,22); 45,1(N.IV,24); 50,6(N.V, 15); 52,3(N.VI, 35); 64,4(N.XI, 23); 68,8(N.X, 12); 69,4(N.VI, 17); 71,2(N.IV,10); 75,9(N.VII, 7) 79,1(N.VI, 4); 79,3 N.V, 3); 82,4 (N.VI, 15).
45. RV.I,24,10(N.III, 20); 50,3(N.III,15); 84,7(N.IV, 17); 89,1(N.IV, 19); 89,10(N.IV, 23); VI,47(N.VI, 7); 44.21(N.VI, 17); 50,5(N.VI, 6); 59,4(N.V, 22); 63.8(N,VI, 29); 71,2(N VI, 7); etc.
46. VS.15,32(N.III, 21); 7,38(N.IX, 8); 11,27(N.VI, 1) 3,24(N.III, 21); 3,26 (N.V, 23); 12, 68(N.V, 28).
47. Indices and Appendices of the Nirukta.
48. Op. cit., pp. 5ff.

8

Modern Studies in Vedic Exegesis

The keen interest of occidental intellectuals in the religion, culture and literature of ancient India led to introduction of Sanskrit Studies in the West in the eighteenth century. In the initial stages of acquainting themselves with the Sanskrit language and literature the European students of Sanskrit were naturally pre-occupied with the study of Classical Sanskrit and had no clear concept about the nature and scope of the Vedic language and literature. The first European to acquire a little knowledge of the Vedas was Henry Thomas Colebrooke who in the year 1805 A.D. published in the *Asiatic Researches* (Vol. VIII) a lengthy essay entitled "On the Vedas, the Sacred Writings of the Hindus" supplying some rudimentary information about the scope and importance of the Vedic literature. However, due to his impatience and lack of adequate proficiency in the nuances and subtleties of the Vedic language and literature Colebrooke failed to assess accurately the wealth of ideas embodied in the Vedas, and consequently made in his above-mentioned essay the following disparaging and misleading remarks about the Vedas: "They (the Vedas) are too voluminous for a complete translation of the whole; and what they contain would hardly reward the labour of the reader, much less that of the translator. The ancient dialect in which they are composed and especially that of the first three Vedas, is extremely difficult and obscure and, though curious, as the parent of a more polished and refined language (Classical Sanskrit), its difficulties must long continue to prevent such an examination of the whole Vedas, as would be requisite for exacting all that is remarkable and important in these voluminous works." (Colebrooke's, *Essays*, Vol. I, p. 113).

As a result of the discouraging conclusions drawn by Colebrooke with regard to the Vedas no British Sanskritist evinced interest in the study of the Vedas for nearly a quarter of a century. And afterwards the first European to be attracted towards the Vedic studies was a German scholar named Friedrich Rosen, Professor in the University of London, who in 1830 published his *Rig-Vedae Specimen* and undertook the task of editing and translating the Ṛgveda. However, the premature death of Rosen in 1837 cut short his plans and consequently only the first Aṣṭaka of the RV. edited and translated into Latin by Rosen with notes appeared posthumously in 1838. In the infancy of Vedic studies in the West Sāyaṇa's commentary on the RV. was the only guide of the students of the Veda. So Rosen's Latin translation of the first Aṣṭaka of the RV. was based on Sāyaṇa's commentary. In keeping with the then prevalent practice of following Sāyaṇa H. H. Wilson, Boden Professor of Sanskrit in the University of Oxford, translated into English the whole of the RV. in six volumes (London, 1850-88) on the basis of Sāyaṇa's commentary. In the Introduction to his English translation of the first Aṣṭaka published in 1850 Wilson acknowledges his debt of gratitude to Sāyaṇa and stresses the importance of Sāyaṇa's commentary as follows: "The scholia of Sāyaṇa on the text of the Ṛgveda comprise three distinct portions. The first interprets the original text, or, rather, translates it into more modern Sanskrit, fills up any ellipse, and if any legend is briefly alluded to, narrates it in detail; the next portion of the commentary is a grammatical analysis of the text, agreebly to the system of Pāṇini, whose aphorisms, or *Sūtras*, are quoted; and the third portion is an explanation of the accentuation of the several words. These two last portions are purely technical, and are untranslatable. The first constitutes the basis of the English translation; for, although the interpretation of Sayāṇa may be, occasionally, questioned, he undoubtedly had knowledge of his text far beyond the pretensions of any European scholar, and must have been in possession, either through his own learning, or that of his assistants, of all the interpretations which had been perpetuated, by traditional teaching, from the earliest times."

In spite of such high compliments paid by Wilson to Sāyaṇa

the Western students of the Veda were not fully satisfied with Sāyaṇa's interpretation of the R√. and began to feel their independent path in the field of Vedic exegesis. Rudolph Roth of Germany, who received instruction in the Vedas from Eugène Burnouf at the College de France Paris, blazed a new trail in the domain of Vedic exegesis. In the year 1846 Roth published his epoch-making work entitled *Zur Literature und Geschichte des Weda* (On the Literature and History of the Veda). He may be rightly described as the pioneer of the deductive and scientific method of Vedic interpretation. He put forward the view that an interpreter of the Veda should not rely upon the interpretations suggested by ancient Indian commentators and should himself interpret the Veda with the help of the Veda itself. In other words, in order to determine the meaning of a Vedic word an interpreter should first of all examine all the Vedic passages where the word occurs and then let the concerned passages themselves suggest the meaning. In the famous seven-volume *Sanskrit-Wörterbuch* popularly known as St. Petersburg Dictionary on account of its publication from St. Petersburg between 1852 and 1875 Roth who was entrusted with the task of compiling its Vedic part entered under each Vedic word all the Vedic passages concerned for determining its meaning in accordance with his deductive method of Vedic interpretation. In the preface to the St. Petersburg Dictionary Roth has made the following observations with regard to the ancient Indian commentators of the Veda and about his own arduous task in ascertaining the meaning of Vedic words: "As regards one of the branches of Vedic literature, the treatises on theology and worship, we can desire no better guides than these (ancient Indian) commentators, so exact in all respects, who follow their texts word by word, who, so long as even the semblance of a misconception might arise, are never weary of repeating what they have frequently said before, and who often appear as if they had been writing for us foreigners rather than for their own priestly alumni who had grown up in the midst of these conceptions and impressions . . . The case, however, is quite different when the same men assume the task of interpreting the ancient collection of hymns . . . Here were required not only quite different qualifications for interpretation but also a greater freedom of judgment and a greater breadth of view and of historical intuition. However, priestly learning was wanting in freedom of judgment, while no one in India has ever had any conception of historical development. The very qualities, which have made those commentators excellent guides to an understanding of the theological treatises, render them unsuitable conductors on that far older and quite differently circumstanced domain. As the so-called Classical Sanskrit was perfectly familiar to them, they sought its ordinary idiom in the Vedic hymns also. Since any difference in the ritual appeared to be inconceivable to them and the current forms were believed to have existed from the beginning of the world, they fancied that the patriarchs of the Indian religion must have sacrificed in the very same manner. As the recognized mythological and classical systems of their own age appeared to them unassailable and revealed vsrieties, they must necessarily (so the commentators thought) be discoverable in that central point of revelation, the hymns of the ancient Ṛṣis who had indeed lived in familiar intercourse with the gods and possessed far higher wisdom than the succeeding generation . . . It has never occurred to any one to make our understanding of the Hebrew books of the Old Testament depend upon the Talmud and the Rabbins, while such scholars are not wanting as consider it to be the duty of a conscientious interpreter of the Veda to translate it in conformity with Sāyaṇa, Mahīdhara etc. Consequently we do not believe like H.H. Wilson that Sāyaṇa, for instance, understood the expressions of the Veda better than any European interpreter; but we think that a conscientious European interpreter may understand the Veda far better and more correctly than Sāyaṇa. We do not esteem it our first task to arrive at that understanding of the Veda which was current in India some centuries ago, but to search out the sense which the poets themselves have put into their hymns and utterances. Hence we are of opinion that the writings of Sāyaṇa and the other commentators do not form a rule for the interpreter, but are merely one of those helps of which the latter will avail himself for the execution of his undoubtedly difficult task, a task which is not to be accomplished at the first onset, or by any single individual . . . We have, therefore, endeavoured to follow the path prescribed by philology, to derive from the texts themselves the sense which they contain, by a juxtaposition of all the passages which are cognate in diction or contents—a tedious and laborious path in which neither the commentators nor the translators have preceded us. The double duty of exegete and lexicographer has thus devolved upon us."

No exception can be taken to the principles of the deductive method of Vedic interpretation enunciated by Roth. However, all the meanings of Vedic words proposed by him have not met with the unanimous approval of the Vedic scholars, and his German translation of certain hymns of the RV. has also been criticised by some scholars like A. Bergaigne and F. Max Müller.

It must also be mentioned here in this connection that in collaboration with his pupil W.D. Whitney Roth accomplished the most arduous task of editing the AV. (Śaunakīya) which was published from Berlin in 1856. Moreover, Roth edited and published for the first time Yāska's Nirukta in 1852.

Roth's pupils among whom the names of W.D. Whitney, H. Grassmann, K.F. Geldner, Charles Lanman, Richard Garbe and H. Zimmer deserve special mention made notable contributions to the realm of Vedic studies. Whitney who collaborated with Roth in editing the AV. translated this Veda into English with critical and exegetical notes. Whitney's translation of the AV. published posthumously in volumes VII and VIII of the Harvard Oriental Series is a monumental work and solid contribution to Vedic exegesis.

Roth's another pupil, H. Grassmann who was also a well-known mathematician, compiled a dictionary of the RV. entitled *Wörterbuch Zum Ṛgveda* (Leipzig, 1873) in which the various meanings of each word have been classified and numbered, and the meaning of each form of a word indicated against it by the relevant number. Grassmann's dictionary which has got no parallel in the field of Vedic lexicography is definitely an improvement upon Roth's famous dictionary. After the publication of his dictionary Grassmann translated the Ṛgveda into German and published the translation in two volumes in 1876-77. However, it is a matter of surprise that in several cases Grassmann's translation differs from his dictionary with regard to the meanings of Ṛgvedic words. See, for instance, the German translation and the dictionary meaning of *sūnṛtā* occurring in RV. I, 134,1 and 135,7; and of *mārutasya vedhasaḥ* (RV. I, 156, 4). It is interesting to note that in all such cases the meaning suggested by Grassmann in his dictionary is more appropriate. It may be mentioned here that with regard to the meanings of the Ṛgvedic words entered in his *Sanskrit-English Dictionary* Monier-Williams generally follows Grassmann's dictionary.

While Roth and his eminent pupils together with several other distinguished Vedic scholars were making important contributions to Vedic exegesis in Germany, Eugene Burnouf's another brilliant pupil, F. Max Müller, was working in England to place in proper perspective the ancient as well as modern approach to Vedic exegesis. The credit of editing for the first time the entire RV. with Sāyaṇa's commentary goes to Max Müller who published it from London in 6 volumes between 1849 and 1875 together with a comprehensive and learned Introduction and several indices. As he was endowed with a versatile genius, Max Müller ably edited the English translation by eminent scholars of the important religious scriptures of the Hindus, Muslims, Buddhists, Jains and Zoroastrians published in 50 volumes from Oxford in the Sacred Books of the East Series. In volume 32 of this Series Max Müller translated with critical and exegetical notes the Ṛgvedic hymns addressed to the Maruts, Rudra, Vāyu and Vāta. In this work he has also quoted side by side the translations of each verse attempted by Wilson, Benfey and Ludwig. Besides, he wrote a number of books on the religious, cultural and historical aspects of Sanskrit among which his *History of Ancient Sanskrit Literature* published in 1859 from London ranks foremost, as it embodies the results of his critical and historical studies of the Vedic literature. The importance of this epoch-making work of Max Müller may be gauged from the fact that even after a lapse of over a century the frame-work of Vedic chronology proposed by him in this work still holds sway over the minds of most of the modern Indologists. It may be mentioned here that Max Müller has been gravely misjudged by several later scholars in respect of his views on Vedic chronology. He never claimed to have fixed the date of the RV. around 1200-1000 B.C. as misunderstood by several scholars. What he meant to say was that the date of the RV. cannot be later than 1200-1000 B.C., and that he did not know how much earlier it can be further pushed back. In his Gifford lectures on "Physical Education" in 1889 Max Müller clearly stated his position as follows with regard to the date of the Vedic hymns: "We cannot hope to fix a *terminus a quo.* Whether the Vedic hymns were composed 1000, or 1500, or 2000, or 3000 years B.C.. no power on earth will ever determine." In spite of this unequivocal statement of Max Müller several later scholars have continued to entertain the erroneous notion that Max Müller had proved 1200-1000 B.C. as the date of the Ṛgveda.

Max Müller's approach towards the Vedas and Indian culture was marked by sympathy and understanding. He was in favour of giving due credit to the ancient Vedic commentators like Sāyaṇa for their contributions to Vedic exegesis (see note 24 of Chapter VII). Max Müller opposed the tendency of some Western scholars to propose emendations in the Vedic text to obviate the difficulties of interpretation. He was of opinion "that a mere translation of the Veda, however accurate, intelligible, poetical, and even beautiful, is of absolutely no value for the advancement of Vedic scholarship, unless it is followed by *pieces justificatives*, that is, unless the translator gives his reasons why he has translated every word about which there can be any doubt, in his own way, and not in any other." (SBE, Vol. 32, Introduction, p. x). He admits that although he translated some Vedic hymns into German in metrical form, yet he felt in honesty bound to confess that a metrical translation is often an excuse only for an inaccurate translation; and he cited Grassmann's metrical German translation of the RV. as an example.

Although Roth expressed the opinion that a translation of the RV. is a task for the next century, translators had no patience to wait till the meaning of all the Vedic words has been precisely determined. A. Langlois of Paris made an ingenious and arbitrary French translation of the RV. which was published from Paris in four volumes between 1848 and

1851 and re-edited in one volume in 1870; and which has been described by Max Müller as thoroughly uncritical and guess-work of a man of taste. Theodor Benfey published between 1862 and 1864 a German translation of the RV. I, 1-130 with scholarly notes in which he traced the history of some important words. But he assigns to most of the words the meanings suggested by Sāyaṇa or conjectural meanings without an intercomparison of relevant passages. The translations of the RV. made by Wilson and Grassmann have been already mentioned above. K.F. Geldner and Adolf Kaegi, two illustrious pupils of Roth, published in 1875 from Tübingen a metrical German translation of seventy hymns of the RV. with contributions from Roth also in accordance with the principles of Vedic interpretation enunciated by him. In the opinion of several scholars including M. Winternitz this translation is much preferable to Grassmann's translation. A French translation of *Forty hymns of the RV.* together with annotations was published by A. Bergaigne in the *Memoires de la Societe de Linguistique* (VIII, 1; 264; 348; 393; 479). Similarly A Hillebrandt published from Göttingen in 1913 a German translation of about 140 Hymns of the RV. under the title *Lieder des Rigveda* with notes. We have already mentioned above the English translation of selected hymns of the RV. published by Max Müller in vol. 32 of SBE.

Alfred Ludwig published in six volumes from Prag between 1876 and 1888 a German translation of the whole of the RV. with a comprehensive commentary and a lengthy Introduction discussing the various problems relating to the RV. In addition to fully availing himself of the modern aids to interpretation Ludwig thoroughly utilized Sāyaṇa's commentary in the task of his translation. Thus his translation follows a middle course: it is neither wholly dependent upon Sāyaṇa like Wilson's nor fully arbitrary and ingenious like that of Langlois. Some scholars rate Ludwig's prose translation higher than Grassmann's metrical translation of RV. Assessing the merit of Ludwig's translation H. Oldenberg opines that though Ludwig in his translation of the RV. and in its supplements had undoubtedly seen the meanings of many Vedic passages better than Roth, Ludwig's contribution to scholarship lacked thoroughness and a method; that in his case everything was a chance, a hunch—occasionally a lucky brain-wave, a dashing off of well-conceived ideas amounting occasionally to genius—a mixture of a grain of reason with a bushel of audacity; and that Vedic scholars have to accept loyally even today some of the interpretations of Ludwig, but on the whole no one would ever feel the need to have anything to do with the methods followed by Ludwig (Vedic Research, pp. 8-9). There is no doubt that Ludwig's translation bears ample testimony to the erudition and hard work of the translator. However, it does not stand the test of critical and objective scholarship; for instance, in many places Ludwig has made arbitrary rendering without caring for the context and the Vedic idiom (see note on RV. VII, 83,1 in my previous work *Vaidika-Vyākhyā-Vivechana*), and has also suggested many untenable emendations to the Vedic text in a number of verses to conform to his arbitrary interpretation. Most of Ludwig's emendations have been rejected by Oldenberg in his *Noten.*

R.T.H. Griffith published from Benares in four volumes in 1889-92 the first metrical English translation of the RV. which is mainly based on Sāyaṇa's commentary and Wilson's English translation, although Griffith has also derived some help from the translations made by Ludwig, Grassmann, Benfey, Max Müller, etc. Griffith's translation which is on the whole a medley of earlier translations lacks clarity in several places on account of its meterical composition, and illustrates Max Müller's above-referred dictum that a metrical translation is often an excuse only for an inaccurate translation. However, the brief footnotes added to his translation are illuminating as they mostly refer to the exegetical contributions of his predecessors.

H. Oldenberg published in 1897 in volume 46 of the Sacred Books of the East Series an English translation of 130 Ṛgvedic hymns addressed to Agni with exegetical notes in which he refers mostly to the views of his precedessors in the field of Vedic exegesis. In comparison with Max Müller's translation elucidated with critical notes published in volume 32 of the same Series Oldenberg's translation is very inferior and his exegetical notes are very sketchy. In numerous places Oldenberg seems to have borrowed the wording of Wilson's or Griffith's translation of the Vedic verses.

K.F. Geldner who had previously translated into German in collaboration with Adolf Kaegi Seventy selected hymns of the RV., as pointed out above, later prepared a German translation of the whole of the RV. which was posthumously published in volumes 33-35 of the Harvard Oriental Series. In the Preface to his translation Geldner says modestly that he has endeavoured a faithful linguistic translation which is again only a renewed attempt at explanation and an additional aid to the readers of the original text but a poor substitute for it for those unacquainted with the Sanskrit language. The translation is accompanied by a very helpful and illuminating commentary abounding in references to parallel passages of the RV. It goes without saying that Geldner's translation of the RV. is not only the last but also the best of all the available translations of this Veda. In India the only worth mentioning attempt in this direction was made by Prof. H.D. Velankar, who, following in the footsteps of Geldner, translated into English the Second and Seventh Maṇḍalas of the RV. and made a Hindi rendering of 108 Ṛgvedic hymns in a selection entitled *Ṛk-Sūkta-Vaijayantī*. C.R. Lanman, Bergaigne, Peter Peterson, A.A. Macdonell and many others have translated some selected hymns of the RV. for the guidance of beginners in Vedic studies. Most of such translations generally lack originality, though they offer some useful suggestions here and there.

Of the remaining three Vedas the Sāmaveda which is mostly (excepting 75 Mantras) a collection of the Mantras culled from the RV. for the purpose of singing at sacrifices has been edited and translated by various scholars. J. Stevenson edited and translated into English the Rāṇāyanīya recension of the Sāmaveda published from London in 1842. Stevenson's translation is a free rendering of Sāyaṇa's paraphrase of the Sāmaveda. The *Kauthuma* recension of the Sāmaveda was edited and published by Th. Benfey in 1848 from Leipzig with a metrical German translation, a complete glossary and annotations. Benfey's translation and annotations bear ample testimony to the erudition of the author. A metrical English rendering of the Sāṃaveda with a popular commentary containing references to the RV. wherefrom the verses have been derived was published by R.T.H. Griffith from Benares in 1893. In fact the interpretation of the Sàmaveda is dependdent upon that of the RV.

Among the Samhitās of the Yajurveda the Vājasaneyi-Saṃhitā (Mādhyandina) of the Śukla-Yajurveda was the first to be edited and translated. Albrecht Weber first published from Breslau in 1846 his *Vājasaneyi-Saṃhitae-Specimen* containing a Latin translation of Adhyāyas IX and X with annotations in Latin, and later published in 1852 from Berlin and London the complete text of the V.S. with the commentary of Mahīdhara. In his *Indische Studien* Vol. II A. Weber later published a German rendering of the 16th Adhyāya of the V.S. The 40th Adhyāya of the V.S. which is also known as *Īśopaniṣad* has been translated by several eminent scholars including Max Müller, P. Deussen, William Jones, E. Roer, Ram Mohan Roy, R.E. Hume, S.C. Vasu, etc. J. Eggeling in his English translation of the Śatapatha-Brāhmaṇa (published in the Sacred Books of the East series) has made valuable contributions to the interpretation of the V.S., because the first nine Books of the S. Br. constitute a sort of a commentary on the first 18 Adhyāyas of the V.S. R.T.H. Griffith published in 1899 from Benaras a metrical English translation of the whole of the V.S. under the title "The Text of the White Yajurveda", which mainly follows Mahīdhara's commentary as admitted by Griffith in the Preface to his translation. An English Translation of the Taittirīya-Saṃhitā with a lengthy Introduction and brief notes by A.B. Keith was published in volumes 18-19 of the Harvard Oriental Series in 1914. Keith's translation which generally follows Sāyaṇa's commentary is on the whole literal and accurate. L.V. Shroeder, who had earlier published for the first time between 1881 and 1886 from Leipzig the text of the Maitrāyaṇī-Saṃhitā, published a German translation of numerous passages of this Saṃhitā in his work entitled *Indiens Literatur und Kulitur* (Leipzig, 1887, pp. 110-162).

The first attempt to translate the AV. into German was

made by Th. Aufrecht and A. Weber. A German translation of Kāṇḍas I-V and XIV of the AV. with exhaustive notes by Weber appeared in volumes IV, V, XIII, XVII and XVIII of the Indische Studien between 1858 and 1898, while a German translation of Kāṇḍa XV had been previously published by Aufrecht in vol. I of the Indische Studien in 1850. Moreover, Weber published from Berlin in 1895-96 a German translation of Kāṇḍa XVIII in the Proceedings of the Royal Prussian Academy. J. Grill published from Stuttgart in 1879-88 a German translation of 100 selected hymns of the A.V. with annotations under the title *Hundert Lieder des Atharva-veda*. C.A. Florenz translated into German 1-50 hymns of the 6th Kāṇḍa (Göttingen, 1887). A French translation of Kāṇḍas VII-XIII with a commentary was published by Victor Henry from Paris between 1891 and 1896. Ludwig published in Vol. III (pp. 428-55) of *Der Rigveda* (Prag, 1878) a German translation of about two hundred and thirty of the most important hymns of the AV. without any commentary. L. Sherman translated into German 13 philosophical hymns of the AV.—mainly from Kāṇḍas X, XI, XIII, and XIX in his work entitled "*Philosophische Hymnen aus der RV-und AV.*" in 1887. Maurice Bloomfield first translated into English and critically discussed seven hymns of the AV. from Kāṇḍas I, II, and VII in Volume VII of the American Journal of Philosophy (pp. 467 ff); and later on in 1897 he translated into English nearly one-third of the entire Atharva-Veda with a learned and detailed commentary under the title "*Hymns of the Atharva-veda*" in volume 42 of the Sacred Books of the East Series. In this commentary Bloomfield has thoroughly discussed the interpretations suggested by Sāyaṇa and modern exegetes, and furnished concordances with the other works of Vedic literature. No student of the Veda in general and of the AV. in particular can afford to ignore this scholarly work of Bloomfield. R.T.H. Griffith published in 1895-96 from Benares a metrical English translation of the AV. with a popular commentary. As we have pointed out above, Roth's pupil W.D. Whitney who collaborated with his teacher in the editing of the AV. translated it into English with illuminating and critical notes about the readings and interpretation of the text, but unfortunately he died in 1894 and could not see his translation through the press. Therefore C.R. Lanman edited Whitney's translation and published it in 1905 as volumes VII and VIII of the Harvard Oriental Series. It is a happy coincidence that both Whitney and Bloomfield who made most significant contributions to the studies of the Atharva-veda were American scholars.

In addition to the dictionaries of Roth-Böhtlingk, Grassmann and Monier-Williams mentioned above, some other lexicographical studies also deserve special mention. A. Bergaigne published in the Journal Asiatique his learned paper on *Etudes sur le Lexique du Rigveda* in 1883-84 dealing with some important words beginning with *a* and discussing in the Introduction the methodology of lexicography. C.C. Uhlenbeck published in 1899 from Amsterdam a small Vedic dictionary under the title *Kurzgefasstes etymologisches Wörterbuch der altindischen Sprache*. In the field of lexicographical studies W. Neisser's *Zum Wörterbuch des Rigveda* published from Leipzig between 1924 and 1930 deserves special mention as it examines important words philologically and etymologically. The other two important Sanskrit lexicons of the 20th century are M. Mayrhofer's *A Concise Etymological Sanskrit Dictionary* (Kurzgefasstes etymologisches Wörterbuch des Altindischen) being serially published from Heidelberg (Vol. I, 1956: Vol. II, 1963; Vol. III upto the word *śvaśuraḥ*, 1970) and *the Dictionary of Sanskrit* (on historical principles) being published by the Deccan College, Poona. Although L. Renou's *Etudes sur le vocabulaire du Rigveda* (Pondicherry, 1958, 69) cannot be termed as a lexicon in the strict sense of the term, it is useful for determining the sense of 35 Ṛgvedic words or forms discussed therein.

As the meanings of cognate words of the related Indo-European languages such as Latin, Greek, Avesta, etc. can sometimes prove helpful in determining the sense of Vedic words, it would not be beside the point to mention here a few such lexicons as attempt a comparison between Sanskrit and some other important languages of Indo-European family. A. Fick published a comparative dictionary of principal Indo-European languages from Göttingen between 1868 and 1876 under the title *Wörterbuch der indogermanischen Grundsprache*.

Ch. Bartholomae's dictionary of ancient Iranian language published from Strassburg in 1904 under the title *Altiranische Wörterbuch* serves as a comparative dictionary to the extent that it cites corresponding Sanskrit words. Similarly A. Walde's *Lateinische etymologisches Wörterbuch* (2nd edition, Heidelberg, 1906-10) contains an index of Sanskrit words at the end; and his three-volume comparative dictionary entitled *Vergleichende Wörterbuch der indogermanischen Sprachen* including an index was edited and revised by J. Pokorny (Berlin-Leipzig, 1926-30 onwards). J. Pokorny's comparative and etymological dictionary entitled *Indogermanisches etymologisches Wörterbuch* (Berne-München, 1957 onwards) can be a useful aid to a Vedic interpreter. B. Schlerath has attempted a scholarly comparison of Avesta and Sanskrit in his Avesta-Dictionary entitled *Awesta*-Worterbuch (Wiesbaden, 1968), the second part of which contains a list of Vedic-Avestan parallels and quotes about 450 Vedic passages and about 350 Vedic words in the concordance.

It is also important to mention here briefly those Vedic indices and concordances which have proved helpful to lexicographical studies of the Vedas. Max Müller's Word-Index to the RV., which first appeared in two instalments in 1872 and 1874 as appendices to the last two volumes of his edition of the RV., ranks foremost among such works. Next comes Whitney's *Index Verborum* to the AV. published in 1881. R. Simon published in 1912 an Index Verborum to the Kāṭhaka-Saṃhitā edited by Shroeder. The *Vaidika Padānukrama Kośa* which was undertaken in the beginning of the 20th century by Svāmīs Viśveśvarānanda and Nityānanda and which wa completed by Dr. Vishva Bandhu in 1963 is a complete word-index of all the Vedas. It is in fact more than a mere word-index because its learned editor Dr. Vishva Bandhu has grammatically analysed all the word-forms, suggested their derivation and also briefly indicated their sense and disputed interpretations in the footnotes. No student of Vedic exegesis can afford to ignore this monumental work of the 20th century. Another monumental work of this type is M. Bloomfield's *Vedic Concordance* published as volume X of the Harvard Oriental Series in 1905. It is an alphabetical index to every line of every stanza of the Vedic texts published till then, and it also records their liturgical formulae (Mantras) and gives an account of the variants in the different Vedic texts. This work is indispensable for every student of the Vedas and is an outstanding aid to Vedic exegesis.

Apart from the translation, lexicons and concordances of the Vedas, the systematic, comparative and historical studies conducted by eminent scholars on various aspects of the Vedic language and thought have made significant contributions to the domain of Vedic exegesis. For a complete alphabetical account of such studies the readers should consult Prof. L. Renou's *Bibliographie Vedique* (Paris, 1931) and Prof. R.N. Dandekar's *Vedic Bibliography* in 3 volumes (I, Bombay 1946; II, Poona 1961; III, Poona 1973), because it does not lie within the scope of the present work to catalogue all publications on the subject. Our principal aim is to give a general survey of important trends and tendencies in the field of Vedic exegesis and to mention some outstanding and epoch-making publications by way of illustration.

In the initial stages of Sanskrit studies in the West the Vedic language was not accorded any special and separate treatment; and consequently the pecularities of the Vedic language were shown as mere exceptions to general rules in the grammars of the Sanskrit language. And this tendency continued for quite some time. For instance, Whitney's *Sanskrit Grammar* (Leipzig, 1879) deals mainly with Classical Sanskrit and treats the special features of the Vedic language as irregularities. However, the Vedic scholars began to feel the necessity of presenting a full and systematic account of the Vedic language, and Grassmann's *Wörterbuch* gave an impetus to the Vedic scholars to undertake a special study of various aspects of the Vedic language. In 1874 B. Delbrück published from Halle his grammatical treatise entitled *Das Altindische Verbum aus den Hymnen des Ṛgveda* which gives an account of all verb-forms of the RV. with an index. In the article entitled *Verb-Inflection in Sanskrit* published in 1875 in Vol. X of the Journal of American Oriental Society John Avery gave a complete and systematic account of the verb-forms of the RV. covering the forms of tenses, moods, infinitives and gerund. In the same volume of the JAOS. C.R.

Lanman published his article entitled *Noun-Inflection in the Veda*, in which the inflected forms of substantives, adjectives and participles contained in the RV. have been systematically presented. An important work entitled *Altindische Nominabildung* dealing mainly with the language of the RV. was published by B. Lindner from Jena in 1877. Delbrück's another important contribution to the study of the Vedic language was his *Altindisches Syntax* (Halle, 1888) which discusses the syntax of important Vedic works including the RV., MS., S. Br. and Ait. Br. A work of similar nature was published by J.S. Speijer (Speyer) in 1896 from Strassburg under the title *Vedische und Sanskrit Syntax* in the Encyclopaedia of Indo-Aryan Research. A monograph on the verbal system of the AV. was published by J.V. Neglein in 1898 from Berlin under the title *Das Verbalsystem des Atharvaveda.* A very ambitious and comprehensive grammatical project entitled *Altindische Grammatik* was undertaken by J. Wackernagel in the end of the 19th century with the publication of its Ist volume (Lautlehre) in 1896 from Gõttingen. Its IInd volume part 1 (*Einleitung Zur Wortlehre*; *Nominalcomposition*) appeared in 1905, and volume III (*Nominalflexion*) in 1930. After Wackernagel's death in 1938 his work was continued by A. Debrunner who published in 1954 part 2 of volume II (*Die Nominal suffixe*) and also brought out in 1957 a second edition of the first volume of the work together with an appendix prepared by himself and with anelaborate Introduction by L. Renou. However, the work is still incomplete and after the death of Debrunner in 1958 some German Sanskritists are said to have undertaken to complete it. In the opinion of Louis Renou (Introduction to its Ist volume, second edition), the *Altindische Grammatik* practically replaces all the previous works and combines in a masterly manner the results of historical linguistics with those of descriptive grammar and philology.

E.V. Arnold, who had previously published a number of articles on the Vedas, such as *Historical Vedic Grammar* (JAOS, XVII, 2), *Rigveda and Atharvaveda* (JAOS, XXII, pp. 309-320) and *Literary Epochs in the Rigveda* (KZ, XXXIV, pp. 297-344), brought out in 1905 from Cambridge his most outstanding work entitled *Vedic Metre in its Historical Development.* Even those scholars who do not accept Arnold's conclusions cannot afford to ignore this monumental work. A.A. Macdonell's *Vedic Grammar* published from Strassburg in 1910 in the Encylopaedia of Indo-Aryan Research is a significant contribution to Vedic exegesis, as it embodies the results of important researches accomplished upto the beginning of 20th century. *A Vedic Grammar for Students* (Oxford, 1916) by the same author not only summarises the contents of the previous work but is also an improvement upon it on account of certain additions including three appendices, viz. List of Verbs, Vedic Metre, and Vedic Accent. *Grammaire de la Langue Védique* (Paris, 1952) by L. Renou is a concise grammatical treatise which succinctly deals with the distinguishing features of the Vedic language in respect of phonology, formation of nouns, declension, conjugation, indeclinables and syntax. Among the modern works on Vedic Grammar may be mentioned the present writer's *Vaidika Vyākarṇa* (Hindi) in two volumes (Delhi, Vol. I, 1965; Vol. II, 1969), which embodies in an integrated form the views of the Padakāra, Pāṇini, Patañjali, Kātyāyana, Prātiśakhyakāras and Bhāṣyakāras on important aspects of the Vedic language along with the results of modern researches on the subject. Reviewing our *Vaidika Vyākarṇa* L. Renou remarks: "It is the first time, I think, that in India such a work is produced and it is a good achievement indeed."

Like comparative lexicons the comparative grammars of Indo-European languages are also an important aid to a student of Vedic exegesis. The first work of the kind was published in 1816 from Frankfurt by Franz Bopp, the founder of Comparative Philology, on the conjugation system of Sanskrit in comparison with that of Greek, Latin, Persian and German under the title *Über das Conjugation-system der Sanskritsprache, in Vergleichung mit jenem der griechischen, lateinschen, persichen und germanischen Sprache*. Later Bopp brought out a 3-volume comparative grammar of Sanskrit, Greek, Latin, Persian and German (Berlin 1833-49). M. Rapp's *Vergleichende Grammatik* in 5 volumes was published from Stuttgart between 1852 and 1858. A Schleicher's work entitled

Compendium der Vergleichenden Grammatik der indogermanischen Sprachen appeared in 1861 from Wiemar. K. Brugmann and B. Delbrück published a comprehensive work on the subject in 5 volumes under the title *Grudnriss der Vergleichenden Grammatik der indogermanischen Sprachen* (Strassburg, 1886-1900). A.V.W. Jackson's work entitled *An Avestan Grammar in comparison with Sanskrit* (Part I dealing with phonology, inflection and word-formation) appeared in 1892 from New York. A. Meillet brought out his work entitled *Les dialectes indeuroepéennes* from Paris in 1908. H. Hirt's *Indogermanische Grammatik* in 5 volumes was published from Heidelberg between 1921 and 1929. J. Kurylowicz who has made substantial contributions to the comparative study of Indo-European languages has edited a 4-volume work entitled *Indogermanische Grammatik* (Heidelberg, 1968 onwards).

For a complete account of the studies of Vedic words and concepts contributing to Vedic exegesis, the Vedic bibliographies mentioned above may be consulted with profit. The most outstanding and epoch-making work on the subject is the *Vedische Studien* by R. Pischel and K.F. Geldner in 3 volumes (Stuttgart, 1889-1901) in which the learned authors have thoroughly examined and philologically traced the meanings of about 70 obscure Vedic words through various stages; have mythologically treated some important Vedic names such as *Viśpalā*, *Purūravas* and Urvaśī; and have discussed the problem of Vedic interpretation and put forward the view that, since the RV. is essentially an Indian product, the Indian commentators are best qualified to interpret the Veda. In the opinion of Pischel and Geldner, the Vedic as well as post-Vedic Indian literature in its collective aspect is the best guide to Vedic interpretation. The learned scholars observe that the Indian people in their thoughts and feelings still remain what they were in the past, and so long as they live in history they are Indians and possess an Indian spirit which we meet in the hymns of Viśvāmitras and Vasiṣṭhas, no less than in the Kādambarī of Bāṇa (see vol. I, p. xxxii). In sharp contrast to the views held by some other distinguished Vedic scholars such as Roth and Oldenberg, Pischel and Geldner have expressed the opinion that the true character of the RV. has been far more correctly interpreted by Sāyaṇa than by European interpreters. Pischel and Geldner undoubtedly supported the modern deductive method of Vedic interpretation and were in favour of deriving all possible help from Comparative Philology, but they did not agree with those Western scholars who indulged in an outright condemnation of the Veda-Bhāṣyakāras, and recommended a sympathetic appreciation of their interpretations.

The eminent French savant Abel Bergaigne has made a valuable contribution to Vedic exegesis through his well known work *La Religion Vedique* (3 vols., Paris, 1878-83, English translation by V.G. Paranjpe, Poona, 1973) in which he has endeavoured to solve some riddles of Vedic exegesis by explaining the metaphors implied in the Vedic verses. In the Introduction Bergaigne explains the nature and scope of his work as follows: "After a comparative study of the different uses of each word of the Ṛgveda, which has resulted, on the one hand, in the Vedic part of the St. Petersburg Dictionary due to M. Roth and, on the other, the complete *index verborum* which has been published by M. Grassmann under the title of *Wörterbuch Zum Rigveda*, I thought that a comparative study of the different forms of each deity might contribute in its turn to the solution of some of the difficulties, some recognised as such, and others avoided rather than solved, which the exegesis of the most ancient literary monument of India still presents. I have therefore undertaken to give to the public a sort of *index rerum*, or better, an index of the ideas of the RV."

To illustrate Bergaigne's method of Vedic interpretation through the explanation of metaphors employed in the Vedas, we may refer to his explanation of the enigmatic *vṛṣabha* (lit. bull) of RV. IV, 58,3 which has been variously interpreted by the ancient Indian exegesis (supra). On page 231 of Vol. I Bergaigne observes that a mythical bull, which has three bellies, three faces and in so far as he is confounded with a female, three udders, (III, 56,3) is also connected with three places (IV,58,3) which is the same as saying that it has three homes (Cf. III, 56,5), and he has penetrated all the mortals (IV, 58,3); and that his last detail, like the triplicity of forms, suits fire as well as the sacrificial beverage equally well. Bergaigne further explains on the same page that in RV. IV, 58,3 are attributed to the bull, along with three feet and two heads, suggestive of the division of the universe into two and three worlds, four horns, corresponding to the four cardinal points, and seven hands, which according to him (see Chapter on *Mythological Arithmatic*) refer to another division of the universe into seven worlds. So in his view the seven hands of this being, tied in a *three-fold* manner, also his two heads, three legs and four horns correspond to different systems of the division of the universe. In this way Bergaigne suggested some rational Vedic explanations which militated against the Vedic interpretations attempted by his contemporary Vedic scholars of the West, particularly eminent German scholars, who therefore chose to ignore his monumental work. Irked by this 'conspiracy of silence' Bergaigne in conclusion (Vol. III, p. 273ff) criticises the Vedic translations and interpretations suggested by Roth, Grassmann and Ludwig, and expresses his anger and anguish as follows:

"I have taken this occasion, while translating this hymn to expose to public view the miserable plight—this expression has certainly to be used here—of the present interpretation of the RV. I have done it sometimes in a tone of which the vivacity might appear excessive. Along with acerbity of criticism I might be also blamed for the self-confidence which I have imported into my own affirmations. But I have to request the reader to consider that I have been fighting single-handed against a powerful school, which might claim almost all the contemporary Vedic scholars as belonging to their number, and M. Ludwig himself probably may be one of them, although he has taken a more independent attitude than any other. I am living far away from my adversaries who are writing and teaching, almost all of them, on the other side of the Rhine. I may be allowed to add that, if here is not exactly a conspiracy of silence in regard to my first volume, they have generally confined their notice of it to merely a very vague praise hemmed in by restrictions which are in no way precise, and that in short they have hardly regarded it as worthy of consideration. —My 'contribution', as they call it in Germany, to the study of the RV. consists essentially of three new ideas, new at least by reason of the importance which I attach to them, of which two are concerned with the Vedic expressions and the third with the Vedic words, these three being very intimately connected with one another. The first two are: *liturgical contaminations of the myths* and a taste for incoherent metaphors amounting to a paradox and for the enigma properly so called. The third involves the necessity of an energetic reaction against the tendency to multiply indefinitely the meanings of one and the same word; and it is inseparably connected with two other conceptions; for the complexity of the expressions and that of the vocabulary are, and will always remain, on account of the very nature of things, in inverse ratio to one another. In short, the essential question between my adversaries and myself comes to this: would it be desirable to introduce a new meaning for words whenever we come across a new idea, howsoever strange it be, or would it be desirable, on the contrary, to admit the strangeness of the idea (—, but this strangeness ought never to be isolated and there must be some analogies to be found for it in some portion of the Vedic Saṃhitā,—) every time when we find that we can escape it only by multiplying to an inordinate degree and with too few outside parallels the meanings of words?...At the same time with utmost sincerity I once again give expresson to the high esteem which I feel for the scholars against whom I have launched such a vigorous polemic. The chief of the school against which I am fighting is also my master in a certain sense. Which one of us has not been guided in his first steps of Vedic learning by the dictionary of M. Roth? I am sorry to be obliged to say that the defects in the translation of M. Grassmann appear to me to be more and more serious as I have the occasion to verify some portions of it. But I cannot without a veritable ingratitude towards his memory fail to recognise the services which he has rendered, in spite of its imperfections, by his *Wörterbuch Zum Rigveda*. Lastly, I have already on several occasions expressed my main grievance against M. Ludwig: too often he stops in the middle of what has appeared to me to be the right way. But this criticism itself, in my opinion, contains a praise. I recognise, what cannot be contested I think by any impartial mind, that his translation has contributed to a notable progress in Vedic studies." (Vol. III, pp. 319-321)

Appreciating Bergaigne's procedure Oldenberg (Vedic Research, p. 9) observes that there is no doubt that the procedure indicated by Bergaigne appears to be the correct one from various points of view; that Bergaigne was completely justified in his criticism of his predecessors; and that his own interpretations which are lexicographically original are for the most part quite conclusive.

Besides his earlier work entitled *Die Religion des Veda* (Berlin, 1894) dealing with various aspects of Vedic religion, Oldenberg's two other publications, viz. (1) *Die Hymnen des Rigveda* Vol. I, *Metrische und textgeschichtliche Prolegomena* (Berlin, 1888) and (2) *Rigveda, Textkritische und exegetische Noten* in two volumes (Berlin, 1909, 1912—Vol. I covering Maṇḍalas 1-6 and Vol. II Maṇḍalas 7-10) are notable contributions to Vedic exegesis. In the *Prolegomena* Oldenberg discusses the metrical peculiarities of each hymn of the RV., the arrangement of the RV., Saṃhitā and its relationship with the other Saṃhitās, the Brāhmaṇas and the Sūtra-literature. In the *Noten* which is a sort of a critical commentary on the RV. with a good bibliography Oldenberg deals with the grammatical and exegetical problems of the RV., makes copious references to the views of other eminent scholars on the subject; and thus this work serves as a compendium of modern exegetical studies on the RV.

In order to elucidate Vedic thought several modern scholars have discussed in various articles the nature and chief characteristics of Vedic deities from different points of view. In this connection Alfred Hillebrandt's contributions deserve to be specifically mentioned here. He published from Breslau between 1891 and 1902 his three-volume work entitled *Vedische Mythologie*, whose first volume (1891) deals with Soma and related deities, Volume II (1899) discusses the Vedic deities Uṣas, Agni and Rudra, and Vol. III is devoted to the discussion of the other Vedic deities. The second edition of this work appeared in two volumes in 1927-29 and the same was reprinted in a single volume in 1965 from Hildesheim. Although many propositions put forward by Hillebrandt have been rejected by the later scholars, yet his treatise retains its importance as a pioneering work on Vedic Mythology. Another important work on the subject is A.A. Macdonell's *Vedic Mythology* published from Strassburg in 1897 in the Encyclopaedia of Indo-Aryan Research, which succinctly embodies the results of previous researches on the Vedic deities and is more systematic and objective in approach. *The Vedic Index of Names and Subjects* (London, 1912) in two volumes authored jointly by A.A. Macdonell and his pupil A.B. Keith is an epoch-making work which authoritatively explains the meaning of Vedic names and gives a succinct account of the Vedic subjects on the basis of the original Vedic texts, and frequently refers to the views of other researchers in the field.

In the galaxy of topmost Vedic scholars of the 20th century who have made outstanding and substantial contributions to the realm of Vedic exegesis may be mentioned the names of Professors Louis Renou and J. Gonda. Professor Renou has translated with critical and exegetical notes a considerable number of Vedic hymns, interpreted the meaning of a large number of difficult Vedic words, and exhaustively and brilliantly discussed various important problems of Vedic interpretation in his numerous publications among which *Etudes Védiques et pāṇinéennes* in 17 volumes (Paris, 1955-69) deserves special mention. Prof. Renou is one of those few Western Vedists who are against suggesting emendations to the Vedic text. Prof. J. Gonda's contributions to Vedic exegesis range from the interpretation of important Vedic words and concepts to the elucidation of some significant aspects of the Vedic language in his manifold publications which include *Four Studies in the Language of the Veda, Epithets in the Ṛgveda, Stylistic Repetition in the Veda, and the Vision of the Vedic Poets.* In his numerous articles Dr. A. Esteller has subjected the text of the Ṛgveda-Saṃhitā to a metrical rhythmical criticism in support of his hypothesis that the present Saṃhitā-text redacted by the Saṃhitākāra in accordance with his later notion of euphonic combination does not represent the original *Kavi-text* which can be reconstructed by applying the principles of metre and rhythm to the *Saṃhitā-text*. However, Dr. Esteller's view has been hotly contested by several scholars who are not in favour of suggesting any emendation to the traditional Vedic text on any ground.

When the Indian intellectuals became aware of the keen interest evinced by the Western scholars in the study of the Vedas, it aroused a feeling of national pride among the Indian people and created a new awareness about the importance of their ancient scriptures. Thus the revival of Vedic studies in modern India is in no small measure due to the Vedic researches of Western scholars. And a new interpretation of the Vedas attempted by the Western Vedists gave an impetus to the enlightened and unorthodox Indian scholars to make a fresh and rational approach to the Vedas. In fact the new and rational interpretation of the Vedas formed the basis of social and religious reforms among the Hindus in the 19th century. In the eastern part of India this movement of social and religious reforms was led by Raja Ram Mohan Roy who authored a number of books including the English translation of several important passages and texts of the Vedas, Upaniṣads and the other Hindu scriptures. And from the western part of India arose Svāmī Dayānanda Sarasvatī who attempted a fresh and rational interpretation of the Vedas in his several works including the *Ṛgvedādibhāṣya-bhūmikā* (1877), the *Śukla-Yajurveda-bhāṣya* (1878-79) and the *Ṛgveda-bhāṣya* (I, 1, 1, to VII, 61, 2 only) basing his interpretation on the etymological method of Yāska and on the Pāṇinian aphorism (III, 1, 85) "*Vyatyayo bahulam*". Moreover, Svāmī Dayānanda Sarasvatī also emphasized the importance of explaining the Vedic metaphors. Almost at the same time a laudable attempt was made by Shankar Pandurang Pandit who in his *Vedārtha-Yatna* (5 vols., Bombay, 1876-83) undertook to give a rational interpretation of the RV. on modern lines together with Padapāṭha, Sanskrit paraphrase, translation in Marathi and English, and exegetical and critical notes. But due to his premature death this important project could not proceed beyond the third Maṇḍala.

Dr. A.K. Coomarsvami in his work entitled *A New Approach to the Vedas: An Essay in Translation and Exegesis* (London, 1931) suggested the mystic interpretation of the Vedas arguing that the real import of the Vedic verses can be understood on the basis of a thorough study of the thoughts of the mystic saints of the entire world. Similarly Sri Aurobindo in his several publications including *Hymns to the Mystic Fire* (Pondicherry, 1952), *the Vāmadēva Hymns to Agni* (Pondicherry, 1951) and the *Secret of the Veda* (published serially in the monthly Ārya) has suggested an esoteric interpretation of the Vedic verses on the plea that the Ṛgvedic hymns were writtern by the mystic seers in an age when there was a double face to the current religion, an outer face for the general public, *profanum Vulgus*, and an inner face, esoteric one, for the initiates. T.V. Kapalisastri in his Sanskrit commentary entitled *Siddhāñjanā* on the Ist Aṣṭaka of the RV. published from Pondicherry in 1950-51 expounds the esoteric interpretation of the Vedic Mantras suggested by Sri Aurobindo. In order to further expound Sri Aurobindo's method of esoteric interpretation A.B. Purani published from Varanasi in 1963 his treatise entitled *Studies in Vedic Interpretation* (on the lines of Sri Aurobindo), excerpts from which are quoted below to illustrate his approach to the Veda : "Rivers, waters, oceans (seas) stand for the current of consciousness—movement of consciousness. Indra frees the current of Rivers from the above mental plane and the waters of the rivers of light flow down into human consciousness. These are the Sarasvatī and other rivers." (p. 179)

"Dyaus and Pṛithivī represent the pure Mental and the Physical consciousness; between them is the Antarikṣa, the intermediate or connecting level of the vital or nervous consciousness." (p. 190)

Similarly a metaphysical interpretation of the Vedic verses has been suggested by Dr. V.S. Agrawal in his several publications including *Sparks from the Vedic Fire* (Varanasi, 1962) and *Vision in Long Darkness*. It may be pointed out here in this connection that almost all the scholars including Dr. Coomarsvami, Sri Aurobindo together with his followers and Dr. V.S. Agrawal base their mystic interpretations on the literal meanings of the Vedic words suggested by Sāyaṇa. In other words, they superimpose their own esoteric meaning on Sāyaṇa's linguistic interpretation. Therefore if Sāyaṇa's linguistic interpretation falls, their mystic explanations also vanish. No serious attempt seems to have been made by them to correlate such explanations with the totality of Vedic idiom, usage and thought.

Most of the translations of the Vedas in modern Indian languages are based on Sāyaṇa's interpretation, but one or two in Hindi follow the line of interpretation adopted by Svāmī Dayānanda Sarasvatī.

Some of the modern scholars have subjected a few isolated words, passages or hymns of the Vedas to astronomical, physiological, historical, social, geographical, geological, political or anthropological interpretation according to their ingenuity. For instance, H. Jacobi in an article entitled *Über das Alter des Ṛgveda* published in *Festgruss an Rudolf von Roth* (pp. 68-73) in 1893 from Stuttgart placed an astronomical interpretation on RV. VII, 103,9 along with X,85,13 and put forward the view that the proposed astronomical interpretation of these Vedic passages coupled with the non-mention of the Polestar in the RV. points to the high antiquity of the RV. which can be placed at about 4500 B.C. Simultaneously Lokamānya B.G. Tilak in his *Orion or Researches into the Antiquity of the Vedas* (Bombay, 1893) published in the same year picked up some passages from the RV., TS. and Sat. Br. for astronomical interpretation to prove his thesis "that the traditions recorded in the Ṛgveda unmistakably point to a period not later than 4000 B.C., when the vernal equinox was in Orion," and that the earliest period of ancient Vedic literature is the Aditi-Period or Pre-Orion Period extending roughly from 6000 B.C. to 4000 B.C. In another work entitled *the Arctic Home in the Vedas* (Bombay, 1903) he placed geological and geographical interpretation on certain Vedic passages to postulate a new theory of the Arctic Home of the Aryans in the Ṛgveda, which failed to elicit the approval of modern scholars. Dr. V.G. Rele in his monograph entitled '*The Vedic Gods As Figures of Biology* attempts an ingenious interpretation that the Vedic gods symbolize different centres of activity in the nervous system of the human body : e.g., the Rudriyas are the sensory-motor cerebral nerves; the god Parjanya is the reflex activity that excites the sexual organs; and the god Viṣṇu is comparable to the spinal cord. This interpretation totally banishes divinity and spiritualism from the Vedas and turns them into ordinary books of biology, which is the height of sheer absurdity. Another facet of similar absurdity is displayed by those pseudo-Vedists who interpret the Vedic word *Viṣṇu* as "a social reformer". Max Müller has aptly observed that a casual reader of the translation of the Veda has done so much harm by meddling with Vedic antiquities (SBE, vol. 32, Introduction, p.xxiii). It is, in fact, these casual readers of the Vedic translations who have spun out ludicrous and fantastic theories about the Vedic history, thought and culture on the basis of their confused understanding arising from tentative and conjectural translations of the Vedas without ever opening the original Vedic Saṃhitās to verify independently the ground on which they are going to build a superstructure out of their imagination. Among such casual readers of the Vedic translations may be mentioned the name of Sir Leonard Wooley who dubs the Ṛgveda "the epic of destruction of one of the great cultures of ancient world". (supra II). No serious Vedic scholar, who has been able to understand even a small portion of the original Vedic texts without the aid of a commentary or a translation and who has attained the proficiency of correcting a wrong translation, would ever pass such a judgment on the RV. It is not a mere coincidence that the authors of all sorts of fantastic theories about the Vedic history and culture are only such persons as are not able to understand even a single Vedic verse without the aid of a translation in a modern language. In this respect the hasty and conjectural translations of the Vedas have done a positive disservice to the cause of Vedic exegesis.

9

A Comparative Assessment of the Bhāsyakāras and the Modern Interpreters of the Vedas

In order to take a balanced and impartial view of the exegetical attempts made by the ancient Indian Bhāṣyakāras and the modern interpreters of the Vedas it is essential to make a comparative assessment of their merits and demerits so that the future interpreters of the Vedas may take full advantage of the good points and cautiously avoid their shortcomings. It may be pointed out at the outset that in my humble opinion the ancient Indian and modern systems of Vedic interpretation cannot be considered as entirely opposite and contrary to each other in spite of their known differences of approach and emphasis. Both the systems of interpretation share several points of strength and weakness. Historically speaking, the modern method of Vedic interpretation is indebted to the works of the ancient Indian exegetes. It would be a fallacy to class all the ancient and mediaeval Bhāṣyakāras of the Vedas into one category and to place all the modern Vedic interpreters and translators into another. I have no hesitation in saying that all the Vedic Bhāṣyakāras mentioned in the preceding Chapters are not equal in their calibre, erudition and outlook. And similar is the case with the modern Vedic interpreters among whom some are original, erudite, exact, sincere and cautious in their approach to the subject, while others choose to project their prejudices and preconceived notions into the Vedas with the aid of second-hand translations without caring to read the original text. I may add that such faddists who are found in all times and climes should not be taken seriously.

The Merits and Demerits of the Bhāṣyakāras

Among the ancient and mediaeval Veda-Bhāṣyakāras described above in Chapter VII Sāyaṇa has produced the maximum number of Bhāṣyas and has incorporated in them, to a very large extent, the main results of Vedic exegesis achieved by his predecessors. So Sāyaṇa does not represent an individual Bhāṣyakāra but the principal school of traditional interpreters of the Vedas. Since Sāyaṇa's Ṛgveda-Bhāṣya is most exhaustive and comprehensive not only among his own Veda-Bhāṣyas but also among all the available Bhāṣyas on the Vedas, it may be justifiably selected as a representative Bhāṣya for the purpose of discussing in a general manner the merits and demerits of the Veda-Bhāṣyakāras, although Sāyaṇa's interpretation in numerous cases is different from that of his illustrious predecessors like Skanda and Veṅkaṭamādhava who sometimes suggest a better meaning; Cf. e.g., their Bhāṣyas on RV. I,1,7; 25,10; 25,20; III, 59,7; VII, 83, 2 etc. Sāyaṇa is on the whole the best and the most representative Bhāṣyakāra who has embodied in his commentary the gist of a substantial portion of the Vedic interpretations of his predecessors.

The most salient feature of Sāyaṇa's Ṛgveda-Bhāṣya is that in his commentary he endeavours to supply all available exegetical information about each hymn. For instance, in the beginning of his commentary on each hymn Sāyaṇa first of all informs us about the Pratīka (the introductory words), the number of verses, the Ṛṣi, the deity and the metre of the hymn according to Kātyāyana's Sarvānukramaṇī. Then he refers to the ritual application of the hymn and its individual verses, and cites the relevant passage of the Brāhmaṇa (Ait. Br.) or the Śrauta-Sūtra (Asv. S.S.) in this connection. If he is aware of any *Itihāsa* connected with the hymn, he cites the concerned *Itihāsa* together with its original source such as the Bṛhaddevatā and the Śāṭyāyana-Brāhmaṇa in the beginning of his commentary on the hymn. While explaining a verse, Sāyaṇa first paraphrases its each word in simple Sanskrit. If the verse under explanation or any part of it or the idea contained in it is found explained or alluded to in an earlier work such as a Brāhmaṇa and the

Nirukta, Sāyaṇa cites it in his Bhāṣya to eluciate his interpretation. In order to explain difficult and obscure Vedic words Sāyaṇa refers to the relevant portion of the Nighaṇṭu, and quotes its etymologies suggested by a Brāhmaṇa-text or by Yāska. In support of his interpretation Sāyaṇa sometimes cites or refers to the analogous Mantras from the RV.,TS. and AV. In order to explain the formation and accent of the Vedic words Sāyaṇa completely relies upon the Pāṇinian grammar and often refers to its Sūtras and Kātyāyana's Vārtikas; and he also cites the Uṇādi-Sūtras wherever necessary. It is important to mention here that with regard to the grammatical explanation of several Vedic words Sāyaṇa's views differ from those of such celebrated grammarians as Vāmana and Jayāditya. See, for instance, our *Vaidika-Vyākaraṇa*, Vol. II, p. 703 notes 150 and 157 and p. 716, note 245, etc.

Some of the alternative interpretations of a Mantra offered by Sāyaṇa in his Bhāṣya represent the views of the earlier Bhāṣyakāras irrespective of the fact whether he names them or not. There is no doubt that Sāyaṇa's Ṛgveda-Bhāṣya which represents a synthesis of different exegetical traditions of ancient India is not the work of a single author. This is why it is marred by several contradictions which cannot be easily reconciled. For instance, his Bhāṣya on RV. I,25,10 explains *Pastyāsu* as "*daivīṣu prajāsu*", whereas the same word is interpreted as *Yajamānānām gṛheṣu* in his Bhāṣya on RV. IV,1,11 and as *Yāgagṛheṣu* on X,46,6. The commentator seems to have relied upon the Nighaṇṭu III,4 for the second interpretation, but there seems to be no justification for the first interpretation. One fails to understand why Sāyaṇa offered such a baseless interpretation of the word *Pastyā*. Another serious shortcoming of Sāyaṇa's commentary is that although he offers many alternative explanations of a verse or a word on the basis of its current interpretations or etymologies, he does not indicate his preference for any of them. Still another drawback of Sāyaṇa's Bhāṣya is that even when there is a grave doubt about the meaning of a verse or a word he attempts its interpretation and does not state explicitly that its explanation needs further investigation. Such doubtful and half-baked interpretations hinder the future progress of Vedic exegesis, because the current interpretation of a doubtful verse or word is bound to influence the future interpreters and thus impede the course of fresh and independent interpretation. Not only Sāyaṇa but almost all the Bhāṣyakāras lack historical outlook and therefore fail to see the anachronism in utilizing the legends or events of the later times for Vedic interpretation. For instance, Sāyaṇa in his Bhāṣya on RV. X,142,7 imports the legend connected with Arjuna's act of burning the *Khāṇḍava* forest narrated in the Mahābhārata.[1] Similarly Sāyaṇa suggests the interpretation of some Vedic verses or words on the basis of ideas or meanings current in the later works and Classical Sanskrit only. The most glaring defect of Sāyaṇa's commentary is that whenever he is faced with any difficulty in interpretation he unhesitatingly resorts to such sweeping Pāṇinian Sūtras as *Vyatyayo bahulam*, *Vā Chhandasi*, or *Bahulam Chhandasi* in order to interpret the grammatical form of a Vedic word to conform to his choice. Through the arbitrary application and gross abuse of these Pāṇinian Sūtras the Bhāsyakāras sometimes take the liberty of interpreting the case-ending, gender and number of a noun or a pronoun, and the person and number of a finite verb to fit into their pre-conceived interpretation. For instance, Sāyaṇa in his Bhāṣya on RV. I, 143,3 interprets the nominative case-ending of *Aktuḥ* in the sense of the accusative (*dvitīyārthe prathamā*). If the Bhāṣyakāra's proposition is accepted, the obvious inference would be that the Vedic language does not observe any rules of declension, conjugation, number, gender, person or syntax. However, such an assumption is far from the truth as shown by the modern scholars in their works on Vedic Grammar[2].

It would be gratuitous to assume that the other ancient and mediaeval Veda-Bhāṣyas are free from the above-mentioned shortcomings found in the Bhāṣyas ascribed to Sāyaṇa. In fact, most of these drawbacks are common to almost all the Veda-Bhāṣyakāras, and difference between one Bhāṣyakāra and another is only quantitative and not qualitative. For instance, Veṅkaṭamādhava's Ṛgartha-dīpikā does not suffer from so many contradictions as are met in Sāyaṇa's Ṛg-Bhāṣya, because besides being the composition of a single author the former is very brief and does not contain detailed exegetical and grammatical notes. In comparison with Sāyaṇa some of the later Bhāṣyakāras of the selected Vedic hymns or verses show scant regard for the Vedic idiom and thought, and attempt to project their own sectarian views into the Vedic text; compare, for instance, the Veda-Bhāṣyas composed by Nīlakaṇṭha, Kāśīnātha Upādhyāya, Ānandatīrtha and his followers. Among the mediaeval Veda-Bhāṣyakāras Ātmānanda offers the mystic interpretation of the *Asya-Vāmīya-Sūkta* and Dyā-Dviveda's efforts are devoted exclusively to the legendary interpretation of the selected Vedic verses, while most other Bhāṣyakāras attempt a ritualistic interpretation of the Vedic Mantras on a much narrower base than that of Sāyaṇa. None of the later Bhāṣyakāras can claim superiority over Sāyaṇa in respect of technique of interpretation, depth of scholarship, or width of vision; and most of them are indebted to Sāyaṇa.

Although no impartial scholar will seek to gloss over the shortcomings of the ancient and mediaeval Veda-Bhāṣyas, yet it would be crass ingratitude on the part of the later generations of scholars to belittle and ridicule the achievements of the ancient Bhāṣyakāras who accomplished their works with the aid of their memory only under difficult conditions in an age when the modern facilities of printing and aids to research such as lexicons and indices were non-existent. However, some of the modern scholars such as Benfey, Roth, Oldenberg, etc., decry and contemptuously treat the Veda-Bhāṣyas of Sāyaṇa and the other Indian commentators. For instance, Roth in the Preface to his St. Petersburg Dictionary arrogantly remarks that a conscientious European interpreter may understand the Veda far better and more correctly than Sāyaṇa. But how many European interpreters of the Veda can be considered to be more 'conscientious' than Sāyaṇa? Similarly Th. Benfey, disparaging the Bhāṣyakāras and indulging in self-praise of the Western interpreters of the Vedas, makes the following biased remarks in the Introduction to his edition and translation of the Sāmaveda: "Quite irrespective of all particular aids, the Indian method of interpretation becomes in its whole essence an entirely false one, owing to the prejudice with which it chooses to conceive the ancient circumstances and ideas which have become quite strange to it so many centuries later, from its own religious stand-point; while, on the other hand, an advantage for the comprehension of the whole is secured to us by the acquaintance (drawn from analogous relations) with the life, conceptions, wants and popular songs of ancient peoples, which we possess,—an advantage which, even if the Indians owed to tradition more details than they actually do owe, would not be eclipsed by their interpretation." Biased exaggeration in Benfey's comparison of the two systems of Vedic interpretation is too obvious to need any comments. It is shocking to note that an eminent scholar like Oldenberg is not prepared to concede any credit to the Bhāṣyakāras for their contribution to Vedic exegesis, and spares no invectives to condemn them. Irked by the praise showered by Geldner and Pischel on the Veda-Bhāṣyakāras Oldenberg in his *Veda-forschung* (English translation entitled *Vedic Research* by V.G. Paranjpe, Poona, 1973) dubs their Veda-Bhāṣyas as "a monstrous heap of rubbish" and condemns them as follows: "It was a bold undertaking (on the part of Geldner and Pischel) to rehabilitate the indigenous Vedic exegesis, highly discredited as it has been since the beginning of Roth's literary activity. Whenever we come across the interpretations of the old commentators, they have appeared to us as a monstrous heap of rubbish, a gelatinous mass, being very similar in their outlook and their essentials to each other, while in some other details being guilty of endless mutual contradictions" (pp. 15-16 of the translation). Decrying the Veda-Bhāṣyakāras Oldenberg further observes: "These interpreters continually indulge in etymologies of words, as good or as bad as their wild etymological technique would allow them, and through them they betray their lack of real solid knowledge. Or, they simply indulge in conjectures. Naturally they may thereby occasionally hit the correct explanation: this is not absolutely difficult to happen many times. But they shoot past the target endlessly and hopelessly and exhibit their shallowness and perversity in endless succession." (p. 16 of the translation). Elsewhere in the same book Oldenberg denies all credit to Sāyaṇa for any correct interpretation of the Veda and dubs him a "*fool*" in the following strong words :

"I would first of all emphasize—and this will be done in the shortest possible manner—the fact that in my opinion a much greater prudence than the V.S. (*Vedische Studien*) are accustomed to show is needed in coming to the conclusion that an explanation of Sāyaṇa which is correct must be based on an authoritative tradition. This commentator, whom we see constantly indulging in guesses about the meanings of words,—this guessing may be by himself or by the authority on whom he relies—, would really be much more of a fool than he actually was if he had never surmised a meaning correctly." (page 67 of the translation).

As is evident from the foregoing quotations, Oldenberg was very much pained by the praise and appreciation which Geldner and Pischel expressed in their work *Vedische Studien* for the Indian interpreters of the Vedas. Therefore, Oldenberg devoted a considerable part of his monograph entitled *Veda-forschung* to the criticism and condemnation of Indian commentators (see pp. 12-24, 67-82 of the translation). Roth, Oldenberg and other Western scholars of their ilk had through their vituperations against the Indian commentators created such a vicious atmosphere of revulsion and hatred against Sāyaṇa that even very sane and rational Western scholars were afraid of admitting publicly that they had ever consulted Sāyaṇa's Veda-Bhāṣyas or that their interpretation is in conformity with Sāyaṇa's. Bergaigne's following statement testifies to this fact : "Some readers may possibly think, because in my interpretations I am constantly introducing Soma, the sacrificial butter and prayer, that I am going back to the Indian interpretation. But I declare in the most formal manner that, if ever I happen to agree with Sāyaṇa (it happens rarely), it is always without meaning it, and in the majority of cases (why should I not confess it) without knowing it.... I have studied the commentary of Sāyaṇa, I say this in all humility, only in fragments—." (Vedic Religion, Vol. III, p. 282).

The intensity of a feeling of revulsion aroused in the West through constant propaganda against Sāyaṇa's commentaries can be gauged from the following remarks of Dr. E.J. Thomas in his Foreword to Dr. V.G. Rele's monograph entitled "The Vedic Gods as Figures of Biology" : "The first step was made by Rudolf Roth (1821-1895). He saw that what Sāyaṇa tells us is not final, and this famous utterance *Los von Sāyaṇa* ('get rid of Sāyaṇa') had led or misled scholars for a long time. I have met a noted Vedic scholar, a pupil of Roth, who refused to look at Sāyaṇa."

However, there were some sober and sympathetic Vedic scholars in the West, who valued and appreciated the contributions of the Indian commentators to Vedic exegesis. Among such Western scholars H.H. Wilson, Boden Professor of Sanskrit in the University of Oxford, was the first to pay compliments to Sāyaṇa in the Introduction to the English Translation of the first Aṣṭaka of the RV. as follows : "Although the interpretation of Sāyaṇa may be occasionally questioned, he undoubtedly had a knowledge of his text far beyond the pretensions of any European scholar, and must have been in possession, either through his own learning or that of his assistants, of all the interpretations which had been perpetuated by traditional teaching, from the earliest times."

F. Max Müller also did not agree with those Western scholars who indulged in outright condemnation of Sāyaṇa. Max Müllar held the view that despite known drawbacks in his Bhāṣyas Sāyaṇa's contributions to Vedic exegesis must be ungrudgingly acknowledged (supra, note 24 of Chapter VII). As we have pointed out above, Geldner and Pischel, the joint authors of the *Vedische Studien*, were ardent admirers of the Indian commentators, and countered the vicious propaganda unleashed against the Veda-Bhāṣyākaras by Roth and his pupils. In fact, Geldner and Pischel went a step further and advocated the view in their above-mentioned work that while interpreting the Veda according to the modern method of interpretation due help must be derived from the Veda-Bhāṣyas of the Indian commentators who could understand the Veda better, because the RV. is uniquely an Indian product and the same spirit pervades in the entire range of Indian literature from the RV. to the Kādambarī of Bāṇa (supra, VIII).

The above observation made by Geldner and Pischel that the RV. is uniquely an Indian product cannot be lightly brushed aside by any interpreter of the Veda, because until and unless a Vedic interpreter is thoroughly acquainted with the topography.

mountains, lakes, rivers, climate, flora and fauna of the region where the Ṛṣis saw the vision of their hymns, he cannot understand the subject-matter of the Veda nor can he appreciate the beauty of Nature, dawn, sun-rise, sun-set, thick dark clouds, strong winds, and lashing torrential rains, etc., vividly described in the Vedic hymns. No amount of Comparative Philology and inter-comparison of Vedic passages can help an interpreter of the Vedas visualise the geographical background of the Vedic hymns unless he has actually lived for a considerable period of time in the land of the Vedas to witness and experience the natural phenomena described by the Ṛṣis. Most of the Western interpreters of the Vedas were faced with this difficulty as admitted by Oldenberg who observes in his Vedic Research (p. 7) that the Veda fell to the share of those who remained in Europe, in a preponderant measure to the share of the German and French scholars, who had never trodden upon the Indian soil. In the absence of thorough acquaintance with the geographical background of the Vedas the Indian commentators including Sāyaṇa also experienced the difficulty of interpretation in respect of certain words and passages. For instance, Sāyaṇa in his commentary on RV. III, 23,4 explains the rivers *Dṛṣadvatī* and *Āpayā* as certain rivers (*Kāchīn nadī*) without identifying them and offers an utterly baseless interpretation of *Mānuṣa*,[3] the lake *Mānuṣa*, situated between these two rivers in the Kurukṣetra region, as he was not familiar with them. An Indian commentator is, on the whole, in a better position to understand the geographical and cultural background of the Vedas than his Western counterpart. Therefore, commending the valuable contributions of the Indian commentators to Vedic exegesis, Prof. Goldstücker remarks[4]: "Without the vast information which those commentators have disclosed to us,—without their method of explaining the obscurest texts,—in one word, without their scholarship, we should still stand at the outer doors of Hindu antiquity." Similarly E.B. Cowell in his (p. 11 of Poona edition, 1927) Preface to the 4th volume of H.H. Wilson's English translation of the RV. admires the Veda-Bhāṣyas and recommends their interpretations in preference to the arbitrary conjectures of the European scholars as follows : "It is easy to depreciate native commentators, but it is not so easy to supersede them; and while I would by no means uphold Sāyaṇa as infallible, I confess that, in the present early stage of Veidika studies in Europe, it seems to me the safer course to follow native tradition rather than to accept too readily the arbitrary conjectures which continental scholars so often hazard."

As pointed out above, despite certain drawbacks in their interpretation the Veda-Bhāṣyakāras deserve due credit for keeping alive the tradition of Vedic exegesis under trying circumstances, and for facilitating our first entry into the citadel of Vedic learning. It must be borne in mind that the ancient Bhāṣyakāras of the Vedas had already prepared different types of indices relating to the Vedic language, religion and mythology as essential aids to Vedic interpretation. The Ṛgveda-Bhāṣyakāra Mādhava (supra, Chapter 7) claims to have composed 12 Anukramaṇīs dealing with the conjugation, declension, indeclinables, derivation, syntax, accent, euphonic combinations, Ṛṣis, metres, deities, Itihāsas and the interpretation of the RV. It shows that the ancient Bhāṣyakāras had subjected the original Vedic text to a minute and thorough investigation for the purpose of its systematic interpretation. It is, therefore, a biased and baseless allegation to say that the Vedic interpretation suggested by the Veda-Bhāṣyakāras is all arbitrary and conjectural without any solid base. Although we do not mean to defend the shortcomings and mistakes found in the Veda-Bhāṣyas, at the same time we do not approve of the campaign of condemnation and calumny let loose against them by some biased modern scholars. There is no doubt that if the ancient Vedic exegetes had got at their disposal all the results of modern researches, they would have unhesitatingly revised and made up to date some of their interpretations, because some of the principles of Vedic interpretation enunciated by them are as rational as the systematic approach of modern scholars. In this connection the principles of Vedic interpretation enunciated in the Mādhavānukramaṇī as well as in the introductory verses of Veṅkaṭamādhava's commentary on each Adhyāya of the RV. are really worthy of note and cannot be ignored by any student of Vedic exegesis.

The Merits and Demerits of the Modern Interpreters of the Vedas

It may be pointed out at the outset that just as the Indian commentators of the Vedas express divergent opinions on the interpretation of certain words and passages so the eminent Western interpreters also hold different views in such cases; and complete unanimity on any point is out of question. It can not be gainsaid that the modern, rational and critical interpreters of the Vedas have definitely improved upon the old and traditional Indian method of Vedic interpretation in some respects, and have availed themselves of the aids provided by Comparative Philology and modern tools of research such as systematic and comparative lexicons, grammars, word-indices, concordances, and historical, critical and comparative studies pertaining to the words and ideas of the Vedic language and literature and of the cognate languages. The contributions of the modern scholars to these branches of learning, as enumerated succinctly in the preceding Chapter, must be duly acknowledged and made full use of by every student of Vedic exegesis. Some Western scholars have achieved commendable results in determining the meaning of individual Vedic words through inter-comparison of related passages, in tracing historically the various stages of the meanings of important Vedic words, in tracing the various stages of development of certain Vedic concepts, and in ascertaining the chronological relationship among important works of Vedic literature. The systematic, comparative and historical approach made by the modern scholars to the problem of Vedic exegesis is worth emulating.

However, in spite of these merits the Vedic interpretations and translations rendered by the modern scholars are not entirely free from flaws. Their claim for complete originality and independence of judgment is not corroborated by their translations of the Vedic Saṃhitās. We are giving below a sample of the originality of the English translation of the Vedic Hymns published in SBE Vol. 46 by H. Oldenberg who has made the most scathing criticism of the Indian commentators of the Vedas. Prior to Oldenberg's above-mentioned English translation, the hymns under reference had been translated into English by Wilson and Griffith who avowedly owe their debt of gratitude to Sāyaṇa for their interpretation. Oldenberg in his English translation of these hymns relies mostly upon the translations of Wilson and Griffith, and presents in a very few cases the new interpretations suggested by his predecessors such as Roth, Grassmann, Ludwig and Bergaigne. Oldenberg's own contribution to the translation of these hymns is thus quite insignificant. Oldenberg's translation of RV. I, 1, 1 may be compared with its English renderings made by his two illustrious predecessors, Wilson and Griffith, to judge the originality of Sāyaṇa's bitterest critic in modern times :—

Wilson "I glorify Agni, the high priest of the sacrifice, the divine, the ministrant, who presents the oblation (to the gods), and is the possessor of great wealth."

Griffith "I laud Agni, the chosen priest, God, minister of sacrifice,
The hotar, lavishest of wealth."

Oldenberg : "I magnify Agni, the Purohita, the divine ministrant of the sacrifice, the Hotri priest, the greatest bestower of treasures."

Now I leave it to the readers to compare these three translations of the same verse and judge whether Oldenberg, the last translator, has in any way improved upon the preceding translations or has simply rehashed the same in an inferior way. Such examples abound in Oldenberg's translation. Moreover, Oldenberg often refers to Sāyaṇa's views in his notes on the translation (Cf. pp. 84, 85, 93, 97, 144, 168, 174, 200, 235, 249, etc.) and also endorses Sāyaṇa's interpretation (Cf. pp. 84, 144, 168, 249, 284, etc.). Whenever Oldenberg encounters any difficulty in interpretation, he resorts to arbitrary conjectures. For instance, finding it difficult to explain the nominative form *aktuḥ* of RV. I, 143, 3 Oldenberg emends it to the accusative form *aktūn*, taking a cue from Sāyaṇa who also explains it in the sense of the accusative saying "*dvitīyārthe prathamā*" under the sweeping Pāṇinian Sūtra "*Vyatyayo bahulam*", though both Oldenberg and Sāyaṇa are equally wrong here.[5] These examples show that Oldenberg's translation and interpretations are not marked by any originality which may justify the use of his caustic remarks against the Indian commentators like Sāyaṇa.

Although the Western interpreters of the Vedas enunciate the principle that the meaning of Vedic words should be determined with the help of the Vedic text itself in accordance with the Vedic idiom, usage and thought without importing the later non-Vedic notions and prejudices into the Veda, in actual practice the Vedic translations and interpretations attempted by the Western scholars do not conform to this principle; and some of them are marred by the tendencies of text-emendation, cultural bias and vaguely literal rendering.

Text-Emendation

The tendency of some Western scholars to condemn the Indian commentators of the Vedas encouraged the other workers in the field of Vedic studies to view with suspicion all the Indian traditions including the one concerning the preservation of the Vedic texts. Whenever such scholars faced any difficulty in interpreting any Vedic word or verse, they attributed their difficulty (rather ignorance) to the supposed incorrect reading of the text, and emended it to suit their desired interpretation on the specious plea that with their knowledge of Comparative Philology they can correct the incorrect readings of the text. Accordingly Ludwig and Grassmann in their translations of the RV. suggested a large number of emendations to the Vedic text to suit their interpretations. In our work entitled *Vaidika-Vyākhyā-Vivechana* some of their emendations have been discussed and found untenable. That these modern s holars resorted to the expedient of text-emendation in haste without a thorough investigation of the subject is conclusively proved by an examination of their emendations. For instance, when Grassmann failed to interpret the locative form *mānuṣe* of RV. III,23,4, he emended it into the nominative form *mānuṣa* to suit his interpretation, and Oldenberg (SBE, Vol. 46, p. 288) endorses this emendation. But I have thoroughly discussed this emendation and shown that the locative form *mānuṣe* is correct (see my article mentioned in Note 3).

Most of the emendations suggested by Ludwig have been rejected by Oldenberg in his *Rigveda-Noten.* Pischel and Geldner also do not accept most of the emendations suggested by Ludwig and Grassmann, and prefer to interpret the Veda according to the traditional text. Nevertheless, Geldner himself has suggested some emendations. Similarly Oldenberg who has rejected Ludwig's emendations has himself suggested some other emendations.[6] We are surprised to find contradictions in Oldenberg's stand-points and statements. As pointed out above, he severely criticises Sāyaṇa and at the same time follows and refers to his commentary with approbation. Similarly suggesting emendations to the Vedic text and not regarding it as wholly correct, Oldenberg rejects the text-emendations of his predecessors and expresses his views on the subject as follows[7]: "Scholars, under the influence of views, formed too hastily and subjective in the extreme, believed that the traditional text as handed down to us consisted of constant deviations from the type to which they ought to have conformed and they, on the whole, did not find it particularly difficult to reinstate the texts in their suitable forms.... No philologist could possibly fail to recognize the wonderful accuracy with which the Ṛg-Veda text has been handed down to us. But we have certainly to make an exception above all of certain details of the phonetic tradition in respect of which grammatical theorists have imposed their views and falsified what was correct; in many instances we can—especially with the help of the metrical rules—restore the phonetically correct text.... Many of the mistakes, believed by us to be in existence for a long time, have disappeared or will certainly disappear, when in the meantime our progressive grammatical knowledge and our exegetical talent has found or will find a justification for the traditional text. On the other hand, we can correct many—not very many—of these mistakes or conjecturally restore the original text. Altogether, however, where there is an actual mistake in the text, our chances of restoring the original text are not very favourable."

Several Western scholars including Bergaigne, Max Müller and Renou are opposed to the tendency of text-emendation. Bergaigne criticises the emendations suggested by some Western scholars and expresses himself on the subject as follows:[8] "M. Roth will kindly allow me to reply that the translation which he has proposed presents at least in some portions a very clear example of the way how the sense of Vedic expressions, which are absolutely clear and have been preserved perfectly (he does not propose himself any correction for this passage), might have been misconceived by the European exegesis, when it is under an obsession to remove all bizarre things and to bring the hymns of the Ṛṣis in line with our own aesthetic sense, in a word to transform their theosophic lucubrations into small pieces of simple and sane poetry. *I have to add that most often it is this same spirit, which makes people discover textual corruption in texts which are perfectly free from corruptions, when the other expedients of which a misuse has been made by them even to a greater degree, such as the multiplication of the meanings of words and the hypothesis of homonyms, do not suffice to suppress from the Vedic texts something which they do not want to see there.*"

Max Müller is a staunch supporter of the traditional text and a bitter critic of the modern tendency of text-emendation. In the Preface to his English translation of the selected Vedic hymns published in vol. 32 of the SBE., Max Müller has thoroughly discussed this problem. Regarding the authenticity of the present text of the Ṛgveda-Saṃhitā Max Müller observes[9]: 'I may say that the text as printed by me is more correct than any MS. now accessible, more trustworthy than the text followed by Sāyaṇa, and in all important points identically the same with that text which the authors of the Prātiśākhyas followed in their critical researches in the fifth or sixth century before our era. I believe that starting from that date our text of the Veda is better authenticated, and supported by a more perfect *apparatus criticus*, than the text of any Greek or Latin author, and I do not think that diplomatic criticism can ever go beyond what has been achieved in the constitution of the text of the Vedic hymns." The same scholar further (ibid. p.11) opines that by the time of the Ṛgveda-Prātiśākhya both the Pada and the Saṃhitā texts were so firmly settled that it was impossible to omit a single short *a* for the sake of uniformity or regularity; and then he poses the question: who is the critic who would dare to tamper with a canon of scripture of which every iota was settled before the time of Cyrus, and which we possess in exactly that form in which it is described to us by the authors of the Prātiśākhyas? Max Müller vehemantly opposes the very idea of suggesting any emendation, saying (ibid. p. Lxxii): "I should deem it reckless to alter one single letter or one single accent in an edition of the hymns of the Ṛgveda. As the text has been handed down to us, so it should remain; and whatever alterations and corrections we, the Mlechhas of the nineteenth century, have to propose, should be kept distinct from that time-hallowed inheritance—, a text so ancient and venerable that no scholar of any historical tact or critical taste would venture to foist into it a conjectural reading however plausible, nay, however undeniable."

Some Western scholars including Grassmann, Kuhn and Arnold suggest emendation of the text to restore the so-called metrical regularity of the Vedic verses. But Max Müller does not approve of any such emendation and argues that the supposed metrical regularities, for which all this "*carnage*" has been committed, are not based upon any *a priori* principles, but deduced by ancient or modern metricians from those very hymns which seem so constantly to violate them. Louis Renou was a staunch supporter of the Vedic text handed down by tradition, and in his exegetical studies he treated with regret the text-emendations suggested by Geldner or Oldenberg who opposed emendations in principle but suggested in practice.

Cultural Bias

Although all the Western interpreters of the Vedas cannot be accused of cultural bias, it would also be unrealistic to assume that all the Western scholars have been entirely free from prejudices and preconceptions in interpreting the Vedas. If the Indian commentators consider the Vedas to be the eternal and divine source of all knowledge under theological bias, most of their Western counterparts, obsessed with the superiority of their race and culture, look down upon the Vedas as the outpourings of a primitive priestly class, and are not prepared to concede that the Vedas contain any eternal truth or philosophical or scientific ideas of any consequence. The number of the Western scholars, who have endeavoured to understand the Vedas with impartiality and sympathy, has been very small indeed. Most of the Western Orientalists have striven to findin the Vedas such primitive and puerile ideas as could be compared with the practices and beliefs of the most primitive and uncivilized tribes of the world. For instance, H. Oldenberg in his well-known work *Religion des Veda* (Berlin, 1894, p. 3) dubs the Ṛṣis of the RV. as "barbarian priests invoking barbarian gods"; and in the Introduction to his *Veda-forschung* he clearly refers to the religious distance of Western Vedists from the Vedas: "The Vedic texts, moreover, do not stand in those intimate relations with our religious literature to awaken in our minds associations of a deeply moving character, on one set of people amounting to fascination, and perhaps of a disquieting nature on another." Similarly some other Western scholars also give vent to their cultural bias, while comparing the Vedas with their religious scriptures. For instance, Griffith in the Preface to his English translation of the RV. expresses his religious bias as follows[10]: "I must beg my European readers not to expect to find in these hymns and songs the sublime poetry that they meet with in Isaih or Job or Psalms of David," and further adds[11]: "The great interest of the Ṛgveda is, in fact, historical rather than poetical." No impartial student of the Vedic literature can accept Griffith's assertions that the Vedic hymns are devoid of poetical beauty and that the RV. has got only historical importance. Similarly the well-known Vedic scholar M. Winternitz expresses his bias against the Vedas while comparing them with the religious poetry of the Hebrews, as follows[12]: "It is true, the authors of these hymns rise but extremely seldom to the exalted flights and the deep fervour of, say, the religious poetry of the Hebrews." Although Max Müller was more sympathetic to Indian literature and culture than most of the Western scholars, yet he has also expressed the following biased opinion about the Vedic hymns[13]: "A large number of Vedic Hymns are childish in the extreme; tedious, low and commonplace."

Most of the Western scholars are inclined to compare the customs, rites and culture of the Vedic people with those of the most backward and primitive tribes of the world, and feel uneasy if any of their colleagues praises the Vedic civilisation. For instance, Oldenberg makes such comparisons and places the funeral rites of the Vedic people at the same level as the customs of savage and semi-savage tribes[14]; and he is particularly irked by the attempts of *Zimmer*, the author of the *Altindisches Leben*, and of Pischel and Geldner, the joint authors of the *Vedische Studien,* who paint in their works an idealistic picture of Vedic civilisation. However, the progress of Vedic studies in the West produced a sense of moderation among the Western students of the Vedas who gradually began to take a more balanced view of the Vedic civilisation. This sense of moderation is reflected in the following remarks of M. Winternitz[15]: "We need not, therefore, imagine the people of the Ṛgveda either as an innocent shepherd people, or as a horde of rough savages, nor, on the other hand as a people of ultra-refined culture." Similarly A.A. Macdonell also dispels the erroneous notion of the earlier Western scholars about the RV. and observes[16]: "The Ṛgveda is not a collection of primitive popular poetry, as it was apt to be described at an earlier period of Sanskrit studies."

Most of Western scholars are not prepared to accord a high antiquity to the Vedas and are, on the contrary, anxious to assign them as low a date as possible. This tendency of the Western scholars is aptly described by Winternitz as follows[17]: "It became a habit, a habit already censured by W.D. Whitney, to say that Max Müller had proved 1200-1000 B.C. as the date of the Ṛgveda. It was only timidly that a few scholars like L. Von Schröder ventured to go as far back as 1500 or even 2000 B.C. And when, all at once, H. Jacobi attempted to date Vedic literature back to the third millenary B.C. on the grounds of astronomical calculations, scholars raised a great outcry at such heretical procedure, and even today most of the Western scholars shake their heads wondering how Jacobi could venture to assert so exaggerated an opinion on the age of the Veda. Strange to say, it has been quite forgotten on what a precarious footing stood the 'opinion prevailing hitherto', which was so zealously defended." Similarly, on the discovery of certain clay tablets of the 14th century B.C. at Boghazköi in 1907, containing the names of certain important Vedic deities such as Mitra, Varuṇa, Indra and Nāsatyau among the gods of Mitani, a number of Western scholars including Oldenberg, Giles, etc., took the view that this discovery does not provide any justification for assuming a greater antiquity for the Veda, because, in the opinion of these scholars, the gods mentioned in the said tablets are not the Vedic gods, but "these are the gods of some Western Aryan tribe akin to the Indians, inherited from some common past, as the Indians on their part had inherited from the same source", although a number of eminent Western scholars including Jacobi, Konow, Hillebrandt and Winternitz regard them as the names of Indian Vedic deities on account of the particular grouping and forms of these names[18].

Vaguely Literal Translations

It is a serious defect of the modern method of Vedic interpretation that some scholars resort to a vaguely literal translation of the ancient texts and thus create confusion in the minds of the readers about the real meaning of the Mantras of the Vedas. Although it is a very difficult job to convey correctly the original idea of an ancient text into a modern tongue through the inadequate medium of translation and the pioneers of the modern exegetical studies such as Roth and Max Müllar had already cautioned against rushing into the stupendous task of translating the Vedas, several Western scholars have ventured to translate the Vedas and the other ancient texts and the results of their translations are in most cases far from gratifying. A few samples of vaguely literal translations are cited below. R.T.H. Griffith makes the following metrical rendering of the RV.IV, 2,18:

> "Strong one! he marked them—and the gods before them—
> like herds of cattle in a foodful pasture.
> There they moaned forth their strong desire for mortals, to
> aid the True, the nearest One, the Living."

I am very sceptical if any English-knowing person can make out what the translator wants to convey in the above-cited piece of the translation of a Vedic verse. Will it be possible for the readers to understand fully the import of Oldenberg's following English translation (SBE., Vol. 29, p. 22) of two benedictory Mantras of the Śāṅkhāyana Gṛhya Sūtra (1,6,6) : "Offspring I put into thee, cattle I put into thee"? In fact, it is a mistranslation of the benediction: "I bestow offspring upon thee, I bestow cattle wealth upon thee." Such misleading and vague translations of the Vedic texts cause a lot of confusion in the minds of the readers about the contents of the Vedas. This is why M.

Winternitz was constrained to make the following observation about such translations of the RV.[19]: "The outsider who takes a translation of the Ṛgveda in his hand often wonders that so much in these hymns is unpoetical, indeed unintelligible and senseless. But the reason is frequently only that the translators do not content themselves with translating that which is intelligible, but that they think they *must* translate *everything*, even that which has up till now not been rightly interpreted."

The upshot of the whole discussion is that although the Western interpreters of the Vedas have made outstanding contributions to Vedic exegesis, yet their works especially translations are not the models for Vedic interpretation and leave much to be desired. The shortcomings of both the systems of Vedic interpretation, Indian and Western, should be cautiously avoided and the best features of both of them should be synthesized to arrive at the exact meaning of the Vedas in a systematic manner. In order to achieve this object the maximum aid must be derived from the ancient Indian works which sometimes throw a good deal of welcome light on the interpretation of obscure Vedic passages. I have exemplified this approach in the interpretation of the word *mānuṣa* of the Ṛgveda III,23,4 in my paper published in the Journal of the Ganganatha Jha Research Institute (see note 3). In order to resolve the difficulties arising from the doubtful form of a Vedic word, one should neither resort to the facile explanation of *Vyatyayo bahulam* or *chhandasi bahulam* offered in the works of the Indian commentators, nor to the ingenious escape of *emendation* adopted in the works of some Western scholars. Since a vaguely literal translation of the Vedas seldom succeeds in conveying the precise import of the Mantras, an attempt should be made to elucidate the exact acceptation of Vedic words which are in most cases used in a figurative sense. The terminology of the Vedas should be explained in its own special sense and it should not be confused with similar words of Classical Sanskrit.

A comparative analysis made by me of the Veda-Bhāṣyas and the modern exegetical studies in respect of selected forty hymns of the RV., the first half of which has already been published under the title *Vaidika-Vyākhyā-Virechana* (Delhi, 1976), reveals that most of the modern attempts at Vedic exegesis are little more than a rehash and translation of the meanings already suggested by the Veda-Bhāṣyakāras, and that the study of the Veda-Bhāṣyas is as important as that of the modern interpretations and lexicons for determining the correct meaning of the Veda (see *Introduction* to the *Vaidika-Vyākhyā-Vivechana*).

Notes and References

1. See my article entitled *Vedic Sources of the Śārṅgaka Legend of the Mahābhārata* in MM. Dr. Umesh Mishra Commemoration Volume, pp. 397-401.
2. Cf. note 71 on p. 698 of my *Vaidika Vyākaraṇa* Vol. II with regard to the scope of *Vyatyayo bahulam* (see also p. 493 article 223 of the same work).
3. For the interpretation of *Mānuṣa* see my article "*A New Interpretation of the Vedic Word Mānuṣa*" in the Journal of the Ganganatha Jha Research Institute, Vol. XVII, parts 3-4.
4. See p. xvii of the Preface to the First Edition of Griffith's *Hymns to the Ṛgveda*.
5. See my work *Vaidika-Vyākhyā-Vivechana* (pp. 65-68) for its correct interpretation.
6. Cf. SBE., Vol. 46, pp. 69,80,158,190,288; Contra, pp. 40,68,190, 249-50.
7. *Vedic Research* (English translation of Veda-forschung), pp. 31 ff.
8. Vedic Religion, Vol. III, p. 329.
9. Preface to the First edition of SBE, Vol. 32, pp. xliv-v.
10. Op. cit., p. xii.
11. Ibid., p. xiii.
12. A History of Indian Literature, Vol. I, p. 79.
13. Chips from a German Workshop, II Edition, 1866, p. 27.
14. Vedic Research, pp. 50-54.
15. Op. cit., p. 65.
16. A History of Sanskrit Literature (5th edn.), p. 65.
17. Op. cit., pp. 293-94.
18. Cf. Winternitz, op. cit., p. 305.
19. Op cit., p. 69.

10

The Principles of Vedic Interpretation

The subject of Vedic interpretation is highly technical requiring a specialised knowledge of not only the language of the Vedas but also of the vast Vedic and post-Vedic literature together with a thorough grounding in the exegetical, grammatical, religious, cultural, philosophical, philological, lexicographical, mythological and historical studies connected with them. It is not meant for amateurs and casual readers of the modern translations of the Vedas, nor should it be used as a ploy by politicians, demagogues, or partisan preachers. Even though the Vedas being the most ancient and holy scriptures of the Hindus have an important bearing on the religion, philosophy, art, literature, history and culture of the subcontinent, the interpretation of the Vedas should be academically pursued in an impartial and dispassionate manner to arrive at the truth. It is, therefore, imperative for every student of Vedic exegesis to keep in view the following general principles for interpreting the Vedic texts.

1. The Intellectual Equipment of an Interpreter

It is a truism to say that the Vedas are composed in a highly developed and refined language which follows a set of well-defined rules and diction. So any attempt to interpret the Vedas, without a thorough knowledge of the grammar of the Vedic language, with the help of the later Sanskrit language is analogous to the venture of a person who tries to understand Kālidāsa's *Meghadūtam* with the help of a modern Indian language like Hindi or Marathi. Although there are numerous apparent similarities between the Vedic language and Classical Sanskrit, differences between them in respect of grammar, vocabulary, style, matter and spirit are very conspicuous. Even those words which appear to be common to both the languages denote different meanings in the earlier Vedic language and the later Sanskrit language. For instance, such common words as *Aśva*, *Go*, *Ratha*, etc., mostly convey entirely different figurative meanings in the Vedic language according to their context. Moreover, the meanings of even ordinary words of common usage have to conform to the spirit and matter of the Vedas. So long as an interpreter is not fully conversant with the sum total of Vedic concepts, he cannot do justice to Vedic exegesis. In order to acquaint himself with the development of Vedic thought through various stages in all its ramifications an exegete must thoroughly master not only the original texts of the Vedic Saṃhitās, Brāhmaṇas, Āraṇyakas, Upaniṣads, Vedāṅgas, Smṛtis, and Epics, but must also familiarize himself with all the available Bhāṣyas and modern exegetical studies detailed in the preceding Chapters. No single individual can accomplish such a stupendous task by himself without availing himself of the labours of his co-workers past and present. While taking full advantage of the contributions of his predecessors, an interpreter has to guard himself against their errors and utilize their exegesis with an open mind without either blindly following them or prejudicially rejecting them. Casting aside all preconceptions, prejudices and preferences, an interpreter must accept the Vedic text alone as the final arbiter of Vedic exegesis. If he is unable to interpret satisfactorily any Vedic word or passage he must frankly admit this fact and keep the question open so that the future exegetes may further pursue the subject with an open mind.

2. Authorship and Genesis of Vedic Hymns

If an interpreter knows the Ṛṣi, i.e., the author of a Vedic hymn, and the genesis of its composition, this knowledge will definitely prove helpful to him in the interpretation of the hymn. This is why the ancient authorities on the Vedas require every Vedic student to learn the Ṛṣi, the metre, and the deity of every hymn. For this purpose the ancient Indian Vedists composed during the Sūtra period indices called *Anukramaṇīs* listing the names of Ṛṣis of every Vedic hymn. Kātyāyana's *Sarvānukra-*

maṇī and Śaunaka's *Ārṣānukramaṇī* give a complete account of the Ṛṣis of the Ṛgvedic hymns. Similarly *Anukramaṇīs* for the other Vedas also were composed. The Bṛhaddevatā contains the names of the Ṛṣis of the RV. and the legends connected with them. In self-composed verses in the beginning of his commentary on each Adhyāya of the Fifth Aṣṭaka Veṅkaṭa-mādhava has discussed the question of the Ṛṣis of the RV. A comparative analysis of the various traditions concerning the Ṛṣis shows that none of them is fully reliable which could be helpful in Vedic interpretation, as most of the available traditions seem to be based on mere conjectures which are conflicting in some cases. For instance, there are different traditions about the Ṛṣis of the Ṛgvedic Hymn VIII, 67. According to the Nirukta VII, 27 (Cf. Bṛhad. VI, 88-89), some fishes caught in a net are the seers of this hymn, but Kātyāyana's *Sarvānukramaṇī* says that the seer of the hymn is either *Matsya Sāmmada*, or *Mānya Maitrāvaruṇi*, or that many fishes caught in a net praised the Ādityas. The Sat. Br. XIII, 4, 3, 12, mentions a king named Matsya Sāmmada who might have been the real Ṛṣi, but due to confusion in tradition he was later confused with a fish. It shows how traditions regarding the Ṛṣis became confused and unreliable, and later metamorphosed into legends contained in the Brāhmaṇas, the Nirukta, the Bṛhad, the Epics, etc. If any Vedic hymn is interpreted in accordance with such legends[1], its interpretation is bound to be only *Aitihāsika*, mythological, in character but not necessarily in keeping with the original meaning intended by the seer. A student of Vedic exegesis should carefully and critically examine the tradition handed down by the *Anukramaṇīs* to ascertain its dependability regarding the seer of a particular hymn, because the authors of the Anukra-maṇīs did not seem to have inherited any uninterrupted and reliable tradition in this regard; otherwise they would not have named animals and inanimate objects, mentioned in certain hymns, as their Ṛṣis. For instance, *Kapota* "a dove" mentioned in the RV. X, 165 has been named as its Ṛṣi. Similarly *Hiraṇya-garbha* occurring in the beginning of the RV. X, 121 has been declared as the seer of this hymn. Thus the *devatā* (the subject-matter) of a hymn is named its Ṛṣi in several instances. For example, Viśvāmitra and the rivers are declared to be the deities as well as Ṛṣis of RV. III, 33; Purūravas and Urvaśī in respect of RV. X, 95; Paṇis and Saramā in respect of RV. X, 108; and Yama and *Yamī* for RV. X, 10. It does not stand to reason that the deity of a hymn could have been its Ṛṣi. Moreover, how could animals such as a dove, a bitch or a falcon be the seers of Vedic hymns? All this leads us to the conclusion that the ancient traditions concerning the Ṛṣis of the hymns cannot be fully relied upon to explain the authorship and genesis of Vedic hymns. However, the tradition with regard to the Family Maṇḍalas (II-VII) is reliable to the extent that the hymns comprised in each of these six Maṇḍalas were composed mostly by the Ṛṣis belonging to the particular family to which the ancient tradition ascribes that Maṇḍala. Nevertheless, the legends contained in the later works with regard to the Ṛṣis of the Family Maṇḍalas cannot be made the basis of Vedic interpretation, unless and until they are corroborated by internal evidence of the Vedic texts.

This state of affairs concerning the authors and genesis of the Vedic hymns has made the task of a Vedic interpreter all the more difficult, because he has to sift facts from fiction jumbled up in the mass of ancient traditions and legends in order to attempt a correct interpretation of the Mantras.

3. Ritual Application of Mantras

Besides the Ṛṣi and the legends connected with him, the ritual application of a Vedic hymn or any of its Mantras is supposed to throw light on its genesis according to some ancient and modern scholars, who favour a ritualistic interpretation of the Vedas. However, the problem of ritual application of Vedic verses is very complicated as discussed above in Chapter III. Without blindly following the ritual literature on this point an interpreter has to decide on the basis of evidence available from the Vedic Mantras themselves and from the historical development of the ritual concerned whether the Mantra under interpretation was originally composed for that very ritual or was later on tucked to the ritual due to some apparent and misleading similarity of a word or a syllable. Since the entire interpretation of a Mantra will depend upon the question of its ritual application, an interpreter has to be very judicious in deciding this matter.

4. Metre

It is not unlikely that some scholars might raise the question how the form of a Mantra—poetry or prose—is concerned with Vedic exegesis. However, it is an irrefutable fact that the metre of a Mantra plays an important role in its syntax and thus renders valuable help in determining the meaning of Vedic verses. The Prātiśākhyas, Pāṇini and modern scholars accept the *Pāda* (verse) of a stanza as a definite unit for the purposes of Sandhi and accent. It must be noted that the *Pāda* of a stanza also serves as a syntactical unit in the Veda; and if this factor is kept in view, it proves helpful in arriving at the correct meaning of Vedic Mantras. For instance, the metre requires that for the correct interpretation of RV.I,1,1 the word *Yajñasya* of its second Pāda should be syntactically construed with the following word *devam* of the same Pāda rather than with the preceding word *purohitam* of the first Pāda as is taken by several interpreters[2]. The ancient Veda-Bhāṣyakāra Veṅkaṭa-mādhava also corroborates the view that the Pāda of a stanza generally contitutes a syntactical unit[3]. In conformity with this principle each *Pāda* of a stanza should be treated as a separate unit and written in a separate line, if possible, to facilitate the interpretation of its words, as has been done by Macdonell in his *Vedic Reader for Students* and in my *Vaidika-Vyākhyā-Vivechana.*

5. Devatā (Subject-matter)

It is imperative for an interpreter to have a general view about the subject-matter of the hymn or Mantra he is going to explain. The ancient Indian exegetes such as Yāska, Śaunaka and Kātyāyana employ the term *devatā* to describe the subject-matter of a hymn or a Mantra[4]. It has been aptly observed in the Bṛhad. that he who knows the devatā of the Mantras understands their meaning[5].

Now the question arises as to how an interpreter can know the devatā of a Mantra unless and until he has fully understood its meaning by going through the complete process of interpretation. The ancient Indian interpreters of the Vedas such as Yāska, Śaunaka, and Kātyāyana made a study of this aspect of Vedic exegesis and briefly recorded their findings on the subject in their celebrated works. Śaunaka's Bṛhaddevatā contains a detailed account of the deities of the RV. Although Kātyāyana's Sarvānukramaṇī is mainly based on the Brhad., it (Sarvā.) is comparatively more concise and precise. A *Devatānukramaṇī* ascribed to Śaunaka, which might have contained a comprehensive account of the deities of the RV., is not available now, and only a few quotations from this work are found cited here and there. Some Anukramaṇīs dealing with the subject-matter of the AV., VS., and TS. are also found. But it appears that some of the commentators of the Vedas did not fully rely upon the traditional indices of the subject-matter of the Vedas and preferred to make their own independent judgment about the *devatās*, as is evident from the introductory verse in the V.S. Bhāṣya of Uvaṭa (supra, note 16 of Chapter 7) who claims to have mentioned the Ṛṣis, deities and metres of the Mantras on the authority of the Sat. Br., his teacher and his own reasoning. The ancient Indian indices and exegetical works dealing with the problem of Vedic deities must be invariably consulted by every interpreter of the Vedas but should not be blindly followed, because these works represent a medley of facts and fiction. An interpreter may take due help from those facts which accord with the Vedic text, but reject such extraneous legends as might have accumulated in course of time around the names of the Vedic deities as a result of misinterpretation of some portions of the hymns concerned. In fact these legends prejudice the mind of an exegete in favour of the mythological interpretation and thus hinder the independent and correct interpretation of Vedic Mantras. It may be pointed out that many modern interpreters also have been influenced by such legends in their interpretations of the Vedic hymns. The traditional legendary interpretation of the Ṛgvedic hymn VIII, 91 accepted and endorsed by most of the modern scholars is a case in point. In my article entitled *A Non-legendary Interpretation of the Apālā-Sūkta* published in the VIJ., 2(1), 1964, pp. 755-72, it has been shown that the legends pertaining to this hymn actually mislead an interpreter and hinder its correct and independent interpretation. It is also important to bear in mind that many a legend connected with the Vedic deities owes its origin to the misinterpretation of allegories implied in the Mantras. For instance, the legend of Prajāpati and his daughter, which several modern scholars including Geldner believe to be alluded to in the RV. I, 71, 5, is an allegory according to several ancient authorities such as the MS., Ait. Br., P. Br., and Sat. Br. Similarly the *Urvaśī-Purūravas* legend, which according to the ancient tradition, forms the subject-matter of the RV. X, 95, is also explained as an allegory in some ancient works. Therefore, an interpreter must critically examine the traditional legends associated with the Vedic hymns and find out the truth.

A critical analysis of the Nirukta., the Brhad, and the Sarvā. reveals that the ancient traditions recorded in them with regard to the subject-matter of the Vedic Mantras are not based on reliable and solid facts, but are conjectures; otherwise Yāska (N. VII, 4) would not have made such a disappointing and sweeping statement as the following one with regard to the problem of ascertaining the deity of those Mantras whose deity has not been indicated by tradition or by any words contained in them: "Such Mantras belong to the deity of the sacrifice or part of the sacrifice at which they are to be recited; if such Mantras are not found associated with any ritual act, then they belong to Prajāpati according to the Yājñikas, but to Narāśaṃsa in the opinion of the Naruktas; or any deity at will may be fancied for such Mantras." However, the standpoint of the author of the Brhad. in this connection is more rational, as he opines that an interpreter should ascertain the deity of a hymn by identifying its (deity's) characteristic features in the hymn[6]; and that an expert in Mantras should determine the deities of the hymns by minutely investigating the incident or occasion relating to the deity praised by the seers in the beginning and at the end of the hymns[7].

The apparently paradoxical and seemingly preposterous statements in the Mantras with regard to the mutual relationship of Vedic deities present a riddle which can be solved by deciphering the code skilfully employed by the Ṛṣis. For instance, it is enigmatically said in the RV. that Indra created from His own Self the *Mother* and the *Father* simultaneously[8]. Almost all the Vedic interpreters ancient and modern are unanimous in accepting the interpretation of the *Mother* as Earth and that of the *Father* as Heaven in this context. In the Vedic terminology Heaven is often described as *Father* and the Earth as *Mother* for producing and sustaining creatures. In fact, the terms father, mother, son, daughter, brother and sister are employed in the Vedic language for various deities to express the relationships of anteriority, posteriority, concomitance, space and importance among the deities. Thus a natural phenomenon preceding another in terms of time is called father or mother of the subsequent phenomenon. For instance, *Uṣas* (Dawn) is spoken of as the Sun's *mother* to express her priority in appearance; as the *daughter* of Heaven who is considered to be her source in term of space; and as the *sister* of the Sun who is regarded as the son of Heaven. The words *duhitṛ* "daughter" and *Pitṛ* "father" denote a similar relationship between Dawn and Heaven in the ancient legend, the later version of which alludes to Prajāpati's desire for his daughter. An interpreter must keep in mind this important aspect of the Vedic language.

It is also important to bear in mind that the limbs, weapons, vehicles, etc. of the deities spoken of in the Vedas are in fact metaphorical descriptions of their various aspects and functions. For instance, the rays of the sun symbolize his horses.

6. Pada-Pāṭha

As the Vedic texts are now available in the Saṃhitā form, a Vedic student has to analyse the words of the Saṃhitā into separate words in accordance with the rules of Sandhi to explain the form of each individual word. Although a greater part of the Vedic texts presents no difficulty of euphonic analysis to a serious student of Vedic grammar, some of the euphonic combinations which can be analysed in more than one way strain the nerves of Vedic interpreters and have been variously explained by both ancient and modern authorities on the subject as discussed above (supra, chapter 5 First of all an interpreter must consult the Padapāṭhas composed by the ancient authorities such as Śākalya and Ātreya (supra, chapter 5 then consider the objections raised against their views by the later scholars like Yāksa, Grassmann and Oldenberg, and finally make his own independent judgment in keeping with the Vedic idiom and usage. Unless and until the independent form of each individual word of the Saṃhitā is known, its interpretation cannot proceed smoothly. Therefore an interpreter must pay particular attention to this important aspect of the problem, if he is not going to base his interpretation entirely on the ancient Pada-pāṭhas.

7. Grammatical Explanation of Words

After the analysis of euphonic combinations an interpreter is faced with the problem of explaining the grammatical formation including syntactical relationships of the individual words of the Vedic text. An erroneous impression is prevalent among some people that anyone familiar with the grammar of Classical Sanskrit can explain the grammatical formation of Vedic words. The sooner this impression is dispelled, the better it would be for the progress of Vedic studies. It is undoubtedly true that though Classical Sanskrit being the descendant of the Vedic language has inherited a considerable part of the grammatical structure of the latter, yet the former is much different from the latter in many respects. Therefore, a student of Vedic exegesis must free himself from the notions of Classical Sanskrit and fully familiarize himself with the system of Vedic grammar as discussed above in Chapter VIII. The Prātiśākhyas and the Pāṇinian Grammar, which render good help for the grammatical explanation of Vedic words to some extent, do not constitute a complete Vedic grammar as understood in the modern sense of the term. In fact, the unwarranted application of such sweeping Pāṇinian Sūtras as *Vyatyayo bahulam*, *Bahulam Chhandasi*, *Vā Chhandasi*, etc., leads to the misinterpretation of Vedic forms[9]. For instance, some ancient Indian grammarians misapply the above-cited rules of the Pāṇinian Grammar to interpret the form *bāhavā* (RV.VII,62,5) as an instrumental singular, whereas it is actually an accusative dual of *bāhu*[10]. Similarly ancient Indian commentators resort to the unwarranted use of such Pāṇinian Sūtras to impose any type of grammatical explanation on a Vedic word which they cannot explain satisfactorily[11]. While an interpreter has to guard himself against such unwarranted grammatical explanations attempted by the ancient Indian commentators, he has to remain vigilant at the same time to eschew the temptation of text-emendation indulged in the interpretaions of some eminent modern scholars mentioned in the preceding Chapter. In addition to the knowledge of Vedic grammar, an inter-comparison of Vedic passages containing similar forms is a sure guide to the correct grammatical explanation of Vedic forms. For instance, the form *nāvaḥ* (RV.I,25,7) may be explained either as a genitive singular or accusative plural of *nau*, but only the context and the comparison of the related Vedic passages can dispel this doubt[12]. Without a minute examination of the Vedic usage some indeclinables are interpreted as nominal forms by some scholars; see, e.g., the interpretations of *guhā, satyam, sādhuyā, amuyā*, etc., occurring in the RV[13]. The accent of words must also be taken into account while explaining their grammatical formation, because accent proves quite helpful in deciding whether a particular word is a noun, a pronoun, a compound, or a finite verb. The knowledge of Comparative Philology will undoubtedly help an interpreter in identifying the phonetic variations of the same word; compare, e.g., *tanvam* and *tanuvam, svargam* and *suvargam, trayambakam* and *triyambakam, śatavalśaḥ, śatavaliśaḥ* and *śatavaleśaḥ, śukra*, and *Śukla, roman* and *loman, rohita* and *lohita*, etc. A student of Vedic exegesis must possess an historical outlook to understand the various phases of development through which the Sanskrit language has passed so that he may apply only those rules to explain the grammatical formation of Vedic words which are germane to them.

8. The Meaning of Words

The problem of explaining the meaning of Vedic words is twofold: (1) to explain, in accordance with the context, the meaning of such words as are common to both the Vedic language and Classical Sanskrit; and (2) to find out the meaning of obscure and rare Vedic words, which the ancient exegetes had compiled in the 4th Chapter of the Nighaṇṭu. Although the meaning of common words seems apparently to present no difficulty of interpretation to a casual reader of the Vedas, those acquainted with the intricacies of the problems of Vedic interpretation realise the magnitude of the difficulties involved, because the common words do not always denote the same meaning in the earlier and later stages of the Sanskrit language and have undergone tremendous semantic transformation in some cases. Take, for instance, the earlier and later meanings of the words *Asura* and *Mṛga*. The inclusion of common words in the list of synonyms compiled in the first three Chapters of the Nighaṇṭu testifies to the fact that the ancient exegetes of the Vedas were aware of the different meanings expressed by the common words in different contexts. Therefore, the most important factor in determining the meaning of a word is its context. The meaning of even common words must be decided in keeping with the nature and characteristic features of the deity for which they are employed. For instance, the common word *go* which ordinarily denotes "a cow" in Classical Sanskrit may mean in the Vedic language *waters*, *rays of light*, *stars*, etc., according to its context. In the case of common words the ordinary lexicons are not of much avail, though they could be consulted for removal of doubt. On the other hand, the Nighaṇṭu, the Nirukta, the Veda-Bhāṣyas, the modern exegetical studies and the Vedic lexicons must be consulted before finally determining the correct meaning of an obscure and rare word. However, the final decision in the matter should be taken after carefully examining the context and the Vedic usage on the basis of an inter-comparison of parallel passages. And if the meaning of such words still remains doubtful, an interpreter should honestly admit his inability rather than advance unwarranted conjectures.

9. Accent

As accent plays a very important role in determining the meaning of Vedic words, an interpreter of the Vedas must fully master the rules of Vedic accent before embarking upon the most technical and arduous task of Vedic interpretation. Various problems concerning the declension, conjugation, number, gender, person, etc., of Vedic words can be solved by examining their accent. A Vedic word without accent belongs to any one of the following categories which must be determined according to its form and context:

(a) vocatives which are not in the beginning of a Pāda;
(b) certain particles such as *cha, vā, iva*, etc.;
(c) finite verbs in certain syntactical positions; and
(d) certain pronominal forms such as *mā, me, naḥ, vaḥ*, etc. (For details, consult my *Vaidika-Vyākaraṇa*, Vol, II, pp. 845-46).

In certain Vedic words the position of accent determines their meaning and gender. For instance, certain nouns ending in *-as* and denoting a neuter gender accent their first syllable but denote an adjective when their accent shifts to the final syllable e.g. *ápas* "action", *apás* "active", *yáśas* "glory", *yaśás* "glorious". Similarly the change of accent in compounds leads to the change of their meaning. For instance, a Tatpuruṣa compound *Rājaputrá* having accent on the final syllable means "the son of a king", whereas a Bahuvīrhi compound *Rā́japutra* which accents its first syllable would mean "the father of a king". Therefore, an interpreter must carefully examine the accent of a word before determining its meaning.

10. Etymology

That etymology often provides the best key to the original and correct meaning of a Vedic word is proved by the fact that the Ṛṣis themselves hint at the derivation of certain words. For instance, it is said in the RV. III, 29,11 that when Agni is formed in the atmosphere (*Mātari*) he is called *Mātariśvan*. Similarly the RV. VI, 15,13 hints at the etymology of *Jātavedas* as follows: he, *Jātavedas*, knows all the births, i. e., all those born (*Viśvā veda janimā Jātavedaḥ*). The employment of the word *purohita* in its etymological sense is evident in the RV. VI, 70, 4-5; VII, 53, 1, etc. In several verses of the RV. the god *Pūṣan*, "the Sun", is significantly described as *Jāra* "consumer" of his sister, the Dawn[14]. If the same phrase is translated according to its later connotation prevalent in Classical Sanskrit it would mean "the paramour of his sister", which is not its real meaning, as is evident from the context. Most of the modern scholars recognize the importance of etymology in Vedic interpretation and suggest the etymological meanings of Vedic words in their interpretations, lexicons and translations. Therefore, in accordance with this widely accepted principle an interpreter must take full advantage of etymology to determine the meaning of a word. However, a meaning based on the etymology of a word must be tested on the touchstone of Vedic idiom and usage. Moreover, the meanings of cognate words in the related languages (see Chapter VIII for such lexicons) can prove helpful in confirming the etymological meaning of a word. While deriving due help from etymology, an interpreter must avoid the temptation of suggesting fanciful and unwarranted etymologies of words (supra, chapter 5) The etymology of a word should be attempted within the four corners of the Vedic idiom, usage and thought. If the usage of various forms of a root is attested in the Vedic language, the derivation of a Vedic word from that root is justifiable and helpful in Vedic interpretation.

11. Metaphors

Since the seers are very fond of metaphorical expressions, an exegete should not always interpret the Vedic words in their literal sense but should try to ascertain if any metaphor is implied in the expression under discussion. As pointed out above, the words of kinship such as mother, father, brother, sister are metaphorically employed in the RV. to express the relationship of anteriority, posteriority and concomitance among natural phenomena. Similarly the various interpretations—ancient and modern—of the metaphorical expression alluding to a *Vṛṣabha* having four horns, three feet, etc. (RV.IV,58,3) have been referred to above in the preceding Chapters. It is also well known to all students of Vedic exegesis that such common words as *parvata*, *samudra*, *aśva*, *go*, etc., are often metaphorically employed in the Vedas. The interpretation of metaphors used in the Vedas is the crux of the problem of Vedic exegesis and a hard nut to crack. A close acquaintance with the thought and style of the Ṛṣis is the only key to the interpretation of the Vedic metaphors. Bergaigne's commendable attempt to explain metaphors in his *Vedic Religion* (supra, chapter 8) is worth emulation by every student of Vedic exegesis.

12. Unattached Epithets

If an epithet is used in conjunction with a noun that it

qualifies, its interpretation is not much of a problem. However, when an adjective is employed alone without the noun concerned, it (the adjective) poses a problem of interpretation. There are numerous instances of this type in the RV. In order to determine the meaning of an unattached epithet an interpreter should study its Vedic usage to find out the noun which it often qualifies, for such an unattached epithet denotes the meaning of that noun together with its own meaning. For instance, the unattached epithet *varīyas* "wider" denotes "wider *space*"[15], and the phrase *ṣaṭ urvīḥ* "six wide" means "six wide *directions*"[16]. On account of their constant association with *Uṣas* the unattached epithets *chitramaghā*, *vājinī* etc., which are enumerated in the Nighaṇṭu, I,8 among the sixteen synonyms of *Dawn*, can be easily recognised as referring to it. On the problem of interpreting Vedic epithets a student of Vedic exegesis may consult with profit Prof. Gonda's well-known work *Epithets in the Ṛgveda* (supra, chaptea 8).

13. Secondary Sense of Words

An interpreter must bear in mind that the Ṛṣis do not always use words in their primary sense and sometimes employ them in their secondary sense. For instance, the word *go* is used in the sense of *cow-milk* in the RV. IX, 46,4—"Cook the exhilarating (*Soma*) with cow-milk"; in the sense of *cow-hide*[17] in the RV. X, 94,9—"They sit on cow-hide, milking *Soma*"; and in the sense of a *bow-string* made of cow-hide in the RV.X,27,22—"The string fixed to each bow clanged loudly." In the last-cited verse the word *vṛkṣa* also is employed in its secondary sense of *a bow made of wood*. Similarly the word *dānu* is found used in its secondary sense of "a son of *dānu*"[18]. Some scholars are apt to explain the secondary sense of such words as instances of their figurative use. Whatever be the mode of explanation, the secondary sense of such words should be clearly brought out by an interpreter and should not be confused with their primary sense.

14. The Veda as its own Interpreter

It has been aptly observed that the Veda must shine with its own light, i.e., the Veda must be its own interpreter. In other words, the obscure words and passages of the Veda must be explained with the help of those passages whose meaning is clear beyond any shadow of doubt. Although the modern scholars like Roth have highly commended—rather propounded—this deductive system of Vedic interpretation and made considerable use of it, the ancient Indian Bhāṣyakāras were not totally ignorant of it. For instance, Veṅkaṭamādhava observes that the wise determine the meanings of Mantras with the help of the other Mantras of clear import contained in the other Śākhās[19]. The Veda-Bhāṣyakāras did make use of this method, but sparingly"[20]. The lack of suitable indices and concordances made it difficult for the ancient commentators to avail themselves fully of this method. But now when the indices and concordances of all the important Vedic texts are available, a student must fully utilize this scientific method to determine the meaning of a word, and must carefully compare all the passages of the Vedic Saṃhitās, the Brāhmaṇas. the Āraṇyakas, the Upaniṣads and the Vedāṅgas wherever the word under interpretation occurs. This method, will not, only illuminate the meaning of the word but will also throw ample light on the various stages of its semantic development. Sometimes the later literature also proves helpful in arriving at the correct meaning of Vedic words. For instance, a comparison of the relevant passages from the Mahābhārata and the Brāhmaṇas proved decisive in determining the correct meaning of *mānuṣe*[21] occuring in the RV.III,23,4. It has been aptly observed both by the ancient and the modern interpreters of the Vedas that unless an interpreter is thoroughly conversant with the style and thought of the Vedas he will not be able to make out the sense of a Vedic Mantra even though he knows the meaning of each word contained in it. Therefore a thorough knowledge of the whole of the Vedic literature is a *sine qua non* for an interpreter of the Vedas. Abel Bergaigne has rightly summed up his conclusions about the best method of understanding the Ṛgveda in the following words[22]: "The more I study this problem, the more compelled I feel to abandon the interpretations which I have so far accepted from M. Roth and M. Grassmann with complete confidence. The more convinced also I am that, without neglecting the light which might be shed by other sources, the best method of understanding the Ṛgveda would be to read it incessantly, not hymn by hymn, but verse by verse, and in a manner even word by word."

Notes and References

1. For legends connected with the Ṛṣis, see *Ṛgvedic Legends* by H.L. Hariyappa, Poona, 1953; *The Seers of the Ṛgveda* by V.G. Rahurkar, Poona, 1964; *Die Sagenstoffe des Ṛgveda* by E. Sieg, Stuttgart, 1902; *Nītimañjarī* of Dyā Dviveda.
2. For a detailed discussion on this point, see my *Vaidika-Vyākhyā-Vivechana*, pp. 2-4.
3. Śloka 15 in the beginning of Veṅkaṭamādhava's commentary on the 8th Adhyāya of 6th Aṣṭaka—"*Pāde pāde samāpyante prāyeṇārthā avāntarāḥ*".
4. Nirukta VII, 1; Brahd. I,6; Sarvānukramaṇī II, 4-5.
5. Bṛhad. I, 2.
6. Ibid. I, 20.
7. Ibid. I, 22.
8. RV.X, 54, 3.
9. See my *Vaidika Vyākaraṇa*, Vol. I, Preface, p. 10; Vol. It, pp. 493,694, notes 70K and 71.
10. Ibid. Vol. I, p. 379, note 174.
11. See my *Vaidika-Vyākhyā-Vivechana*, pp. 67-68 for the explanation of *Aktuḥ*, pp. 167-168 for *Svardṛśaḥ*.
12. See *Vaidika-Vyākhyā-Vivechana*, pp. 35-36 for discussion of *nāvaḥ*.
13. *guhā* is invariably used in conjunction with such verbal forms as √kṛ, √bhū, etc.; Cf. RV. I,123,7; II,12,4; IV, 18,5; X,100,7. See *Vaidika-Vyākhyā-Vivechana*, pp. 13-14 for *satyam*, p. 91 for *guhā*.
14. RV. VI, 55, 4-5; X, 3,3; Cf., supra, chapter 1 note 5.
15. RV. V, 49,5.
16. RV. VI, 47,3; X,14,16; X,128,5. Cf. our *Vaidika-Vyāhkyā-Vivechana*, p. 205.
17. Cf. RV. VI, 47,26; 75,11; AV. VII, 125,1; VS. 29,48; N. IX, 12.
18. RV. I,32,9; X,120,6. In later works such as the Sat. Br. and the Mbh. the variant reading *danu* is found.
19. Introductory verse 7 in Veṅkaṭamādhava's Bhāṣya on the 3rd Adhyāya of the 8th Aṣṭaka, p. 3591 of Vishva Bandhu's edition.
20. For instance, Sāyaṇa in his Bhāṣya on RV. III, 34,5 cites another Mantra (RV.I 143,7) in corroboration of his interpretation of the word *dhiyaḥ* as "*Dawns.*"
21. See my article entitled "*A New Interpretation of the Vedic Word Mānuṣa*" in the Journal of the Ganganatha Jha Research Institute, Vol. XVII, parts 3-4.
22. Vedic Religion. Vol. III. pp. 287-88.

INDEX